Praise for James Hollis:

"Nourishing . . . Like a master chef, James Hollis knows that good food for the soul cannot be ordered to go."
—*The Plain Dealer* (Cleveland)

"Everyone seems to be obsessing about the monetary cost of the graying of the American population, but there's very little talk of the soul. James Hollis . . . has plenty to say about the soul. . . . Erudite and cultured but also accessible."
—*Portland Tribune*

"Hollis speaks to and teaches from the heart. A combination of genuine vision and genuine humanity is a rare and valuable gift."
—Clarissa Pinkola Estés, author of
Women Who Run with the Wolves

"James Hollis is the most lucid thinker I know about the complexities and complexes that interfere with living a full life. . . . He's one of our great teachers and healers."
—Stephen Dunn, Pulitzer Prize–winning poet

Praise for James Hollis's
Finding Meaning in the Second Half of Life:

"Offers insight into the process of finding true meaning later in life. . . . Challenging . . . earnest."
—*Houston Chronicle*

"[A] deep Jungian exploration of individuation. . . . humane and compassionate. . . . [Hollis's] focus on the underlying meaning of life will resonate for many."
—*Publishers Weekly*

"A work of soul-making. It brings solace and wisdom to those of us who find ourselves in a dark wood, in the second half of life."
—Edward Hirsch, author of
How to Read a Poem and Fall in Love with Poetry

"Midlife is a time when people can lose their way and flounder. James Hollis knows this terrain, describes it well, and asks the important questions that can lead to clarity, maturity, and meaning."
—Jean Shinoda Bolen, M.D., author of
Goddesses in Everywoman and *Gods in Everyman*

James Hollis, Ph.D., received a B.A. from Manchester College and a Ph.D. from Drew University. He taught humanities for twenty-six years in various colleges and universities before becoming a Jungian analyst at the Jung Institute in Zurich, Switzerland, where he received a diploma in analytical psychology. He lives in Houston, Texas, with his wife, where he has a private analytic practice and is executive director of the Jung Educational Center of Houston.

WHY GOOD PEOPLE DO BAD THINGS

Understanding Our Darker Selves

JAMES HOLLIS, PH.D.

GOTHAM
BOOKS

GOTHAM BOOKS
Published by Penguin Group (USA) Inc.
375 Hudson Street, New York, New York 10014, U.S.A.

Penguin Group (Canada), 90 Eglinton Avenue East, Suite 700, Toronto, Ontario,
Canada M4P 2Y3 (a division of Pearson Penguin Canada Inc.); Penguin Books Ltd,
80 Strand, London WC2R 0RL, England; Penguin Ireland, 25 St Stephen's Green,
Dublin 2, Ireland (a division of Penguin Books Ltd); Penguin Group (Australia),
250 Camberwell Road, Camberwell, Victoria 3124, Australia (a division of Pearson
Australia Group Pty Ltd); Penguin Books India Pvt Ltd, 11 Community Centre,
Panchsheel Park, New Delhi – 110 017, India; Penguin Group (NZ), 67 Apollo Drive,
Rosedale, North Shore 0632, New Zealand (a division of Pearson New Zealand Ltd);
Penguin Books (South Africa) (Pty) Ltd, 24 Sturdee Avenue, Rosebank, Johannesburg
2196, South Africa

Penguin Books Ltd, Registered Offices: 80 Strand, London WC2R 0RL, England

Published by Gotham Books, a member of Penguin Group (USA) Inc.

Previously published as a Gotham Books hardcover edition

First trade paperback printing, April 2008

10   9   8   7   6   5   4   3

Gotham Books and the skyscraper logo are trademarks of Penguin Group (USA) Inc.

The Library of Congress has cataloged the hardcover edition of this book as follows:
Hollis, James, 1940–
    Why good people do bad things : understanding our darker selves / James Hollis.
       p.   cm.
    ISBN: 978-1-592-40276-2 (hardcover)   ISBN: 978-1-592-40341-7
(paperback)   1. Shadow (Psychoanalysis)   2. Good and evil—
Psychological aspects.   3. Jungian psychology.   I. Title.
BF175.5.S55H65   2007
150.19'54—dc22   200627865

Printed in the United States of America
Set in Galliard, with display in Cresci and Medici Script
Designed by BTD NYC

For Jill,
And our four children,
Taryn, Tim, Jonah, Seah
And for Rob who wanted to see his name in this book

And the people of the
Jung Center of Houston, Texas

My special thanks go to Gotham Books/Penguin,
with whom I am pleased to be associated:
  William Shinker, President and Publisher
  Lauren Marino, Executive Editor
  Hilary Terrell, Assistant Editor
  Sarah Reidy, Publicist

And to Liz Williams,
amie et agent provocateur et extraordinaire

CONTENTS

Preface   xi

Introduction: SHADOW ENCOUNTERS   1

Chapter One: SUNDRY SHADINGS OF SOUL
The Four Forms of Shadow Expression   7

Chapter Two: PAUL'S PERPLEXITY
"Though I Know the Good . . ."   24

Chapter Three: RUNNING INTO OURSELVES
The Personal Shadow   38

Chapter Four: PATHOS
Shadow Invasions in Everyday Life   59

Chapter Five: HIDDEN AGENDAS
The Shadow in Intimate Relationships   83

Chapter Six: ONE MULTIPLIED
The Collective Shadow   107

Chapter Seven: LOWEST COMMON DENOMINATOR
Institutional Shadows   128

Chapter Eight: PROGRESS'S DARK EDGE
The Shadow of Modernism   147

Chapter Nine: DARK DIVINITY
The Shadow Side of God   167

Chapter Ten: LUMINOUS DARKNESS
The Positive Shadow   183

Chapter Eleven: SHADOW/WORK
Encountering Our Darker Selves   202

Bibliography   239

Index   243

Nota Bene:

While based on the stories of real people, all names included herein are fictitious, with genders and professions changed and locales mixed. All dreams are accurately cited and are used with express permission of the dreamers, whom I thank. References to C. G. Jungs *Collected Works* are abbreviated in the text as *CW*, with the volume and paragraph number following.

PREFACE

"Each person is a world, peopled
by blind creatures in dim revolt
against the I, the king, who rules them."
—GUNNAR EKELÖF

The *I* that I know does not know enough to know that it does not know enough. It thinks itself luminescent crystal, when it is mostly grays, mostly vague, oblique shapes, and sometimes stark, opaque obsidian. Who I think *I* am is only the ego talking, a fragile wafer cast upon an immense inner sea. Our language betrays us. When I say *I*, which I is speaking? Which part of the whole is, for the moment, dominant? When I say *myself*, which self is speaking? How can I say *I* know myself, in every . . . or any moment?

How is it that good people do bad things? Why is our personal story, our societal history so bloody, so repetitive, so injurious to self and others, so self-defeating? This book operates from a central thesis that is relatively unknown to the general public but is a truism for depth psychology, namely, that *the human psyche is not a single, unitary, or unified thing, as the ego wants to believe. It is diverse, multiplicitous, and divided . . . always divided.*

It is the delusion of the ego, sometimes a necessary delusion, that this aggregate of splinter selves is under our control, contained within the purview of consciousness, or even knowable at all. These splinter selves, these darker presences, are fractal energy systems, and therefore *have the capacity to act indepen-dently of our conscious intention*. In fact, they are quite active, at almost all moments, and have the power to overthrow con-sciousness, usurp freedom, and enact their own programs, whether we know it or not. If we look at this idea humorously, we would have to say that certain parts of ourselves have never been introduced to the other parts, and if they had, they might not get along very well.

This autonomous world within is the realm of what Jung called the *Shadow*. It is not evil, as such, although it may do things that we or others later judge evil. In the end we are wholly accountable for the actions and consequences of the Shadow, even if we were unconscious of its enactments at the time.

The activities of these darker selves, these shadowy force fields, show up in more than our personal lives. They show up in our social systems, in our politics, in our interpersonal rela-tionships, and even in our theologies. Why would it not be the case that the infinite complexities of the human psyche will manifest in the infinite complexities of the world we have cre-ated, or the world as we have imagined? It is rumored that the secret of the universe was once imparted by Hermes Trismegis-tus ("Thrice-Greatest")* in ancient Egypt. That secret, revealed here at no extra cost to the reader, is that "things above are copies of things below, and things below copies of things above" and "the way up and the way down are the same."

Thus, a sincere exploration of the complexities of our daily lives will require us to bear witness to the variegated human psyche, as well. Explorations of the individual human psyche will necessarily uncover its activities everywhere in groups, and even in its images of the universe. Many in our time do not

---

*His Egyptian name was Thoth, alleged to be the inventor of writing, and, like Prometheus in Greek story, an agent who brings secret knowledge, secret powers from the gods to humans.

bother to examine from whence their daily lives are generated; many do not consider the relationship between the individual psyche and the social and political enmeshments we have spun; many do not consider how our own psyche construes and even transplants its image onto the cosmos. In examining this subject, we must therefore sort through how our complex, multiform human psyche plays out at so many levels—personal, societal, cosmic. The organization of this book, its sequential logic, is to start with the personal and immediate, and then move out in widening circles from the personal to the social, then to the historic, then to the cosmic, and back again to the very personal, for it is at least partially from the personal Shadow that all these other planes of our reality derive. In the end, our work with our personal Shadow largely defines our engagement with the Shadow at all the other levels. What we have ignored within ourselves will sooner or later arrive from outside . . . like a truck headed toward us in the wrong lane.

Those who do not consider the implications of the divided human soul remain unconscious and are therefore dangerous to self and others. Those who do bother to stop and look, and ask *why*, become more and more attuned to the complexity of their own psychological processes; their lives grow more interesting to them; and they become less dangerous to themselves and others. It is for this latter group that this book is written. The field is flooded with so-called self-help books that offer platitudinous programs for rapid transformation. Most of them fail us because they do not take the complexities of the human psyche into account. They seldom consider that much of what runs our lives operates outside the sphere of consciousness, nor do they acknowledge that we are torqued within by contradictory motives, that some part of ourselves does not wish to enact the agenda endorsed by another part, that for all the attainments of ego consciousness we achieve, there are darker "selves" at work in quite contrary ways. This book, *Why Good People Do Bad Things: Understanding Our Darker Selves*, invites us to a more disturbing dialogue with ourselves and our world, one that promises greater, not less complexity, but from which an understanding of self and world cannot help but grow.

JAMES HOLLIS
Houston, Texas
2006

WHY
GOOD
PEOPLE
DO BAD
THINGS

"One does not become enlightened by imagining figures of light, but by making the darkness conscious. The latter procedure, however, is disagreeable and therefore not popular."
—C. G. JUNG, *CW 13*, PARA. 335

INTRODUCTION
Shadow Encounters

Consider these actual occurrences:

- A well-respected accountant finds a way to funnel funds from a charitable nonprofit to her private account. For years she tells her husband that she is being rewarded bonuses for her achievements. Only when they take an extended vacation, and someone else is minding the shop, is she discovered.
- A politician inveighing against gay rights is found to be gay himself. Is his public position self-hatred, or cynical exploitation of the ignorance and bigotry of his constituents? Does holding public office mean that much to him, and, if so, why?
- A woman leaving church turns to see her wealthy neighbor slip and land on her derriere in the middle of a puddle. The woman grows hysterical with laughter. She cannot stop laughing—to the mortification of her husband, her son, and later, herself.
- An educator secretly pillages his children's college savings to fuel a gambling addiction. Only when the first child is accepted to college does this chicken come home to roost.
- Billions are spent by ordinary people on pornography, much of it watched over the Internet by those who piously decry any such interest.
- A televangelist tells his flock that he has spoken to God, and God has told him that they are to be happy *and* contribute to His church— which just happens to coincide with the interests of the clergyman.
- A therapist manipulates people into his practice, despite having signed an ethical code that specifically forbids the solicitation of clients.
- The richest country in the world spends billions on armaments and

foreign adventure while slashing health, legal, and educational services to its disenfranchised, and also cuts taxes for the wealthy while, as recent statistics show, one in six of its citizens faces hunger on a daily basis.

• Valuing relationships so much, we nonetheless find few that are not broken. Can one love the "Other," really, as they are, without self-interest interfering? Is there not a narcissistic interest that reveals itself when we carefully review our behaviors and agendas? Do not even parents, most parents, expect their children to endorse their values rather than find their own?

This list can go on indefinitely, as long as there are human stories to recount. However disparate these examples, what do they all have in common? All are manifestations of the *Shadow*.*

How is it that there can be so many discrepancies between our professed values, our presumptive virtues, and our many embarrassing, often destructive, behaviors?

Perhaps the wisest insight ever uttered by a human being came from the Latin poet Terence, who, nearly two thousand years ago, wrote, "Nothing human is alien to me." But can that be true? Surely the *I* that I know and treasure, the *I* that I present to you, is free of the darker sides of human conduct. How could I imagine that there might be a murderer within me? How could I live with the thought that I might nurse violent, lustful, greedy thoughts toward others?

Plato believed that humans were inherently good, as long as they were fully conscious, or so he argued in *The Republic*. If one does wrong, it is because he or she does not fully understand the consequences of one's acts. In his parable of Gyges in *The Republic*, a shepherd finds a ring, the turning of which on

---

*Throughout this book I will capitalize the word *Shadow* in order to emphasize its relative autonomy, its profound *otherness*, which nonetheless is still a deep part of ourselves.

his finger makes him invisible. Because he is thus rendered invisible, he can rob or exploit his neighbors at will, since he is free from the risk of consequences. Would any of us act morally *if we knew we were not to be held accountable?* Plato argues, through the persona of Socrates, that if Gyges is brought to understand the full consequences of his acts, how his behaviors have an impact on others, and how he will thereafter be obliged to live in a society that he cannot trust, he will act "properly," despite the magical powers granted him.*

Many observers of the human condition, me included, consider Plato's position an idealistic but naive understanding of our much more complicated natures. Yet so much of our culture is based upon the mistaken idea that we can educate our youth into socially correct behaviors. (Even I have spent my entire life in education, seeking whatever "the good" may be and transmitting that "good" through teaching, writing, and therapy.) Our penal system professes to be less about punishment, though it is surely that, than the effort to reform character through public disapproval. Thus, we call them *reformatories.* (The Quakers developed the idea of *penitentiaries,* believing that belonging to community was so spiritually necessary that when one was removed from the community, one would so suffer the pain of exclusion as to be inclined to penitence, and therefore voluntarily modify behaviors and attitudes and be restored to the fold.)

Nonetheless, philosophers today label the apparent naiveté of Plato "the Socratic fallacy." All we have to do is look at the

---

*Interestingly, this argument anticipates the argument twenty-three centuries later of Immanuel Kant, who sought to find a basis for moral conduct not levered on the fear of divine retribution, a purely rational ground for "right conduct." He devised "the categorical imperative," which suggests that we should act *as if* the universalization of our acts would be applied to all, including ourselves. So I would not steal from another not because there is a vengeful god waiting to punish me, but because I do not find it congenial to live in a world in which no one can trust the conduct of another.

headlines of our daily papers, or become more conscious of the hidden agendas through which we engage with one another, to get some sense of a darker hue that colors our conscious journeys.

In the Judeo-Christian tradition this darker cast is called "original sin." For the more literal-minded, the decisions of Adam and Eve, as prototypes of all humanity, permanently tainted humankind, almost as a genetic defect. For the less literal, the tendencies of consciousness to privilege its own position, to fail to see consequences, to be unaware of hidden motives, is "origin-al"—that is, primal—in all of us. (A thoughtful colleague of mine, a nonbeliever in any religious tradition, once observed that the one religious concept that she could affirm, which accounted for the mess of the twentieth century, was the archetype of "The Fall.")

Upon reflection we are led to conclude that what we call *ourselves* contains many fragments, many splinter selves. Some of these darker selves are *complexes*, Jung's term for how our psyche gets charged with programmed energies during our separate histories. Since we share a common humanity, and somewhat common culture, we often share history-driven energies around money, power, sexuality, food, and the like. While our ancestors could project the origin of these splinter selves externally onto a Devil, or an Evil One, the modern has a greater likelihood of recognizing that these darker thoughts and acts come from within us, and that we, in the end, are responsible for them. Still, the thought of "darker selves" operating with impunity within is unsettling. Nathaniel Hawthorne's short story, "Young Goodman Brown," depicts how a naive young man encounters the Shadow in the forest, is so disillusioned that he distances himself from his wife (who is aptly named "Faith"), and spends the rest of his life as a troubled, depressed person who shuns contact with humankind.

It takes a strong sense of self, and no little courage, to be able to examine, and take responsibility for, these darker selves when they turn up. It is much easier to deny, blame others, project elsewhere, or bury it and just keep on rolling. It is at these moments of human frailty when we are most dangerous to ourselves, our families, and our society. *Examining this material is not a form of self-indulgence; it is a way of taking responsibility for our choices and their consequences. It is an act of great moral moment, for it brings the possibility of lifting our stuff off of others, surely the most ethical and useful thing we can do for those around us.* As Jung observed:

> The Shadow is a moral problem that challenges the whole ego-personality, for no one can become conscious of the Shadow without considerable moral effort. To become conscious of it involves recognizing the dark aspects of the personality as present and real.*

What is not made conscious will continue to haunt our lives—and the world. In our short transit on this earth, there is more within each of us than we can ever make conscious and assimilate. And yet our quality of life is a direct function of the level of awareness we bring to our daily choices. This book is a reminder, and an invitation, to a more conscious conduct of our lives.

The poet Maxine Kumin wrote a poem titled "Woodchucks," in which she depicts a gentle, middle-class woman who, finding woodchucks burrowing in her basement, grows agitated and sits through the long nights waiting for them to show their faces, whereupon she can nail them with her .22. She finds herself "puffed with Darwinian pieties" about her inherent superiority, and ends, ironically, by wishing that these intruders

---

*Jung, "The Shadow," *CW 9ii*, para. 14.

would permit themselves to be gassed "the quiet Nazi way." Who wishes to find the Nazi inside each of us? Poet Dennis Slattery, in "Shooting Rats," similarly approaches this place inside himself, recalling firing his .22 while "the scream and screech of life / escaping in shocked heaps / fills the air."* Both poets, sensitive to the nuances, the telluric depths, the complexities of the human soul, are aware of what lurks in their basements. Are we? If not, into what outer venues do our rodents of darker design burrow? Do we repress what lurks in our basement, or project this darkness onto others? And if so, how can we ever deal with others, have conscious, ethical relationships, when we are flooding others with our own darkness denied? In this personal, and collective, engagement with the Shadow that lies within each of us, the quality of life, the tenor and outcome of relationships, and the fate of civilization itself rests.

*Slattery, "Shooting Rats," *Casting the Shadows: Selected Poems*, p. 79.

Chapter One

SUNDRY SHADINGS
OF SOUL
The Four Forms of
Shadow Expression

". . . have you seen the gates of deep darkness?"
—JOB 38:17

Both Sigmund Freud and Carl Jung had much to say about these darker selves. Freud, in particular, by articulating the mixed motives of the psyche, by speaking candidly of sexuality, and by daring to challenge the sacred images of the Western world, brought a firestorm of criticism upon his head. In lifting such topics as infant sexuality, or hidden, narcissistic agendas in the most moral of intentions, into the light of public discussion, his work was widely slandered as "dirty" and his motives suspect. In his first major publication, *Studies in Hysteria*, written with Josef Breuer in 1895, he noted how motives in conflict with consciousness and repressed by the ego could seek a third venue and manifest in the body through somatic disturbances. Pathology theretofore approached primarily within the medical model, and often without success, was found to be a symbolic expression of what was darkly denied by conscious life. In *The Psychopathology of Everyday Life* (1901), Freud examined the hidden agendas that undermine consciousness and produce the apparent mistakes—

the so-called Freudian slips—that he claimed were symbolic manifestations of another darker will coursing beneath the surface of the conscious sea.

Later, forced by the horrors of a world consciously devoted to the delusion of progress yet sacrificing its youth at Verdun, Passchendaele, Ypres, or the Somme—where the British suffered 60,000 casualties in the first twenty-four hours—he was driven to write *Civilization and Its Discontents* (1927–1931). In this work he identified and gave proper weight to the elemental human energies that lead to aggression, violence, and destruction. He noted that the demands of social adaptation produce a countervailing sense of helplessness and frustration with which we cope through diversion, substitutions, and sundry intoxications. Chief among these intoxications is the madness of patriotism and the seductive clamors of war, which cast Freud's son as a POW in World War I and took his four sisters, who perished in concentration camps during the Second World War.*

But it was Carl Jung who devoted much of his life's voyage to the exploration of this darker sea within. Son of a Protestant pastor, and kin to five others, Jung was raised to live the life of a sober, respectable, bourgeois Swiss. Yet, as a child, he dreamt that he was watching the great cathedral spires of his hometown of Basel. From the heavens, golden excrement fell from God, splitting the towers, and bringing the edifice to earth. He was horrified and ashamed that he had produced this dream, and for many decades told no one of its appearance. Only later, when he was in midlife, did he realize that "he," the ego, did not produce that dream, but that something deeper, more autonomous, perhaps even "God," had brought him to under-

---

*Friedrich Nietzsche once ironically noted that it was amazing how good "bad music" and "bad reasons" were when marching off against "the enemy."

stand that his spiritual path would not be the same as his father. This troubling dream recast the biblical metaphor that the rejected stone becomes the cornerstone of the new edifice, that the excrement was divine, inexplicably "golden," and was bent on clearing away the old so that revelation might renew.

Of the many concepts Jung articulated,* few if any are richer than his idea of the Shadow. Expressed in its most functional way, the Shadow is composed of *all those aspects of ourselves that have a tendency to make us uncomfortable with ourselves.* The Shadow is not just what is unconscious, *it is what discomforts the sense of self we wish to have.* It is not synonymous with evil, though it may contain elements that the ego or the culture considers evil. In the old radio days of my youth, a favorite program was called *The Shadow,* featuring one Lamont Cranston. The tagline that opened each show was: "Who knows what evil lurks in the hearts of men? The Shadow knows!" And then this worthy soul would go about confronting evil and restoring good, all within thirty minutes, including commercials for soap, cereal, and floor wax. In fact, as we shall see later, the Shadow just as easily contains what we would consider good, healing, developmental energies, the accessing of which leads to greater wholeness. As Jung explains:

> If it has been believed hitherto that the human shadow was the source of all evil, it can now be ascertained on closer investigation that the unconscious man, that is, his shadow does not consist only of morally reprehensible tendencies, but also displays a number of good qualities, such as normal instincts, appropriate reactions, realistic insights, creative impulses, etc.†

---

*Among them are: *complex, archetype, persona, personality type, synchronicity, anima, animus, individuation,* and many others.
†Jung, "Conclusion," *CW 9ii*, para. 423.

As an aspect of ourselves, the Shadow will not go away simply from the entreaties of our will, nor will moralistic "right practices" prove a stay against its influence upon daily life. The Shadow leaks out into our daily activities and, in fact, is present in all matters, no matter how lofty their tenor or intent.

The "personal Shadow" is unique to each of us, although we may share many features with others around us. The "collective Shadow" is the darker drift of the culture, the unacknowledged, often rationalized, interactions of time, place, and our tribal practices. Each of us carries a personal Shadow, and each of us participates in varying proportion in a collective Shadow.

The Four Forms of Shadow Expression

There are four categorical ways in which the Shadow manifests in our lives. They are found when the Shadow a) remains *unconscious*, albeit active in our lives; b) is disowned by being *projected* onto others; c) usurps consciousness by *possessing* us; or d) broadens *consciousness* through recognition, dialogue, and assimilation of its contents.

1. *The Shadow Remaining Unconscious*

The one question none of us can answer is: "Tell me, of what are you unconscious?" By definition, we do not know what we do not know. We do not know what may in fact be knowing us. Yet what we do not know about ourselves persists and subtly infiltrates our values and our choices. Even if we were to begin to tumble to the fact that we were in the grip of motives and agendas contrary to our professed values, we would likely offer a justification for why we thought what we thought, did what we did. Indeed, one of the surest signs of our defense against our Shadow is our ready rationalizations that surface to justify our position on any subject. How easy it is to criticize entire groups of people: "Those people don't have a work ethic," one says, ignoring the gap between our professed charitable values and love of community, and an insistent self-interest in feeling superior. Shirley has read a couple of books on psychology and enjoys diagnosing her friends. She feels better when she feels superior. Edwina claims a special relationship to God and is free with advice to her circle on how they ought to live their lives. Charles makes a point of taking his colleagues to lunch while he drops hints to the boss that their productivity has dropped off because "they have problems at home." Driven by the wounds of the past, Elena idealizes her friends, pushes them to the limits, and then screams betrayal when they repeatedly "let her down." She never notices that the only one consistently present in each relationship is herself. Having set them up to serve her, she drives them away from her, and then they become the subject of her gossip and vituperation. Each of these persons is caught in the Shadow, silently serving personal agendas and remaining wholly unconscious of how they bring harm to others.

The complexity of the universe, and the complexity of our own souls, is so immense that the fantasy of truly knowing ourselves is like standing on the mountain at dusk and believing that we are encompassing all the stars that wheel in their sidereal orbits through the limitless spaces above us. At best we identify a star here and there. We project upon their obscure orbits our own psychic need for "order" (Greek: *cosmos*) and we see pictures in the sky. We are convinced we see a warrior here, a beast there, a constellation of entities whirling through inky pools. And we believe we know these phantoms, believe that what we are seeing is real, objective, and tangible.

So it is with the Shadow. Little do we know that the patterns we see, the interpretations we construct, the worlds we imagine, begin within us, and then autonomously direct us. The Shadow embodies all that which is troubling to us—that is, foreign to our ego ideal, contrary to what we wish to think of ourselves—or threatens to destabilize the sense of self we can comfortably embrace. As the ego is formed through many shards of splintered experience, so it is easily threatened by even its own "otherness," by whatever contradicts, or even corrects, its elemental agenda. So the ego seldom really knows enough to know that it does not know enough. Thus it is owned, possessed, directed by that which it does not know. Does the fish know it swims in water? Of course not. It is one with its element. Does the ego know that it swims in a sea of competitive, often contradictory, values and energies? Seldom.

Who among us is strong enough to consistently admit shortcomings, hidden agendas, ulterior motives? The woman who laughed when her friend fell in the mud puddle consciously, even compulsively, observed the dictates of her faith, and yet, when her secret envy rose and seized her, she guffawed at her rival's distress. Her schadenfreude, or joy in the misery of another, was an emotion wholly alien to her conscious life. Yet it sprang forth in an instant. And what may spring forth from any of *us* in such reflexive moments?

Who among us is not needy, vain, sometimes narcissistic, hostile, dependent, manipulative? Was Mrs. Gandhi happy to be married to a man whose mistress was India? What Shadow dynamics played out in their marriage? Or, is not someone who devotes his or her outer life to the compulsive service of others not secretly depressed and angry also? Is their reflexive sacrifice of self to the other always a good thing? Is it even a choice? Is the one who wins a citizen of the year award not also serving a need to be needed? Is it cynical to become mindful of the presence of the opposite value in whatever consciousness embraces, or is it a deeper form of honesty? Was a particular person a "saint" because she sacrificed her own journey in service to others; was her life as lived in fact her authentic journey, or was she driven by complexes so powerful as to render her incapable of choosing anything else? Does that make her a saint, or a soul to be pitied? Who among us, outside of her inner psychic constellation, could really make such a judgment? May not good works also exist side by side with a tortured inner life? Is it not possible that the rejected inner life, despite the presence of great light in the outer world, masks a very large Shadow? All we have to do is remember the sordid revelations around so many evangelists, so many politicians, the secret lives of movie stars and sports figures, the revelations that history sometimes casts upon the most favored lives, to acknowledge the power of the Shadow and the insistent demand it makes on even the best of us.

Does the religious zealot spend so much time trying to compel or convert others because he is truly convinced of serving the well-being of others, or is he or she in thrall to the anxiety of inner doubt, a doubt that must be driven away by the achievement of unanimity? As author Nicholas Mosley writes, "people [are] likely to be Muslims or Christians more from a need to belong to a group that would provide emotional reassurance in a difficult world, rather than as a result of a personal search for truth and meaning."* So much for divine revelation, and for personal integrity! But also notice how quickly these questions become offensive to our conscious sensibility. We wish to protest at such slights to our honor, our conscious values, our character, our self-governance. This indeed is the shadow zone where we live more often than we wish to admit.

Yet because the Shadow is most often coursing silently beneath our sight, in seas too deep to plumb, we do not under-

*Mosley, *Inventing God*, p. 3.

stand how it plays out in our outer lives. Where does our frequently professed rectitude come from? Is it the inherent good of humankind? Is it a learned, acculturated complex? Can it beget evil, unintentionally to self and others? Can good without its opposite avoid begetting one-sidedness? And, sooner or later, can one-sidedness not prove oppressive, compulsive, even demonic? Who among us cannot now see, perhaps from the perspective of decades, that even the good we intended was not without its problematic consequences? Who, in the second half of life, with at least a modicum of consciousness and psychological maturity, does not look back upon the past with regret, some shame, and no little dismay? And yet, at the time, we thought we knew ourselves, were choosing wisely, prudently, and with the best of intentions. Coming to accountability for our own history is the first step in recognizing what has hitherto been unconscious, namely, the presence and activity of our Shadow.

Who among us can say of our Shadow, that which is unconscious: "I am conscious of that which is unconscious?" Yet, what is unconscious is eating our lunch, and perhaps someone else's as well. What is unconscious constitutes a shadow government beneath the burnished throne of ego investiture.

II. *The Shadow Disowned Through Projection*

"Consider Cassius . . . he hath a lean and hungry look. Such men are dangerous!" (Who makes this observation in *Julius Caesar* but another ambitious politician?) Consider Joe over there . . . ambitious, vain, self-absorbed. (Who then adds, "like me"?) Consider those heathen there, godless and violent. Let's finish them off! (Who then pauses to reflect how *they* mirror *us* so much?) Consider the animosity toward gays from people who have never felt comfortable with their own sexuality in the first place. Consider the convenience of knowing who the enemy is, always—if the enemy is *there*, they are not *here*, so I have no burden of consciousness, no obligation of self-examination.

To ego consciousness, that thin wafer on a vast, phosphorescent sea, what is beneath its purview either does not exist, or is dormant. In fact, the contents of the unconscious are energy systems, dynamic, active, and quite capable of evading the controlling power of consciousness. The early Patristic Church Father, Origen, felt guilt for thinking too much of dancing girls. So, he chose to solve the problem, to suppress his Shadow, by castrating himself. Shortly thereafter he thought of dancing girls. Is it possible that a man, even a sincere, dedicated man, could eradicate his sexual nature? And if so, at what cost, as so many of the recent scandals of clerical abuse have testified?* And who are the worthies who demand this truncation of the nature that their God has given them? What Shadow lurks thereby?

Simply to deny something does not work. Our unconscious components embody a quantum of energy that has power to leave the dark sea within and enter our world, wholly without our conscious awareness. If this were not true, political propagandists and Madison Avenue admen would quickly be out of a job. In *The Hidden Persuaders,* Vance Packard noted how the tools and techniques of covert disinformation and value manipulation developed by intelligence agencies during World War II were eagerly grasped by commercial interests after the war, specifically to evoke the unconscious and to provoke positive projections onto products ranging from prunes to Pontiacs to politicians.

---

*The word *testify* itself comes from the ancient act of holding one's testicles during a solemn oath, based, as such, on one's core being, and therefore, one's sincerity.

No one projects consciously, for that is a contradiction in terms. No one rises and greets the morning with the intention of projection. Yet invariably, the psychic energy within us, especially that which lies outside the range of consciousness, manifests itself through a dynamic that ego cannot contain. This is how we fall in love, how we fear others who are strangers to us, and how we re-create our relational histories over and over. The psyche is a historically driven analog computer. It searches out analogs, so to speak: "Where have I been here before?" "What do I know about this?" "What does my past experience tell me about this?" Although every moment is absolutely unique in history, our psychic system, in service to historically charged experience as well as anxiety management, floods the new field of experience with the data of the old. So we project our inner life, or aspects of it, onto others, onto groups, onto nations. Accordingly, propaganda, political campaigns, and advertising specifically seek to evoke positive or negative responses from us. Too often the critical capacity of ego consciousness is supplanted by the powers of historic programming and new moments are prejudiced by the old.

One woman found herself reacting violently to a total stranger whom she saw on television. (Who has not had positive or negative energy around a celebrity, forgetting for the moment that they are total strangers to us, and may in any case only be playing a role on screen.) After several such reactions, she realized that the man had the same scowl her mother had so often shown her when she was a child. Though decades apart, with a different gender involved, that scowl was enough to evoke a large, affective reaction.

Thus that which we cannot, or will not, face in ourselves, or that which disturbs the picture we would hold of ourselves, is frequently distanced from the nervous ego by the dissociative mechanism of projection. Since the energy, the valence, the is-

sue is now "out there," I do not have to face it "in here."
Again, we do not project consciously, which is why our projections are so powerful, so compelling. Who could imagine that
that to which we are relating "out there" originated "in here"?
Who could imagine that the reality I see "out there" is an aspect of me? No wonder it is so familiar, so compelling! How
able are we moderns to comprehend the truth, and accept the
challenge, of the ancient Chinese text *Art of the Mind*, which
reminds us of the task:

> What man desires to know is *that*. . . . But his means of knowing is
> *this*. . . . How can he know *that*? Only by the perfection of *this*.*

The *that* is the external world we perceive, little knowing it
emanates from *this*, the internal world of our personal psyche.
How, then, could we ever really know *that*, the real world out
there, if we do not know more of *this*, our internal operations,
predilections, prejudices?

Accordingly, we are forever running into our own Shadow,
and believe it is something out there from which we can distance ourselves. With each Shadow projection, our potential
alienation from reality grows apace; the more we dump our de-
tritus on others, the more we relate to a distorted vision of
reality. Seldom does the world, seldom does the other, ever
prove to be exactly what we expected of them. Wars have been
waged, romances conducted, relationships founded and floun-
dered on Shadow projections, and later one wonders what that
was all about. How many projected so much on Princess Diana, grieved her untimely loss, and later learned of her tangled,
tortured life? Was this not the Shadow projection of their own
unlived lives, their search for magic, their flight from personal

*Waley, *The Way and Its Power*, p. 47.

accountability that landed on this poor, troubled soul? On what else does gossip and envy feed if not our flight from ourselves?

What we do not know, or fear acknowledging, does in fact hurt us, and often others as well. As we will see later, so often the one who receives the Shadow projection of others—be it Hester Prynne of *The Scarlet Letter*, the witches of Salem, the devils of Loudon, the Jews of Poland, gays, or a host of other martyrs to unconsciousness—will be vilified, crucified, marginalized, gassed, burned, or ignored. *They are the carrier of our secret life, and for this we shall hate them, revile them, and destroy them, for they have committed the most heinous of offenses. They remind us of some aspect of ourselves we cannot bear to see.* Sadly, the weaker the ego state, the more intolerable this summons, and the greater the potential for "categorical judgment" of others, which is to say bigotry and prejudice.

III. *Possession by Identification*

Did you ever attend a rock concert and find yourself swept up in the fervor of the crowd, perhaps deliberately seeking to loosen the strictures of your ego with pot or booze? Did you ever scream at the referee or find yourself uttering obscenities at the team across the field? (This writer, as a defensive halfback, once enjoyed getting a fifteen-yard penalty for unsportsmanlike conduct after kicking an end in the ribs who theretofore had successfully screened me from the flow of the ball.) Were you ever flush with righteous indignation, felt full of yourself, and exulted as a sudden servant of this larger energy? Did you ever enjoy losing your mind, for awhile? If you never attended a rock concert, did you ever attend a political rally in Munich? Did you ever join a lynch mob? Did you ever hang a minority? Did you ever say "we should bomb them all to the stone age"? Did you ever enjoy being "bad," convinced that something "wonderful" was occurring? Did you ever walk down Bourbon Street to look at all the strange people? If so, then you have experienced being possessed by, and identifying with, the Shadow.

Rock groups seek to activate and channel the youth's psychological need for separation, and to make a lot of money at the same time. (Your mother wanted you to enjoy the Beatles and the Bay City Rollers, adorable moppets despite what went on backstage, but Elvis and Pink Floyd were suspect.) Politicians seek to exploit fears and garner votes. (Who can forget Lyndon Johnson's ad showing a child counting the petals of a daisy? As she counts down, the scene dissolves into a nuclear cloud and one is warned against the militancy of Barry Goldwater. Who can forget an administration run as a continuing "campaign" by George W. Bush, which distracted the viewer from debacles in foreign adventures and domestic favoritism through repetition of the evocative mantra "terrorism"?)

When we are flooded with the Shadow we generally feel an enormous flush of energy. Little do we know that that energy is an aspect of our psyche that, activated, has the power to usurp the ego and carry us along with the tide. William Carlos Williams, a practicing physician and important imagist poet, wrote a story about how he once visited a sick child in a New Jersey tenement. She resisted his probing attempts to open her sore throat. Finally, exasperated, he seized her and forced open her secret scarlet throat. What began as a benign service quickly became a struggle wherein the power complex, which rests within each of us, rose with a fury. He exulted in his role as a healer, and yet later reflected with sadness on his brutalization of a scared and powerless child.

Was William Blake not right when he noted of John Milton's Christian apologia, *Paradise Lost*, that the only character with any energy, any attractive quality was Satan, and therefore "Milton was of the Devil's party, tho he knew it not." Was not

Milton energized by his approach to the Arch Fiend, and captivated by him in turn? His most compelling lines, stage center,
the cynosure of soulful energy, were given to the Dark Prince,
not the bleached heavenly hosts. Does not the Fiend sometimes possess each of us? My analyst in Zurich had a cartoon in
his restroom that depicted two persons walking toward a city
corner, about to collide. One was a priest grinning because he
was walking his little devil on a leash, and the other was a devil
grinning because he was walking his little priest on a leash.
They were brothers, though they knew it not.

How much evil, intended or not, has come from ordinary
citizens being carried along on the tide of such energies? What
we have denied in ourselves will nonetheless be visited upon
the world, sooner or later. To be possessed by the Shadow is to
bring large energy into the world. No wonder it is so often so
seductive. Sometimes we are left to pick up the pieces; other
times, others have to pick up the pieces for us. And none of us
are more dangerous than the righteous who uncritically believe
they are right, for they are the least capable of knowing the
harm they bring with them into this world. Was it not an
American major standing amid the rubble of the Vietnamese
village of Bien Tre who said, "We had to destroy this village in
order to save it." He saw no contradiction in values. Again, one
of the surest signs of being possessed by the Shadow is the
ready rationalizations we have to make them palatable to our
conscience.

IV. *Integration into Consciousness*

How shattering is it when we find the enemy who stares back
at us has our face? Who does not remember the words of the
cartoon character Pogo, who encapsulated the putatively noble
mission of Vietnam by inverting the saying of Admiral Perry,

"We have met the enemy, and he is us"? Who would not run from such an encounter?

After a lifetime of blaming others, it is exceedingly difficult for us to finally acknowledge that the only person who has consistently been in all the scenes of that long-running soap opera we call our life is us, and, as a necessary corollary, that we bear some large responsibility for how the drama is turning out. Who will not be embarrassed, humbled, even humiliated by such knowledge, which may be why we delay recognizing our Shadow as long as possible? As an old joke in Philadelphia has it, "the Quakers came to Pennsylvania to do good, and did very well indeed."

After all, who wants to devote the energy to watching one's dreams and noticing the corrections to the ego's governance that nightly occurs therein? Who wishes to find him or herself in a compromising position in a dream, the dramatization of what one shuns in conscious life? (Freud once said that people denied his theories by day and dreamt them at night). Who wants to concede that one's partner, or one's children, perhaps know aspects of us better than we know ourselves? Who wants the chickens of our choices to come home to roost in our yards, or in our children? But, as the ancients recognized, and as all history testifies, what we have ignored or kept unconscious is still playing out in our lives, and the lives of others. George Santayana's observation that what is not remembered of the past is doomed to be repeated is surely a truism we all must finally accept.

We protest that we mean well, and attest that we seek self-knowledge, but who can bear the full weight of seeing ourselves in this broadened spectrum of our humanity? Did not our brother Oedipus, having seen the truth, blind himself and ask for quick death? Yet . . . yet, in these moments of humbled vanity lie the seeds of healing, of greater consciousness, and of the redemption of history. In these moments of meeting our-selves in the mirror—seeing in that glass darkly the faint linea-ments of our fuller nature—we may claim a larger humanity, a widened consciousness, and, frankly, become somewhat less dangerous to those around us.

The Shadow, the vast sea within, can never wholly be plumbed. But certain chambers, certain enfilades, certain cur-rents may be opened to the mariner's conscious considerations. What I deny within will sooner or later arrive in my outer world. The more I am able to identify what works within, the less likely this material will need be played out in the outer world. As Jung presciently reminded us, what is denied in-wardly will likely come back to us in the guise of fate. Who could have imagined that "fate," which seems to lie so wholly outside of us, could have strands of origin reaching back into us? (How disturbing is it, for example, when one recog-nizes that one is playing out an old parent/child relational script in a marriage many decades later, and that one might have chosen that person precisely, albeit unconsciously, in or-der to relive that script? How pleasing is it to realize that we continuously sabotage our professed goals in service to an ar-chaic denial of our legitimate entitlement?)

Rendering the Shadow more conscious is always humbling, but it is also enlarging, for therein we begin to engage, to re-spect, and to come to terms with our fuller humanity. This enlargement of our humanity will frankly ask much more of ego consciousness than lies within its comfort zone, but it will help us grow up. Jung once observed that we all walk in shoes too small for us. Stepping into larger shoes is a continuing challenge, and a summons to growth. Sounds simple, sounds desirable—but how much it asks of us! As Jung further noted, our task is not in the end *goodness*—for the good we do may just as often arise from complexes or Shadow or have unintended consequences—but rather *wholeness.* Wholeness can never be approached without the embrace of the opposites. Indeed, the wholeness embodied in "the Self is made manifest in the opposites and in the conflict between them. . . . Hence the way to the Self begins with conflict."*

We carry this huge polarity within us. Some of us flee the tension, others rise to embrace it. As the good gray American poet Walt Whitman wrote, "I contradict myself? So, I contradict myself! I am infinite. I contain multitudes." And so we do. And that is what makes us interesting. Progressively knowing these split-off, buried, projected parts of ourselves, and owning them as ours, deepens the journey and gives us work for a lifetime. As problematic as this Shadow work may seem, it is the only way to experience personal psychological healing, as well as the healing of relationships with others. The work we do brings us not to a more satisfied ego, but to the ego's larger move toward wholeness. Shadow work that we may flee is nonetheless the path of healing, enlargement, and community reparation at the same time. The *tikkun olam,* or healing of the world, begins with ourselves, begins with what we do not wish to know about ourselves. Over time, this conscientious scrutiny ripples out from us to touch those around us. Owning our own Shadow furthers the reparation of the world.

*Jung, *CW 12*, para. 259.

Chapter Two

PAUL'S PERPLEXITY
"Though I Know the Good . . ."

"Though I know the good, I do not do the Good."
—LETTER TO THE ROMANS, ST. PAUL

"What is the main principle of Buddha's teachings?'
The Master replied, 'Do no evil, and perform what
is good.' Bai Juyi said, 'Even a three-year-old
knows that!' The Master responded, 'A three-
year-old may know it, but not even an eighty-
year-old can do it.' The poet bowed and left."
—RECORDED DIALOGUES OF DAOLIN

Though we believe we know the good, we do not do it. Why? A corollary question is: what is *the good*? How is it defined, and by whom? Often a function of context, perception, and normative moral codes, the good shifts and may be hard to discern. Sometimes the good produces unforeseen consequences that are not so good. But the perplexing issue here is that all of us frequently find ourselves experiencing contradictions between our intended values and our behaviors, a troubling discrepancy between expectations for ourselves and the consequences of our behaviors.

We have already seen that our Shadow lives often take over because of the anxiety aroused when confronting real issues directly. So we *avoid, repress, split off, project* onto others, and *rationalize*. These are our elemental, primitive defenses against what seems to threaten our insecure or immature ego. Growing as a moral and psychological being obliges each of us to learn more about our Shadow and take it on in a continuing effort of consciousness and courage. But is that all there is to it, more willfulness, more intentionality? Can the Shadow be *solved*, so to speak, if we intend enough, commit enough? What else might there be that lies in the way of such a felicitous fantasy; what persistently, obdurately opposes our best intents?

Though I know the good, or believe I do, I do not do the good. Why? Is this a moral flaw? An existential blemish? A weak, vacillating, dilatory will? Is it sin?* Paul utilizes the Greek word *akrasia*, which may be translated as moral incontinence, weakness of will, where one knows a thing is good, consciously desires that thing, and yet does not enact it. He uses it in a letter to advocate active marital sexuality, lest one partner be tempted to infidelity with another (1 Corinthians 7:5). In the second book of Timothy (3:3) the same word is used as a warning of last days when humankind will become "unloving, irreconcilable, malicious gossips, without *self-control*, brutal, haters of good." Clearly, for Paul, the discrepancy between intention and choice is a function of sin, which for him is a shortcoming in one's spiritual aspirations.

So why this persistent discrepancy, this gap between intention and outcome?

1. Is this discrepancy a wanton expression of our *narcissistic will*? While some have argued that such radical capacity to choose something other than the good is our deepest and finest freedom, why then would we suffer this freedom as a painful contradiction?

---

*It is useful to remember that the etymology of the Hebrew word *sin* derived from an archery term, meaning "to miss the mark." As such, it sounds a bit less judgmental, for who among us has sufficient keenness of eye, steadfastness of forearm, and totality of focus to always hit the center of the target?

2. Is it *hubris*, the frequent inflation of the ego to believe that it knows what is best, when in fact we never really know enough about the complex consequences of our choices? How often have each of us fallen into the delusion that we are truly conscious when we make major, long-considered decisions, when in fact we are in the grip of powers that are dictating choices to us? Or we rationalize, or dissimulate in the face of our instinct, or override our friend's warning against a particular relationship into which we have cast ourselves. Choices are made, and the piper paid in the end. They saw what we, apparently, could not see.

I recall sitting in the academic portion of a professional society listening to a thoughtful paper on the psychodynamics involved in boundary violations between therapist and client. The speaker concluded her talk by summarizing an expert on the subject who reasoned that when such violations occur, the miscreant is caught in a psychic "inflation," believing he or she knows what is going down, and generally has a very solid rationale for the transgression. Then we broke for lunch. After the break, the business session began with the reading of a letter from a sister professional society announcing that that same expert was being severely sanctioned for precisely the violation about which he had written, an erotic involvement with a patient. So much for the *hubris* of believing we know what we are doing. We sat in silence for a long while.

3. Is it "original sin?" The more literal among us have interpreted the metaphoric fall in Genesis as a primal event that stained the human condition for all time. Our suffering since is a penalty for such transgression of divine will. Others of less concretistic mind see the story as an archetypal metaphor that intimates a flaw in our nature, a proclivity to error from a less than perfect being. Still others see the fall as a necessary move from naiveté and infantility to consciousness and moral capacity. As such it is a *felix culpa*, or fortunate culpability, since it brings the gift of a more differentiated consciousness as a result of the transgression. No matter which way the metaphor of "the fall" or "original sin" is understood, an inherent capacity for capricious choice is our common condition.

Through the years the fundamentalist position is fiercely hortatory ("just say no") and judgmental, always haranguing the ego with the exhortation to more and more control. Plato, through his persona Socrates, stakes out a different position. He argues that none of us would consciously, willingly, do evil. If we do so, it is because we are ignorant of the good. There is a high premium placed on education here, especially in the area of ethics. Plato seems to deny the power of the willfully errant psyche. In *Notes from Underground*, Dostoevsky critiques this premise and concludes that Socrates is hopelessly naive and notes that history is replete with examples of multitudes who willingly, joyfully, pulled the roof down on their heads. "A man can wish upon himself . . . something harmful, stupid, and even completely idiotic. He will do so in order to establish his right to wish for the most idiotic things and not be obliged to have only sensible wishes."* It is hard to accept Dostoevsky's premise that it is precisely our innate perversity, that is, desire to thwart the moral engineering of others, that is our greatest virtue, because it keeps us from becoming programmed robots. But he may be right.

We also recall, long before Dostoevsky, what Miguel de Unamuno later called "the tragic sense of life," which acknowledged this yawning gap between intention and outcome. The classical imagination depicted an ongoing conflict between fate and destiny, with human character sandwiched in between. Fate produces the givens within which we must work, while destiny represents "the will of the gods," a challenge to the fullest incarnation of our possibilities. At the heart of this collision is the human sensibility, with its proclivity to inflation (*hubris*), and its tendency to privilege its biased, refracted vision (*hamartia*) and thereby succumbs to self-defeating choices. From this colli-

*Dostoevsky, *Notes from Underground*, p. 112.

sion of multiplicitous influences the vagaries of choice, and their troubling consequences, arise. As Oedipus summarized this paradox, "Apollo brought this fate upon me, but the hand that wounded me was mine own." So the classical tragic vision is saying to us once again that, despite our ego's certainty in any given moment, we *never* know enough to know that we do not know enough. Tumbling to this humbling is what the Greeks called the *anagnorisis*, or the "recognition." From this humbling of the ego, the great tragedians averred, only humility before the gods and cautious piety in the presence of choice prove necessary for the conduct of a conscious life.

Recall Plato's famous metaphor of the cave, in which humanity is depicted in chains, facing the interior wall. Seeing shadows dance by on that wall, we conclude that reality is what we see in that reflection. Plato affirmed that philosophy, with its careful reasoning, would prove the agency that might break those chains, liberate the prisoners, and turn them toward the light of reality. (Perhaps behavioral psychology and psychiatry have been handed this hope today. The antipsychotic Thorazine was named after Thor in the hopes that this medication might break the chains of madness.) Humanity's hope for liberation from ignorance continues, even as the Shadow insinuates itself into our hyperrational, hyper-superstitious age. Given that our capacity for self-delusion never wanes, and conflicts between intention and outcome multiply, we may still be shackled in Plato's cave.

We cannot, any longer, afford to disregard the power of the unconscious, nor its ubiquitous interruptions. Accordingly, we are obliged to approach the issue of the Shadow from the standpoint of depth psychology. *Depth psychology* is thus called because of its effort to respect and to work with the dynamic powers of the unconscious. Most psychologies today skim the surface, treating behaviors, reinforcing ego strategies, and/or medicating—sometimes to good effect. But the persistent problems of our lives remain intractable, for the problem of really becoming ourselves far transcends the modification of our daily pathologies. As the twelve-step groups have it, what we resist will persist. *The problem with the unconscious is that it is unconscious.* We do not know what it is, or how it is working. The willingness to track its manifestations in our biographical patterns and in our compensatory dream life is quite demanding, and most people will simply not make the effort. So the sub-rosa work of their unconscious Shadow continues, whether they pay attention or not.

THE PSYCHE AS A CONGERIES OF CENTERS

When we begin to look at the Shadow problem—why we do not do the good when we believe we know the good—we are forced to look within for the work of invisible forces. Contrary to the ego's fantasy of sovereignty, of sitting on the high throne of consciousness, we rather are continuously in the presence of discrete energies that have a life of their own and a historically driven agenda of which we have scant awareness. Depth psychology discovered that our psyche is composed of an infinite number of such discrete energies, some organized around a particular experience, forming a "complex," and others enacting an agenda to meet our needs or avoid presumed harm. Rather than regally rule behind an impregnable castle, the ego is daily invaded by these fractal energies, and daily our kingdom becomes an occupied nation. *We are not unitary; we are a multiplicity.* (Remember Walt Whitman's claim that he was infinite, that he contained multitudes, that he was a continuing contradiction. Remember Adam Smith in *The Wealth of Nations* describing how even managed economies were driven by "the invisible hand.")

The ego itself is one such "complex," a cluster of energy tied to a history that begins at birth and is added to daily. When someone calls your name, an entire history is summoned to attentiveness. At this moment, your ego is reading these same lines that my ego is writing. Our egos are in contact through the power of language and mental focus. The ego has many gifts to offer—consciousness, attention, focus, intentionality, and some consistency. Yet the many other powers and principalities that occupy our psychological totality are also present, and in any moment such autonomous powers may occupy the ego's throne. Perhaps my next word will trigger one of those lower powers and it will become a marauding brigand bringing new disorders to the kingdom of your consciousness.

All of us have had the experience of feeling a flush of energy, a somatic change, perhaps an accompanying behavior in the face of a stimulus, whether the stimulant was conscious or not. For example, being called upon to speak at a meeting will cause most folks a rush of anxiety. Why? Is the request so threatening? Seldom, if ever. But the fear of personal disclosure, the possibility of occasioning the displeasure of the other, the threat of humiliation, tracks back to primal experience: the insecurity of the child and its dependence on the good will of those around it. We are far removed from those dependent days, but the charged remnant remains with us as a ghostly occupant of our psychological household.

What we call the *Shadow*, then, is the sum of all those separate energies that operate unconsciously, and therefore autonomously, or that are an affront to what we consciously wish to think of ourselves. So the good that we would do is often tinged with the hidden agenda, the complicit collusion, the manipulative motive.

In the face of its fragility, the ego reflexively employs stratagems to defend its territory. Surely the most common, most protective strategy used to defend the ego is *denial*. We all have large areas of denial. If consciousness were to examine every cranny of our history, repeatedly stub its toe on the Shadow, it would grow even more sorely distressed. So, we say, what we don't know won't hurt us. But it does, and we all know that, too. Allied to denial is *avoidance*. All of us have vast areas of life that we finding troubling or threatening, so we steer as clear of such zones as possible. The biases of our typology, for example, lead us to privilege some areas of reality and avoid others. If I am an intuitive, for example, I will hate to balance the checkbook or do my own home repair. If I am a sensate type, I will tend to avoid speculative theory and wish my reality to be grounded only in observable detail. As such, I may work well with ordinary facts but miss the bigger picture. The Shadow presence of the so-called "inferior functions" will, sooner or later, rise to bite us in the rear.*

Perhaps next in line is *repression*, the reflexive submergence of unpleasant truth. While this is an unconscious, ego-protecting mechanism, forgetting what is threatening to us does not mean that it goes away, as we all learn when we have not paid our bills on time. Following closely is *suppression*, whereby I consciously push away that looming root canal lest I be undermined in attending the present moment. As we have seen earlier, the parts of my own unconscious life that I intuit to be problematic, I can also *project* onto others; therefore, I do not have to own that issue in my own life. Thus, as Jesus reportedly intuited, the splinter in my neighbor's eye conveniently appears larger than the log in my own.

All of these anxiety-management strategies might fall under the general rubric of *dissociative* mechanisms. More severe

---

*In the 1920s Jung developed a typology of introversion/extroversion, with the variable functions of thinking, feeling, sensation, and intuition. While we all have all functions, one dominates, and we tend to rely on its selective powers and avoid the troubling problems of the less developed functions.

forms of dissociation would include *amnesia, fugue states,* and even *multiple personality,** whereby the individual defends himself against painful contents by constructing an alternative reality and escaping there when necessary. (An example of a fugue state might be seen in the film *Agatha,* which speculates that the mysterious disappearance of the mystery writer Agatha Christie early in the last century, just after learning that her husband was going to leave her for another woman, was in fact a fugue state through which she separated from her troubled conscious identity for a more tolerable alternative. She reportedly wandered through rural England in an emotional fog for many days before she was identified and slowly returned to her senses. Many other cases of such non-volitional loss of conscious identity, without any physical trauma, have been reported through the years, nearly all in the face of some threatening emotional situation.)

Interestingly, Paul gets near this idea of dissociation, even that of an "alter," in the Letter to the Romans, Chapter 7, where he speculates: "For that which I am doing, I do not understand, for *I* am not practicing what I would like to do, but I am doing the very thing I hate . . . but if I am doing the very thing I do not wish, *I*† am no longer the one doing it, but sin which dwells in me." So *sin* becomes an "alter," a discrete center apart from the *I* as center. While Paul is of course not privy to the ideas of depth psychology, he is intuitively led to consider that there is an energy system separate from the willing I, the ostensible centrum of consciousness. Just as *Satan* derives from the Hebrew word for "adversary," and *devil* from the Latin for "casting over against," so the ancients were driven to

---

*Multiple Personality Disorder is today called Dissociative Identity Disorder. The splinter "identities" outside the ego state are called "alters."

†The italics are mine to show the separate senses of *I* in Paul's struggle with the *I* that I know, and the *I* that I do not know.

consider the multiplicity of the human soul and the presence of a shadowy "antagonist" within. Rather than such an antagonist being the work of a superordinate power—say, the Prince of Darkness—depth psychology avers that such oppositional energy *is* us, and we *are* it. As Milton's Satan confesses, "Which way I fly is Hell; myself am Hell."

Freud labeled this energy, which is so often separate from and subversive to the ego consciousness, the *Id*. His original German phrase was *Das Es*, or *The It*, namely, *nature naturing*. The ego was translated into English from *Das Ich*, or *The I*, and the *Super Ego* from *Das Ueber-Ich*, or that which stands *over I*. The original German made clearer the conflict between nature naturing, the normative proscriptions of culture, and a nervous consciousness running back and forth trying to keep both sides happy, inevitably producing a neurosis, namely, a painful split in one's service to these competing agendas.

Jung's contribution of the idea of the *complex*—a splinter personality, attached to a quantum of energy, a fragment of history, and including a micro-agenda—is most helpful. Martha Grant has humorously described her encounter with such fractious presences as "The Committee":

> *The rude one is only one of many*
> *who populate my inner committee,*
> *an unruly group of stubborn complexes*
> *who try to run my life.*
> *My vigilant effort to tame these insubordinates*
> *is ongoing, endless.*
> *I've wheedled and flattered*
> *and when that didn't work*
> *actually reasoned*
> *with the most recalcitrant members*
> *but it only makes them more determined.*

Besides, they have my number.
They've sat too often with my therapist,
wringing their collective hands in commiseration,
clucking sympathetically,
when all along they were gathering ammunition.
Now they are doling out assignments—
I can hear the papers shuffling—
and what's more,
calling in new recruits from the streets.*

We all have such an autonomous committee—and all the while we thought we were the CEOs of our personal enterprise.

The metaphor of *complexes* allows us to talk about this infinite divisibility of the psyche, with its multiplicitous agendas. On the collective level, as we will see, this idea of the Shadow and its cosmic penumbra raises for theism the problem of "theodicy," a problem successfully avoided by dualisms and polytheisms. The virtue of the latter is its frank recognition of the contradictions inherent to all forms of life. Life *is* inherently contradictory and conflictual, and any view that seeks to finesse these contraries is operating in bad faith. Polytheism "solved" this problem by honoring the complexities and contradictions of the cosmos through the multiplicitous activities of quite disparate gods. Their pantheon of plenipotentiary powers suffers no contradiction because all forms are honored. (We need to remember at all times, however, that these alleged contradictions and contraries in our view of the universe only arise from the ego's nervous preference for conformity. If all that is merely *is*, then there is no contradiction, and there would prove no need for unification under a single principle.)

In the Eastern theological tradition, the problem of evil, and the problem of contraries, is a delusion of the ego. It is the ego's imperial fantasies that are the root of the problem as it separates itself from the flow of life and seeks to colonize the cosmos. Overthrowing the delusions of the ego is the project of Buddhism and Hinduism. In the Western theological tradition, whether Christian, Jewish, or Muslim, the Other is pathologized as the Evil One who tempts us to "sin." So profound is this temptation, infiltrating even our "good works" with Shadow agendas, that we are "saved" only by grace, or the beneficence of the deity. (The monk Martin Luther struggled with this dilemma, knowing that even in his best moments, he was not exempt from narcissistic agendas; accordingly, he concluded, one was "justified by faith," not by the accumulation of ethically contaminated "good works.") Grace, as Paul Tillich once defined it, is accepting the fact that in the end we are accepted, despite being unacceptable.

Fundamentalism in all its forms merely compounds this problem by haranguing the ego for more and more control. ("Just say 'no.'") If this ego reification really worked, we would not see so many televangelists falling from grace, or so many clerical scandals, nor would we see the genuine turmoil of so many souls trivialized by simple moralizing and gratuitous public posturing. Haranguing the ego will prove of little staying value, no matter how resolute the ego. Such a strategy only drives the Shadow deeper and energizes it more. Remember how the Patristic theologian Origen castrated himself to purge himself of unwanted thoughts? Shortly thereafter, he thought of dancing girls. At least when Augustine prayed for chastity, he also asked his God to not move too quickly on his petition. "O God, make me chaste, but not just yet." At least Augustine valued the Shadow as a part of himself, rather than think that he could surgically remove temptation and the inclinations of nature.

THE CONVERGENCE OF RELIGION
AND PSYCHOLOGY

So where are we left, then? Sanity on this issue requires that we adopt a different ego attitude, that we begin a dialogue with these discrete parts of ourselves. This is a dialogue—what Jung called an *Auseinandersetzung*, or setting one thing over against another—and a sorting through, which will need to last a lifetime. Sanity, heightened consciousness, is conversation with, mediation among, these separate energies. Will we ever get it finished? Will we ever be able to do the good as we see it on a reliable, consistent basis? Can we solve Paul's problem? Of course not. We have to relinquish that inflated fantasy, for it will only delude the ego further. Rather, the ego is called to continuous dialogue, to self-examination, to reconsiderations, to the necessary humility of the Roman poet Terence, that "nothing human is alien to me." Then we are conscious for the moment.

Acknowledging the magnitude of this project inevitably brings us back not only to the psychological task but to the religious, as well. Central to religious insight, to religious experience, and to psychological awareness is the conscious recognition and acknowledgement of one's limits, to know that we do not know. From this insight comes less diminishment than a radical reframing of the ego. We are awed by the immensity of the mystery of the cosmos, and the unfathomable mystery of our own souls. Awe is the benchmark of religious experience and psychological insight. (Think of Job as the prototype of the humbled consciousness.) Only humbled consciousness, with pride's penance, will prove psychologically and spiritually enlarging.

Going back to that professional conference, when a colleague and "expert" was exposed as having a sexual relationship with a patient, is to confess that in his fall we were all implicated. Some were quick to judge him, excoriate his lapse, denigrate his worth, but it was my thought that we all should return to our rooms, reflect humbly on the infinitely tangled skein of human nature, on how all of us skate on such terribly thin ice, and that we all so frequently fall into the holes of what we do not know or remember, out of our *hubris*, our complexity, and our own divided souls.

And that is why, though we know the good, or believe we do, we do not do the good. As an old Eastern European story has it, a village took pity on an elderly pensioner and, to give him a reason to live, appointed him to serve as sentinel at the entrance to the *shtetl* and wait for the arrival of the Messiah. After many harsh seasons at his solitary post, he returned to the council and expressed a certain frustration over this project, whereupon he was told, "But consider, it's steady work!" So, our ongoing effort to know the right thing, *if* it exists, and to do the right thing, *if* we can, is steady work: Shadow work.

Chapter Three

RUNNING INTO OURSELVES
The Personal Shadow

> *"The process of coming to terms with the Other*
> *in us is well worth while, because in this way*
> *we get to know aspects of our nature which*
> *we would not allow anybody else to show us*
> *and which we ourselves would never have*
> *admitted."*
> —C. G. JUNG, *CW* 14, PARA. 706

> *"The sons shaped their feet*
> *with the shoes of their fathers.*
> *To the plight of their mothers,*
> *the daughters surrendered their dreams."*
> —"THE RIVER," LARRY D. THOMAS

Reportedly, I was once an exhibitionist. Between birth and age twelve, we lived about one block from a tractor factory, Allis-Chalmers. At noon, when the secretaries passed by our house, en route to lunch at a local diner, I reportedly would remove my clothing and dance and sing to them. My mother would hear their laughter and run out in huge embarrassment and rush me from the porch. Not only was she embarrassed at my nudity, she was even more embarrassed at my calling attention to myself, to us, to her. Soon I became a virtually pathological introvert as I learned not to call any attention to myself. Not only the body, not only singing, but merely calling attention to oneself was clearly out of bounds.

I understand now that my mother's life traumas had admonished her to avoid being seen, avoid attracting the attention of another. Nonetheless, my mother's issues around these matters soon became my personal Shadow. In short time, I learned to repeatedly, reflexively sabotage my potential, derogate my yearnings, and "hide out." In this case, the Shadow was not about nudity, or public expression, but merely being seen, and therefore vulnerable to the opinion of others. A substantial part of my youthful Shadow was accumulated through learning not to be me at all—expressing the natural exuberance of the child was simply too costly in that setting. For a child, at least that child, the necessity of acceptance by the parent prevails over any instinctual desire to express oneself spontaneously. This kind of event, with its message, was repeated many times. At age five, I came home from kindergarten singing a song I learned on the playground: "I lost my arm in the army / lost my leg in the navy / lost my balls in Niagara Falls / and found them in the gravy." I liked the song because it was catchy, and it rhymed. Mind you, I did not know what "balls" were then, but I soon found out, and . . . another brick in the wall, to use the phrase of Pink Floyd. (Decades later, with the publication of the first book, the direct response to me was: "Why did you do that? What will people say?" Though I was fully in adulthood by then, so to speak, that message whistled home to a very old place in me.) From these, and many similar messages, I grew armored against myself. My Shadow was not evil; it was the defense against being myself, my own—apparently risky, apparently too costly—self.

Recall that the Shadow embraces *all that we do not wish to be*.

Accordingly, it is exceedingly difficult for us to acknowledge, work with, and own our Shadow material. The weaker one's ego, the less likely one is to do this work, and therefore the Shadow energies are pathologized by going underground. Being repressed, they can only bubble up in some unexpected moment or venue, through projection onto others, or by subtly taking possession of us and playing out in embarrassing or destructive ways. Each of us will have humbling recollections of being seized by our Shadow—if we reflect at all on our lives— though at the moment we thought ourselves self-possessed, in control. (I once was brought up very short by the admiring stupidity of a college sophomore student of mine who said to me, "I want to be like you . . . to have no feelings." He meant that as a compliment. At that point I really began to realize just how well I had assimilated the admonition to hide myself.)

Moreover, who among us can fully know what constitutes Shadow material in any objective, identifiable way? When we reflect that what is acceptable and what is forbidden varies from age to age, culture to culture, tribe to tribe, family to family, we acknowledge the relativity of the Shadow issue in the first place. When I lived in Switzerland, I was told by a Swiss friend that a Bavarian acting as a Bavarian in Sankt Gallen, would be considered mad. (The distance between Munich and Sankt Gallen is rather short, and only an invisible line on the map separates their borders.) What he was referring to is that a stereotypical *extroverted sensate* type (a Bavarian) would, upon entering an *introverted sensate* type (Swiss) culture, be considered so eccentric, so outside the collective norm as to be considered mad! Narrowly separated by geography, one culture produces machinery and beer, and once supported Hitler enthusiastically, and another specializes in pharmaceuticals, banking, and precision watches, and considered Hitler bourgeois and *therefore* dangerous. Today, as sensate cultures, both have trains that run on time, truly on time, and yet each considers the other with a certain bemusement and no little condescension. So much for an objective definition of the Shadow!

So what is this Shadow, when looked at on a personal level? Perhaps the best way to see the Shadow at work is in the lives of unique individuals like you and me.

THE WOUNDING OF EROS

Edward was a television anchorman. On screen he was polished, cool, articulate. He had the highest ratings in his community, with the lion's market share always accruing to his channel when the sweeps were finished. Throughout his life he had acted with propriety, decorum, and a genuine regard for the feelings of others. No wonder that he was the first choice of nonprofits to emcee at their annual benefits and to introduce the guest of honor—when he was not himself the honoree. What no one knew was that within and behind this cool facade a seething torment consumed his life. Edward came into therapy unwillingly, as men often do. His wife had insisted, or she was out the door, despite her strong religious convictions against divorce.

His wife sent Edward to therapy not because he was a bad person but because he was compulsively "too good." She was tired of the incessant phone calls. When the phone rang, she flinched: "Here it goes again." When Edward drove to the station, or came home from hosting another benefit on the rubber-chicken circuit, he found it necessary to phone his wife. What he felt compelled to tell her was that he had just seen a pretty girl on the street, and had had a fantasy of being with her, or that, minus an outer stimulus, he had to confess his compulsive masturbation. At first, shortly after they were married, his wife, Emily, found these phone calls almost charming: that he trusted her so much, that his fidelity to her was so clear; then she found them amusing; and then compulsive, interruptive, and finally obnoxious. They had to stop. Her next thought was that she was married to some kind of sex addict and that sooner or later he would act out and bring disgrace upon them all. These days, with the advent of Internet porn, their story is not so uncommon, but when Edward and Emily came to see me, almost three decades ago, they found themselves in a strange and threatening world, quite different from the conventional religiosity in which each had been raised.

This story is the story of two persons, one "disturbed," and one apparently perfectly "normal"—whatever "disturbed" is, and whatever "normal" is. Edward was the child of a very domineering mother and a passive, mostly compliant father. His earliest messages were that the body, strong emotion, and above all, sexuality, were, if not bad, clearly dangerous and forbidden territory. Throughout his youth he was the epitome of his mother's dreams: an A student, altar boy, and idealized by all. His childhood was untroubled, and he remembered it as an idyllic time when he felt loved, secure, and clear about life. When, however, puberty arrived, his life was thrown into chaos. The anarchy of the body, the tenebrous tumult of hormone-driven emotion, the widening circle of moral choices—all led him to confusion, dismay, and near panic.

To treat this psychological malady, otherwise known as adolescence, Edward took himself to his priest, who calmly but firmly reinforced his mother's values: masturbation is a sin, impure thoughts are dangerous, and the turbulence of the body is to be contained at all costs. This double message, from the two authorities in his life—mother, and father-priest, (with the personal father emotionally missing as a compensatory energy), created a yawning split within him. No one had ever raised the possibility with him that the God who created his body—with its desires, its pleasures, and its insistence—deserved at least as much respect as the admonitions of his elders.

For several years Edward believed that he was destined to become a priest. He felt a calling to serve God, to cement the approbation of his community, and most of all to feel the family's acceptance so necessary to him. So he went to college, majored in religion, entered the seminary and took vows. However, the archaic gods of the body, and the polymorphous agendas of the psyche, thrust him into such impossible conflict that he managed to get himself expelled. This blow to his ego, and to his shaming before the family, drove Edward to compensate by entering the public arena and soliciting a ready acclaim from others, which had been his mother's milk for so long.*

Despite learning to gain the approval of others by his smooth, even unctuous persona, Edward was haunted by the old devils. His erotic imagination lay outside the controls of a regulated ego. When he finally married Emily, he found their sexual life initially exciting but shortly after marriage, his eros shut down. For reasons to be explained later, Emily was more or less all right with this disconnection, for she knew that they were living the good life, a life much approved and much desired. Thus, on his way to work, seeing a girl on the street, Edward felt the need to phone Emily and tell her his fantasy. The shapely colleague who broadcast the weather invariably provoked at least two phone calls to Emily, even while the news-

---

*Can we not already see that this seemingly *free* choice of profession is itself driven by Shadow issues? What really drove the priest who counseled him, or his mother's unlived life, or the father failing to compensate for her invasive presence in the life of their child? Was not their Shadow instructive in the formation of his?

cast went on. Mostly these calls were before or after the show, but Emily knew that a line was crossed when Edward once called her while the show was live. She could hear the sound of the commercials from both her TV and from her phone.

What Edward had found when he went to the seminary was that he could not quell his active nature, which he presumed piety, or a devotion to a saintly paradigm, would achieve. He could not compel his own nature into quiescence. The more he tried, the worse it got, and the more he felt guilt, shame, and failure. Sit in any private place and try not to imagine some thought, and notice how persistent and ineluctable that thought will be.

When he finally left his mother's home and entered the seminary, thinking that he was a free, conscious adult, Edward predictably carried this deep Shadow split with him. What he experienced in the seminary* was not a compensatory healing of his split but the company of mother-driven men who were so intimidated by the feminine as to seek to banish its presence altogether by physical separation, celibacy, and by placing the feminine on an impossible celestial plateau as an eternal virgin.

When his insistent nature drove him from the seminary, Edward married Emily, believing once again that the problem would be resolved forever. Prey to what Jung would have called a deep "anima split," Edward suffered great torment. (The *anima*, which is the Latin word for *soul*, was Jung's term for the so-called "inner feminine" that lies at the affective core of every male, although the weight of history and the weight of cultural conditioning frequently separate this energy from his conscious life.†) The anima is the carrier of the male's relational capacity—

---

*The word *seminary* derives, ironically, from *semen*, as does *seminar*, and *inseminate*, and *seminal*, and bespeaks a preserve of male generative energy.

†I treat this subject at length in a book on male psychology called *Under Saturn's Shadow: the Wounding and Healing of Men.*

his relationship to the body, to instinct, to feeling life, to spirit, and finally to the outer woman. Whatever anima energies are not available to consciousness will invariably suffer repression, be siphoned off into the anarchic venues of the body, or go outward through projection or compulsive behaviors. The anima split that most men carry no doubt occasions their higher rate of suicide, alcoholism, and much earlier death than women, but the greatest wound of all is their estrangement from themselves, and from each other. Until men can open to this inner life, their paths will be troubled, and their concourse with other men, and their dialectic with women, will remain tormented.

While Edward would never have been diagnosed as "depressed," to have a vital aspect of one's nature oppressed will invariably prove a depressive weight on the spirit. But his anima, with its inspirited energy, escaped even his repressive history and entered the world as fantasy. To his horror, he fantasized about women, or utilized pornography, where the connection with "the feminine" was seemingly available, inviting, and without the complexities that intimacy requires.* At the same time, that exuberant energy, that eros life force, immediately ran into the stone wall of mother and church. With deliberate hyperbole, William Blake once wrote that it is "better to murder an infant sleeping in its cradle than nurse unacted desires." What this visionary, a century before Freud, meant was that the sustained deflection of eros will sooner or later pathologize in destructive ways. It is better, then, to find a way to honor that energy than to have it enter the world in a distorted form.

---

*Edward is not alone in his attraction to pornography. Only during the height of the 9/11 crisis, when people were seeking immediate news, did hits on the Internet exceed the daily traffic in commercial pornography. At the end of 2005, it was reported that worldwide there were more than 4.2 million sexually explicit websites with more than 372 million pages.

Edward's incessant phone calls to his wife not only violated her emotional integrity through constant interruptions, but unwittingly converted her into a surrogate mother and priest at the same time. Edward was tacitly aware that his behavior would inevitably produce the condemnation that he had grown to expect of himself. He could never escape being a bad boy by trying to be only a good boy. What is so sad about Edward was that throughout his whole life he never felt free to be whomever he was, to feel what he felt, to desire what he desired, and to pursue what his nature intended. Anytime that this natural agenda rose within him, he was obliged to pay for it with guilt—which is to say, anxiety and massive self-recrimination.

Finally, Edward began to gain some insight into the mechanisms of his dilemma. He understood the power of his mother experience, unmediated by a balancing, empowering father figure and further reinforced by the truncated, mother-ridden priest of his childhood. To facilitate his own therapy he invited Emily to join him for a number of sessions. Ironically, she came to the first session with a dream of her own. In the dream she observed that a spider had crawled off the arm of a female whom she had distantly known in earlier years and climbed across and onto her arm. It was a simple dream, without words, but puzzling and a little frightening to her. Her association with this other girl, long past, was that she was a little risqué, perhaps "loose," by the standards of that time, and so different from her as to cause Emily to avoid her during her high school days.

So we have a second person in this pas de deux, called marriage, that has a Shadow issue. Edward and Emily were drawn together in the first place because they mirrored each other. Generally speaking, people are drawn toward intimate relationships either because they are opposites who will compensate each other, or because they are complementary, which means that not only their conscious likes and dislikes line up, but their complexes as well. Edward and Emily found each other because they were both walled off from their eros. Edward had the need to put Emily on the pedestal because he suffered from a variant of the virgin/whore complex, an intrapsychic imago that separates and elevates "the feminine" into its celestial adoration, or delimits her through only her carnal form. This is the deep wedge that mother and priest managed to drive into the soul of this child.

Emily, on the other hand, had a similar history and cultural influence, and so had a strong need to be on that pedestal. When questioned further about this spider she could only associate it with darkness, death, and the dirty slough of bodily things. What came across to the therapist when speaking with these two thirtysomething people was how young they felt, how clean, nice, and unreal their goodness. What the therapist experienced in them was the crippling of eros: for Edward the evisceration of his anima energy by the mother complex, and for Emily the constriction of her animus* energy by the weight of the proscriptive god-image to which she had been exposed. Their Christ, and his elevated Mother, were lacking in body, in sexuality, in earthy virtues, and their worship could only deny the same richly fecund values within them. Sadly, rather than worshiping the complex and comprehensive energies of divinity, seen more commonly in Eastern religions, they were inculcated into a pathologized, enervated *imago Dei* in service to

---

*The *animus* is Jung's term for the woman's "inner masculine" energy. It is associated with her personal sense of *empowerment*, not power over others, but the right to own and live her natural being in the world. The negative animus is disempowering, critical, and denigrating, but the positive animus transforms her inner life into outerworld choices.

the neurotic split between mind and body of the founding theologians.*

The splitting of eros and natural life by cultural imposition is itself a major study, for I know of no one in the modern world who does not share some aspect of this wounding of their nature. How can one not carry such splits, for do we not all internalize cultural complexes that override our natural truths, in order to ease our way in the world and gain the necessary support and approval of the family and communal consensus? Thus the Shadow is born, wounded eros goes underground, and too often breeds monsters like rape, pornography, sexual abuse of minors, and guilt-ridden acts that are at origin as much a part of one's nature as eating and sleeping.

I would like to report that both Edward and Emily worked their way through these issues, that they acquired enough insight into the power of their disabling histories, and gained enough purchase on the possibilities of adult choice, that they freed themselves and their marriage from this bondage to the past. Sadly, conjointly, they decided to quit therapy and work on this matter with their priest. I do hope they were able to break through with his help, but I suspect that each of them saw, truly saw, the immensity of the task before them and fled its summons.

For every story of a therapeutic breakthrough, there are at least as many stories of the resistant, recalcitrant, ineluctable power of core complexes, and of our subsequent flight from the rigor of growing up, preferring instead the familiar sloth of the same old, same old. Growing up means not only dialogu-

*A lecturer in Zurich once said that Christianity could only recover its claim on the modern by developing "a sacrament of sexuality," making sacred that which is central to us all.

ing with and confronting the messages that we carry within, admonitions that would deny us our destiny, but it requires risking being oneself in this world, without guarantee, without consensual approval, and without hope of restoring the old innocence. This risk, this venture, this growing up is, sadly, rare indeed. And so Shadow material grows, replicates itself, and we wander in darkness.

The story of Edward and Emily is of course repeated through a million variations in our culture, for such a primal energy as sexuality, with so much potential for good or for harm, with such a mixture of messages that shape and direct it, cannot help but provide much Shadow possibility. Sexuality is a constant theme and subtheme throughout popular culture: music, film, television. Most sitcoms flirt with sexual themes most of the time, not to mention the soaps. Yes, eros is an archetypal energy, and therefore a fundament of our being, but is it possible that something like sex is *too* important to us? And if it is too important, why is that the case?

Sexuality forbidden, or constrained, is a tempting fruit, to be sure, but I am further persuaded that sex (and its accompanying fantasy of romantic love) is now carrying the burden of much of our lost spirituality. When traditional images, or their contemporary surrogates, cannot link one to a sense of transcendent purpose, to some spiritual locus in this centrifugal cosmos, then we will look to other forms of "connection." Later I will mention the permutations of eros we call *paraphilias*, but for now, let us acknowledge that our preoccupation with sex is putting an awesome amount of spiritual traffic across one bridge. Perhaps we over-esteem that bridge because we feel it is one of the very few. So sexuality is a prime energy field for Shadow expression—including child abuse, rape, pornography, incest, and a general cultural preoccupation—

precisely because it *is* important. It is a primal form of connection, after all—our lives begin with separation, and we experience our lives as progressively separated, and so often lonely. Reconnecting with the other, whether it is divinity, a guiding idea, or a warm body, is a powerful urge. But it becomes especially compelling, even obsessive, when so few other modalities help one connect.

I do not wish in any way to come across as moralistic in these remarks. I am not judgmental of any of these permutations of eros, except for those where someone is victimized. For example, the sad story of men who sit in strip bars has nearly broken my heart. They are in a redundant hell, for their search for connection narrows into such a constrained repetition, with so little sustaining satisfaction from superficial, commercialized connection. (It is for this reason that sexuality so easily becomes addictive.) Theirs is not a failure of morality; it is a failure of imagination. It is Shadow material not for moralistic reasons, but because it is an unconscious defense against the open grieving of their souls. The Shadow is not sex; but its excessive importance represents a failed treatment plan for the soul's desire for healing, for connection, for meaning.

A VISIT TO MARS

In addition to sexuality, anger is another common Shadow issue. No doubt anger and sexuality are especially charged because each is potentially anarchic, each has enormous autonomous power, each threatens ego control, and each has the potential to overthrow any group's ruling attitudes and practices. Wrath is, after all, one of the so-called seven deadly sins. Surely anger can be destructive, be it found in domestic abuse, warfare, or the sullen, cold rage that throbs just beneath the surface of so much of modern life.

As I child, I, and I am sure most readers, was told not to be angry. On one occasion, after another child had hit me and run away, I stood shaking with impotent rage. My mother, seeing me thus, redirected her garden hose onto me, saying, "Here . . . this will cool you off." In addition to feeling even angrier, feeling violated, albeit powerless, I got a clear message— that I was not entitled to the feelings I had, or that having had them, there was something wrong with me. This is one example of the birth of neurosis, one of the many chambers of that very large mansion in which we reside—a naturally occurring feeling state is opposed by a powerful prohibition. (In giving these personal examples, I am not picking on my mother, who loved me in the best way she could, with the best lights available to her,* but as an example of what each of us has to do— namely, to reconstruct the etiology and the elements of our Shadow lives, those naturally occurring instincts that suffer constraint, prohibition).

Freud saw symptom formation, be it a dream image or a somatic disturbance, as the psyche's effort to escape such prohibition by eluding the repressive attitudes and finding a symbolic expression. I never saw this more clearly than the time I tossed a pen to a client who was just leaving, having described her deep hatred of her domineering parent. She had been complaining of a synesthesia of her arm, not fully paralyzed, but tingly and awkward. She caught the pen with her dominant arm and when I asked what her expression meant, she stabbed it downward, as though to knife that parent. In that moment, the somatic interference was relieved and her secret wish expressed. The synesthesia was a symbolic numbing of the power

---

*The measure of "love" at that time was: "Would you lie on the tracks in front of a locomotive for this person?" She would, without hesitation, for me, as I would have for her . . . I think.

of her animosity toward her very controlling and devouring parent. In that reflexive moment, the secret wish leaked out, and the neurosis lifted, though only for a while. Then one is left with the task of what to do with the troubling thought that one has homicidal fantasies. But if they are not rendered conscious, where else might they show up in one's life?

When we recall that the etymological root of the words *anger, anxiety, angst*, and *angina* come from the Indo-Germanic root word *argh*, which means "to constrict," then we realize how natural and normal anger is, how naturally the sensitive organism we are reacts to threats toward its well-being. Yes, every family and every culture has a vested interest in containing the destructive powers of anger, but it is neurosis that forms when anger is inordinately suppressed. Two centuries ago William Blake wrote a poem titled, "A Poison Tree," in which he noted how anger expressed aloud might lead to conflict, but also to possible redress and resolution; but anger deflected inward could only produce poison fruit from a contaminated tree— from which relationship itself would be slain. Accordingly, as constriction is injurious to the organic self, so anger is a natural, epiphenomenal response to this threat to its well-being. Not to have this reflexive arousal of sensibility that anger embodies would leave the person in jeopardy. So we have anger, anxiety, angst, and angina, the constriction of the heart, as by-products of threat, real or perceived, but in themselves natural reactions of an instinctually protective organism.

While we do have the cultural acceptance of righteous anger, or even an angry God, anger is generally seen as an unwelcome presence in our midst, however natural it may be. Although each person, and each society, is charged with how anger is to be appropriately channeled, the denial of anger, or its continuous repression, is a deep source of our psychopathology and

will invariably seek its expression in a less healthful fashion.*
We know that one of the fruits of "anger turned inward" is
depression, that anger tends to leak out into our unwitting
behaviors—how we drive, how we tolerate frustration—that
unexpressed anger will affect the body, at the least with high
blood pressure, and that some fragmentary evidence suggests
that a person who has difficulty acknowledging anger can be
more cancer-prone.

An interesting illustration of this Shadow dance with anger
appeared three decades ago in Switzerland in the form of an
autobiographical book titled *Mars*, named after the Roman
god of anger. The author was a young man who discovered
that he was dying of an aggressive cancer. He signed his book
with the pseudonym Fritz Zorn (*zorn* is the German word for
rage). Zorn quite understandably was enraged by the approaching terminus to his unlived, truncated life. He reached the conclusion that he had spent his life as a proper Swiss bourgeois,
denying the power of his emotions, and that this bottled emotion had turned back upon him in the form of an aggressive re-
venge by his psyche. In other words, his unattended emotional
life, he concluded, was now embodied in a malignant payback,
an unconstrained multiplication of life expression in the form
of raging cells.

Zorn further concluded that he had one chance to live—to
release this large Shadow energy in a storm of anger toward
the repressive, superego–driven Swiss culture, and toward his
socially prominent family in particular. If he could express every
cell of anger, he hoped he might burn out the malignant, car-
cinomic invader that was undeterred by radiation and chemo-

---

*For a further discussion of anger, please see my book *Swamplands of the Soul: New
Life in Dismal Places*.

therapy. *Mars* became a best seller, not only because its author's plight was touching, but because his Shadow dilemma was shared by so many. He raced to finish the book and save his life. One day before he died he was told that the book was going to be published. The tale of his heroic attempt to save his life by expressing his Shadow fully remains cautionary to each of us, a reminder of the fact that the energies of the Shadow do not go away—they always go somewhere.*

Understandably, sexuality and anger are so easily identified as Shadow concerns because all societies have feared their power and exercised powerful prohibitive measures, ranging from punitive laws to invading the mind of the individual through controlling guilt complexes. One patient I once had even expressed satisfaction that he suffered a debilitating physical illness, which he took to be penitentiary compensation for his having had an extramarital affair. The cost to the human spirit by guilt complexes inculcated by parents, communities, and religious authorities cannot be overemphasized, and has soured the putative sweetness of many, many lives.

THE COST OF NECESSARY ADAPTATIONS

But there are many other energies, many issues, many venues in our experience of the personal Shadow. In *Finding Meaning in the Second Half of Life,* I noted that the necessary adaptations of childhood produce governing complexes—that is, affect-laden "ideas" that take on a life of their own and subject the adult to their continuous influence. It is our unwitting service to these historically charged clusters of energy that creates

---

*Interestingly, the real name of Fritz Zorn was Fritz Angst. He died in 1976 at thirty-two, and *Mars* was published in 1977.

our redundancies—when we think we are choosing freely in any given moment—and, because they are adaptive responses to external demands, often lead to our progressive self-estrangement. *How many of us, arriving at midlife* or later, having done all the "right" things, having served the expectations of our family and our tribe, *feel so little at home in our lives? All of that unlived life is now part of the personal Shadow—* that which one learned to keep at bay since its expression might prove costly to one's necessary adaptations. This is why the cliché that we become our own worst enemies is a cliché—it is so repeatedly true.

Adaptation to the conditions of life requires the development of a *persona*, the mask we wear in any given social situation. Sometimes we even believe who we really are is contained, or defined, by these persona roles. But the greater the identification with the persona, the greater that the restive dialectic with the Shadow grows. The Shadow—in this case, the unlived life—goes underground and seeks expression through invasions of affect: a depression, for example, a precipitous action soon regretted, troubling dreams, a physical ailment or psychic enervation. In addition, the obligatory adaptations of the first half of life require a progressive diminishment of *personal authority* to the point that we often cease to know who we are, apart from our roles and our history, lose contact with what we desire, and become strangers to ourselves. The critical summons of the second half of life is to recover a personal sense of authority, explore, thoughtfully express the personal Shadow, and risk living faithfully with the soul's agenda. No easy task, but this is why personal Shadow work is so critical.

In addition, Jung's development of personality typology, introversion/extroversion, with the variable functions of thinking, feeling, intuition, and sensation, also constitute Shadow issues in the second half of life. We tend to cruise on our most readily adapted typology—say, an introverted intuitive thinking type, or, stereotypically in America, an extroverted sensate feeling type. Accordingly, we privilege some aspects of life, embrace some tasks, shun other aspects of life, and avoid certain tasks as much as possible. These areas of neglect, and these issues of personal avoidance, will always rebound and show up in our lives as troubling presences, embarrassments, and self-sabotaging patterns. Such typological adaptations and identifications produce imbalances in the personality. Both outer reality, neglected or devalued, and inner reality, neglected or devalued, will exact their due. Whether outer or inner, what we resist will persist and demand an accounting sooner or later.

Paradoxically, our ability to see something of the Shadow within ourselves sharpens our capacity to recognize shadowy actions around us. If we are unable to discern the con artist in ourselves, or the thief, or the bully, how would we be able to recognize this behavior in others? If we are lacking an awareness of those capacities within us, we are more likely to be betrayed by our naiveté. Even the analysis of our humor will reveal hidden motives that, while repressed by the conscious ego ideal, nonetheless are aspects of our complex humanity wishing to see the light of day. How many jokes have a sharp edge to them, perhaps a racist cast, or an aggressive motive? And if we are confronted by another for our aggressiveness, how many times have we protested that we were just joking?

Thus we see again that the Shadow is not synonymous with evil. The personal Shadow is common to all of us in some areas—such as sexuality and anger—but quite unique in other areas, for the vagaries of our history oblige us to leave substantive parts of ourselves behind, remaining unconscious, or studiously avoided. Since these invisible components are autonomous energies, they are forever active in our lives, in our families, in our intimacies, in our dealings with others, and in our own un-lived life.

Jung once observed that the greatest burden the child must bear is the unlived life of the parent. Internalizing the parental exemplum, the child will also stop short of fullness, or will be driven to overcompensate and live on behalf of the parent, or seek some unconscious treatment plan for this insult to wholeness—be it an addiction, a life of continuous diversion, or a preoccupation with the problem—never grasping that such compulsion derives from the received, unaddressed agenda of another. How many of our lives are thus driven to repetition, overcompensation, or unconscious treatments of someone else's personal Shadow? Jung gave the example of a domineer-ing father whose tyrannical rectitude drove his son to drugs and his daughter to moral dissolution, although all three of them were ignorant of how the children were driven to live re-actively to the unlived life of their father.

We cannot for a moment say that the Shadow of others does not affect us, nor can we ever really argue that our Shadow does not roll onto those around us. Thus, our summons to bring the Shadow to greater consciousness is an ethical service to others, as well as an opening to a larger life ourselves.

The paradox that each of us must face is that to really grow up, to really leave home, one needs to separate from the parental imagoes and to begin to own some portions of one's own rich Shadow. The image of Jesus portrayed in so many Sunday schools is that of the shadowless milquetoast, not the man who said to his mother when she showed up at the mar-riage ceremony in Cana, "Woman, what have you to do with me?" Nor the man who, in a fit of rage, threw the money-lenders out of the temple. Or, even more directly, inviting others along the path of individuation, proclaimed that "Who is with Mother and Father, is not with me." These are not ambiguous words. They are words that say that we have an accountability to something higher than our history, our replicative complexes, even our deepest loyalties! Such talk is revolutionary and inflammatory to this day—and psychologically necessary.

Chapter Four

PATHOS
Shadow Invasions in Everyday Life

"Man, being both free and bound, both limited and limitless, is anxious. Anxiety is the inevitable concomitant of the paradox of freedom and finiteness in which man is involved."
—REINHOLD NIEBUHR

"Three passions, simple but overwhelmingly strong, have governed my life: the longing for love, the search for knowledge, and unbearable pity for the suffering of mankind."
—BERTRAND RUSSELL, OPENING CREDO
OF *AUTOBIOGRAPHY*

A fifty-year-old man drinks himself to sleep every night, indulges in compulsive masturbation, but outwardly leads the life of a frugal, abstemious accountant. His soul is dying by day, and desperately seeks connection with the life force by night. He knows that anesthetizing his pain in ethyl alcohol and fantasy pushes him further and further from himself, and of that he is sorely afraid. His outwardly affable demeanor belies the fact that he is drowning in despair. That he cannot share his desperate yearning to live more fully with his wife is partly his fault, if fault be assigned, and partly that of his wife. His wife spends her soul's energy in obsessing on her adult children and keeping up with the neighbors. She stopped growing as a person, and as a partner, years ago. Her overidentification with these roles allows her to avoid their relationship, avoid engaging social issues, avoid developing a mature spirituality. Both are socially prominent, both generous contributors to the common good of their society, yet each, in a world of abundance, is starving to death. Like the proverbial ships in the night, they pass without really seeing the other. Neither would be considered "pathological" from the outside. Yet they are dying of loneliness, and are both haunted by the Shadow of unlived life.

PSYCHOPATHOLOGY: THE SUFFERING OF THE SOUL

Our existential condition is fragile, perilous. Of all animal species, we are the most incapable of surviving on our own without the care, protection, and nurturance of strangers, namely, those whom we come to call our parents or others. We only survive if fate provides us with resilient internal resources, the good intentions of those around us, and a relatively benign environment. Even so, none of us would survive without a considerable capacity for adaptation. Our adaptations lead us to take on the hues, the values, and the reflexes of that environment, and to internalize the messages of family dynamics and cultural milieu. With each adaptation in service to survival or getting needs met, we risk further alienation from our inherent nature. This is the origin of the Shadow problem. The deeper, more obligatory, more divergent these adaptations, the deeper our pathology.

No judgment is intended by the term *psychopathology*. Psychopathology means, when literally translated, the "expression of the suffering of a soul." We wrap ourselves around our adaptations, tropically bend like plants in search of sustaining light, and come to identify with, even love our distortions—as though they were who we are. Our pathologies, our neuroses, our addictions, and our sociopathies are expressions of suffering obliged by adaptation. With each adaptation we grow further estranged from our soul, and yet we are wed intrapsychically to our tropisms. *We become*, perforce, *our adaptations*; we live them out and embody them through our psychopathologies. Denying them becomes a Shadow problem, even as identifying with them is a Shadow problem. When I first went to Zurich to retrain in analytic psychology more than three decades ago, I reasonably transferred my experience of American graduate schools to my expectations there. In a matter of months I learned that the real test there was not about learning content, passing exams, writing papers, or moving to the next level, as I had believed. Rather, in a more implicit, zenlike way, I was confronted with an existential *koan**, a riddle to address. What I learned in those initial months was that *who I had become was my problem. My pathology was the same as my accomplishments.* No wonder the ego is less than thrilled when it confronts the Shadow. So many of my Shadow issues arose from having overidentified with adaptations, and having left some of the best pieces of the soul behind.

At the beginning of the last century Freud wrote a book titled *The Psychopathology of Everyday Life*. We do not, he argued, need to visit an asylum to see psychopathology; it will be found in our daily activities. His analysis of these mundane occasions revealed the power of the unconscious, the presence of mixed agendas, and the objective interference in daily behavior by the dynamic powers of subjective conflicts. Whatever per-

---

**A *koan* is a paradox given to each novice. It is not to be "answered"; it is to be lived in such fashion that the ego's fantasy of sovereign understanding is overthrown.*

cepts, ideas, or complexes have free reign in our unconscious life will play out as Shadow in our conscious world, often harming others or ourselves.

The human sensibility is extraordinarily sensitive and adaptive. This is why our species has survived, not because we are the apex of creation or because some deity has privileged us above other created species. To think so is nothing but hubris! We are here because we adapted better than all the other forms of life.* And yet, paradoxically, that same adaptive skill is the source of so much of our suffering and so much of our estrangement from our nature.

Just this day I was speaking with a man whose presenting issue is depression. For several years he has allowed his business and personal life to drift, often bringing untoward consequences to himself and his wife. Discerning why he is depressed, whether biologically driven or intrapsychic, is of course the first task. Having ruled out the former, we have focused on the latter.

Joseph is fifty-five, happily married on the whole, and the president of his small construction company. In allowing business and personal tasks to go unaddressed, his company is now at risk of bankruptcy. When we explored why he resists these mundane, often unpleasant but not truly onerous housekeeping details, he could not find a reason for his avoidance. In examining the pattern of avoidance we are obliged to acknowledge that *what we do in the outer world is a logical expression of the premises of the inner world*, whether conscious or not. Avoidance of a task is avoidance of the anxiety that that task somehow activates. On the surface, the unattended tasks do not present an anxiety approaching a casus belli, yet the pattern of systemic avoidance persists. Why? Given the absence of a sub-

---

*No doubt the chief argument against so-called "intelligent design" is the grand mess we have made of things.

stantive, conscious provocation, we are led to conclude that
the avoidant pattern is present because it activates a still deeper
anxiety.

When we probed where in his life he learned to be avoidant,
to push underground, to slip slide away, he recognized that
such was the only mode of adaptation to the invasive presence
and incessant demands of his mother. His father had been successful in his business life, but his domestic passivity had abetted
this avoidant strategy as the child learned that the likelihood of
holding one's own against the mother was not encouraging. In
latter life, when beset by health worries, aging and fatigue, and
the financial anxieties of his wife, Joseph slipped into the old familial pattern, and the problems grew. Soon he was avoiding
opening the mail until a bill collector phoned to demand pay-
ment of an overdue bill.

Joseph's depression derived from a generalized perception of
powerlessness in the face of the other (a direct transference of
past powerlessness before the demanding mother), and, after
repeated avoidance and mounting consequences, he had even
more fuel for the depression. Recognizing that his ordinary
daily tasks had taken on the weight of an old archaic powerlessness in the face of the Other—that perhaps 90 percent of what
he feared, and therefore avoided, derived from that earlier matrix of self and Other, helped him begin to retackle the tasks.
Recalling that he was now an adult, with a power, resiliency,
and decisive capacity lacking in the child, also fueled his recom-
mitment to address the nickel-and-dime issues upon which he
had wasted dollar energies.

How is Joseph's avoidance a Shadow issue? We have to recall
the functional definition of the Shadow as *that which renders us
uncomfortable in confronting in ourselves.* Two Shadow issues
emerge immediately. His "mother complex"—namely, the matrix of "invasive presence," and his powerlessness to oppose

it—is so systemic in his psychological makeup that he transfers this relational dynamic to other demanding situations, even those of mundane significance. Remember that our psyche functions like an analog computer, asking, "Where have I been here before?" which is how we attempt to render the new and unknown identifiable, and perhaps controllable, through the examples of the old. Thus we build on our past, but thus also are we shackled to the archaic data of the past. The Shadow issue of the present is inflamed by, driven by, the unaddressed legacy of the childhood programming. Thus, Shadow issue number one is, "That of which I am unconscious, and/or unwilling to face, now owns a part of my life."

Shadow issue number two arises from the backwash of the first. However one might decry the disempowerment of the depression, fueled as it is by the archaic "search engine" of the present, the task of empowering the present remains. Walking in "shoes too small for us," we all reside within the neuroses that brought us this far, the diminishing adaptations that constrict us to the narrow frame of history. To step out of this past, to revision oneself, to step into the larger possibility, is no easy task. Indeed, it is a Shadow issue, for it is our own enlarged imagination, our own risk of greater possibility that now renders us uncomfortable with ourselves. Thus, we remain both *bound to the disempowering past*, and *apprehensive about the risk demanded by the enlarged possibilities of the present*.

This double task, confronting the past, bringing it up into the light of consciousness, and taking on the responsibility for choosing differently, seems obvious when looking at someone else's life. But when we are swimming in our own fears and disabling past, we may do well to see that each defeat engineered by our history remains a challenge to walk into the abyss of the unimagined future. The problem with the past is that *it has no imagination; it can only repeat its script.* The sociopath is limited to the early perception that the Other is here to hurt him, so he can only hurt the other in return. His wound is his history; his pathology is his constricted imagination. So, too, the bigot. So, too, the fundamentalist, of any stripe. Each suffers an anxiety disorder with a reflexive treatment plan devoted to ridding him of ambiguity. Whether presenting as a person with a personality disorder, a bigot, or a fundamentalist, each is locked into the stunted imagination of his or her complexes, and owned by the anxiety-management plan that he has evolved.

As we will see in the chapter on relationships, each relationship is governed by the archaic mechanisms of projection and transference. What is projected is the anxiety evoked by the complexes, namely, the clusters of autonomous history that breed and brood within, and the transferred dynamics of anxiety management. When breaking free of the constrictive imagination of the complexes to risk new possibility remains too intimidating, the Shadow of the unlived life grows greater as our pathology spills into the world to harm others who are the recipients of our projections, transferred history, and anxiety-management systems.

ANXIETY-MANAGEMENT SYSTEMS

We *all* have anxiety-management systems, for without such, without the psyche's amazingly flexible adaptations, our sensitivities would be overrun by life. We learn to blunt our feelings, lest we feel too much. We learn to deny, to repress, to suppress, to project onto others, to distract, to dissociate—all in service to avoiding what we perceive to be overwhelmingly threatening. It has been argued that the only truly pathological state is denial, which after all is a rejection of reality. Yet we recall the character in T. S. Eliot's "Burnt Norton" who observed that humankind cannot bear very much reality. All of us, at different stages of psychosocial development, certain moments of stress, fatigue, or emotional vulnerability, manifest varying capacities for accepting, absorbing, and relating to burdensome or threatening reality.

Additionally, we often find a painful reality that is overwhelming at an early stage, persists perhaps as a phobia, or a strong aversion, encased as it is in the amber of our history. I recall a friend who had been a refugee from Germany and was unable to look through a book of photographs of ordinary people taken by the photographer August Sander between 1900 and 1940. These photographs were of everyday people—bakers, postmen, mothers—in ordinary circumstances, but even the gray ordinariness of it all brought the original affect rushing back, and she had to close the book. Something in their faces, something in the recall of this mundane world, brought the whole past swinging upward. None of us would judge this person's response, her need to protect herself, for we were not there. For her, the Shadow of history created a charged Shadow issue on the personal level, as it does for all of us.

So we have our ingenious anxiety-management systems. Many of them are so implicit in the matrix of daily life that we would never recognize them for what they are. One of the most ubiquitous yet unseen is *routine*. Life is inherently chaotic and unpredictable, as we are frequently reminded by the disasters we witness on daily newscasts. We bring our own form of, or at least our delusion of, order and predictability to our lives through routinization. We tend to rise the same way each morning, break our fast, read our papers, drink our coffee, drive the same route to work, and so on and so on. What is wrong with this? Nothing, and yet it is a Shadow issue insofar as such routine can also be the enemy of life, of unique response to emergent possibility. In his nineteenth-century essay on poetry, Shelley observed not only that the imagination was our highest faculty, but that habit was the great deadener. Notice our stress when our routine is interrupted. We grow "angry," which is to say "anxious," at such dislocations of our constructed "normality." These "constructs" that support and even carry the day are anxiety-management systems, and as such constitute a potential Shadow task when life would otherwise demand spontaneity, risk, and imaginative alternatives.

Another ubiquitous anxiety-management system is addiction. We all are addicts of one kind or another. An addiction is *a reflexive, conditioned, and often progressively compelling behavior whose enactment momentarily lowers stress.* Once upon a time I allowed people in therapy to smoke, wishing to grant them their freedom after all, and acknowledging their stress in such an emotionally charged setting. One couple finished that forever. Each was a chain-smoker, lighting another cigarette with the dying embers of the former. At the end of the hour there were twelve cigarette butts—I counted them—six from each. If anyone had asked them about this, they would have acknowledged that they had had a cigarette, but they were wholly unconscious of their reflexive habits of chain-smoking. The haze hung in the office for days, even after my changed policy.

But just as routine may be a reflexive anxiety-management system, as described above, so many other reflexive responses infiltrate daily life, whether we know it or not. Food disorders are rampant, for food offers archaic oral gratification and the immediate hint of emotional nourishment. Work addiction is common as we project our well-being upon such abstractions as success, getting ahead, economic security, and sundry other ways of avoiding the existential abyss over which we always hang. How many of us are comfortable with Walt Whitman's invitation to loaf and invite the soul?

Our addictive patterns are much more subtle than merely getting stoned, getting blotto, wiping out the pain of life, temporarily, because the psychopathology of everyday life is everywhere. *In addition to anxiety management, our addictions are efforts to avoid feeling what we already feel.* We wish to "get high" because we feel so low. We wish to get "stoned" because we know a stone feels no pain. All of these quite human ploys to manage our autonomous feeling states are understandable and omnipresent. The Shadow issue comes into play when we ask ourselves *what part of our life we are avoiding.* As natural as it is for a sentient being to avoid pain, sometimes going through the pain is the only way to lift the pain, to grow and develop, or quite simply *to reject the powers of pain to govern our entire life.* The only way to break the stranglehold of an addiction is to feel the pain that it is a defense against, the pain that we are *already* feeling.

The task of therapy inevitably involves going through some suffering if one is to grow, which is why so many avoid this deepened conversation with their own journey. This process is not as grim or forbidding as it might sound, for the reward is renewal and enlargement, if we are willing. W. H. Auden noted the ambivalence we bring to this task:

We would rather be ruined than changed.
We would rather die in our dread
Than climb the cross of the present
And let our illusions die.*

*Auden, "The Age of Anxiety," in *Collected Poems*, p. 407.

I would further attest that the purpose of a serious therapy is not to "solve" the suffering, but to find and *address the task it raises for us,* and *to refuse to be blocked, stuck, constricted by the adaptive stratagem that arose.* Addressing the Shadow issue of avoidance is the only way to have this deepened conversation with the meaning of our lives. Thus, a woman whom I see who never knew her own power, never felt legitimate entitlement, never possessed her own voice in her family of origin, or her marriage, joined a Toastmasters Club. Can you imagine what courage it takes her to face her fear and speak out amid such scrutiny? She is learning, difficult step by difficult step, to address the Shadow of the unlived life, the stifled soul that has been her protective adaptation, and to step into a larger anxiety, and therefore a larger life. Her model is the paradigm for us all. Our constrictive adaptations, as necessary as they were, keep us from ourselves, from the larger being we were meant to bring into this world. How dare we keep who we really are from this world, constrict whomever we were intended to become, because we are governed by fear! As Nikos Kazantzakis expressed it:

Humanity is such a lump of mud, each one of
us is a lump of mud. What is our duty?
To struggle so that a small flower may
blossom from the dunghill of our flesh and mind.*

Behind our addictions lies the summons to a larger, riskier life. As Gerald G. May put it so succinctly, "Addiction exists wherever persons are internally compelled to give energy to things that are not their true desires."† Why is it so difficult to find, affirm, and pursue what we truly desire, then?

*Kazantzakis, *The Saviors of God*, p. 109.
†May, *Addiction & Grace*, p. 14.

Accepting a larger level of anxiety is the price of growth. The failure to grow will produce either depression, or such fixated adaptation as we find in our daily neuroses. Stuck as we may be, something in us longs for larger expression, hence our symptoms, our compensatory dreams, and our wistful, insurgent longing that we fail to identify as the soul's summons. This longing, remaining unconscious, so often translates into romantic infatuation—searching for the "magical other" who will make our life work, or projecting our unlived life onto other people—or there would be no cult of celebrity, as floods our popular media, or sentimentalized, undemanding spirituality, as governs so many of our houses of worship.

MAGICAL THINKING

Still another Shadow issue is found in the "magical thinking" in which we daily indulge. Magical thinking is the province of the child, the primitive sensibility, and *all of us under stress*. It is a failure to engage in a distinction between outer and inner, subjective and objective. The child believes its thoughts govern the world, even as, conversely, his or her "interpretations" of the world govern the child. As a child I believed that getting sick was the result of some act for which I was being punished. (I was not up too much on germ theory in those days.) I internalized being sick, as I often was, as a form of shame, guilt, and culpability. Buried beneath the acquisition of our adult sensibility, such archaic thoughts persist in all of us. Thus we blame others, or we accept a shaming blame, and the variegated forms of life, including the natural sufferings to which our species is given, are subjected to the core complexes again.

How prayer is used by people *can* be a form of magical thinking. (Some would say all prayer is magical thinking; but I think the jury is out on this.* At the very least, it is a form of serious intentionality.) At its worst, prayer can be an understandable yet infantilizing expression of magic—a projection of the child's terrors and search for surcease projected upon a cosmic screen, as Freud charged. Much more mature is the prayer for strength, for insight, for wisdom in which one may more consciously make one's choices in the world, or bear with considered, courageous measure the burdens brought upon us.

Magical thinking, of course, generated the naive sciences of ancient cultures. Inevitably, they were based less on disciplined observation and tested hypotheses (which, from Bacon and the seventeenth century to the present, we have come to consider the elementary requirement for speculation), than upon projection, fear management, and confirmation of complexes. How ironic that contemporary fundamentalism returns to this scientific naiveté because of its unexamined, compensatory ego inflation, and its defense of complexes. Perhaps it was nicer to live in a three-storied universe, where we could be the cynosure of ego sovereignty; perhaps it was nicer to live as the apex of creation, where our ego inflation could be celebrated; perhaps it remains nicer to imagine that we can read, or at least a coifed televangelist with pancake makeup can read, the mind of God, who, strangely, seems to have the same tastes, values, certainties, and neuroses as we do! It is another matter altogether to revision our frangible journey aboard a speck of dust flung by a great wind blowing across the aeons. One Chippewa was willing to acknowledge his place amid the great mystery:

*While studies have varied, the broadest and most recent at this writing suggest little if any correlation between prayer and healing. For the faithful, this can provide the challenge of faith, or radical trust, based not on managing the universe but in honest confession of one's existential limits. The story of Job, treated later in this book, reminds us that our efforts to strike "deals" with the universe is an old, old story, perhaps an old, old hubristic strategy to wrest sovereignty from the gods.

Sometimes I go about pitying myself,
and all the time
I am being carried on great winds across the sky.*

PARAPHILIAS: THE PERMUTATIONS OF DESIRE

When we examine the shadowy nature of intimate relationships, we explore one of the biggest of our secrets, that there is
a very deep, archaic part of us that would wish to forswear life
itself, with its rigors, its loneliness, its battering separations and
losses, and melt into the arms of the beloved. Freud considered
most of our neuroses to have a sexual basis, although his understanding of that was much broader than we conventionally
understood. For him, eros, the life force, was forever seeking
pleasure, avoiding pain, persistently seeking tissue tension ces-
sation, even annihilation. When this "urge to merge" prevails,
we regress in the face of our developmental agendas, twist our
eros around surrogate goals (sometimes called "perversions,"
meaning quite literally, "turned or directed toward a goal"), or
suffer immense pain of frustration unless and until we are able
to sublimate urgency of desire into work, art, or some other
creative form. The necessity of such conversion of eros is the
requisite for civilization. Sadly, the permutations of desire can
also lead to great destruction. Jung also celebrated the power
of eros, recalling that Eros was a god to the ancients, and
counted his multiple manifestations as illustrative of the creative ways in which *psyche* or soul manifests in the world in
search of meaning.

Today the psychiatric world identifies disturbances of desire
as *paraphilias*, namely *philos*, or "love," in all its permutations.
Perhaps *desire* is a better word than *love*, given that love and de-

---

*Bly *et al.*, *The Rag and Bone Shop of the Heart*, p. 496.

sire do not have to coincide. To define a *paraphilia*, however, is to assume a cultural perspective in order to make that judgment. Change the culture and the perspective changes. Some of us are not fond of the idea of killing and eating dogs, but such is quite acceptable restaurant fare in other parts of the world. In Plato's world, adult/child relationships were not only natural but a higher form than that between the sexes because they were purer, less burdened by other agendas. Today we call it pedophilia and clap a person in jail. This judgment is necessary because the psyche of the child is sufficiently fragile as to require protection, but who is to say that such desire is unnatural, since it comes from human nature and has been practiced throughout history.

For many, "the love that dare not speak its name," homosexuality, is considered a pathology. Yet it has been present in all civilizations and evenly distributed throughout the world— one piece of evidence among many of its biological rather than cultural or personal bases. Decades ago it was removed from the realm of the abnormal, depathologized by psychiatric circles, and is only considered abnormal by the ignorant today, or those threatened by any ambiguity in their own nature. What has been practiced in every culture, considered normal in many, and honored in some (such as ancient Greece, Rome, as well as the veneration of the "two-spirit" in Native American cultures), is still a Shadow threat to the insecure.

Or consider frotteurism, for example. The desire to rub against another goes back to the child in each of us, and remains in the adult, or we would not kiss, or spoon, or touch each other. Fetishism chooses an object, a metonymy, to summarize, intimate the larger range of associations. Therefore, a person might treasure a picture of the desired one rather than risk a relationship with them, or an item of clothing, a synechdoche, in which a part represents the whole. What is pathological here as a Shadow issue is not the desire, but instead the person's fear of approaching the real object of desire rather than its symbolic surrogate.

The point of these paragraphs is not to valorize one form of behavior or another, but to suggest that desire is profoundly human. We are ipso facto creatures of desire, or we would have no skyscrapers, no symphonies, no space travel, no sons and daughters. People who might be victimized by our desire do need our community's energetic protection, but it might be useful for all of us to begin to catch the judgmental quality of our response to the desires of others when we ourselves are creatures of desire. Currently the United States has 500,000 registered sex offenders, and many others who are not yet identified. That their victims, past and future, are to be protected is clearly necessary, but *their crime is their failures of relatedness*, not their insurgent desire. Their failures derive from an inability to hear the summons to love and the restraints that love asks of us, which encompass and contain, but do not deny, desire.

The permutations of desire have always been, and remain, great Shadow issues. None of us is free of neurosis around this matter, for none of us is absent the agendas of desire or being torn by sundry contradictory messages that continue to collide in our bodies and our behaviors. Great harm has come through the uncontained acts of desire that victimize others, but possibly even greater harm to the human spirit has come through the brutal repression of desire. (Remember Blake's telling hyperbole that it is better to murder an infant in its cradle than to nurse unacted desires? He must have had a strong pre-Freudian intimation of the price of repression, and the twisting of the soul that results.) This Shadow remains with us always, even in the darkness of our bedchambers. Each of us is summoned to discern the difference between repression, which breeds monsters sooner or later, and restraint, which comes out of respect for oneself and for another.

Most of us remain merely neurotic, that is, carrying the splits between adaptation and individuation as a personal suffering. Paradoxically, the hope of the world is found in the merely neurotic. In 1939, with World War II gathering to unleash the greatest destruction in the history of humankind, Jung gave a speech to the Guild for Pastoral Psychology in London. He noted that our species ill tolerates a meaning vacuum and will drift into or be seduced by powerful ideologies.* On the right, he noted, were the hysterical throngs of fascism, and on the left, the sullen masses of communism. From neither could there be much hope of renewal of the spirit, for each required an abdication of personal responsibility and an arrogation of power to the leaders. Only the "neurotic," he believed, having internalized the struggle, kept hope alive for the tending of the human spirit. As individuals prove willing to work through their personal suffering, so the tendencies of the larger culture are treated and amended. Today, as we have seen, fascism and communism are discredited, but are replaced by a paraphilic consumer culture driven by fantasy, desperately in search of distractions and escalating sensations, and a fundamentalist culture wherein the rigors of a private journey are shunned in favor of an ideology that, at the expense of the paradoxes and complexities of truth, favors one-sided resolutions, black-and-white values, and a privileging of one's own complexes as the norm for others.

The problem with all paraphilias is that they do not connect us in sustaining, satisfying ways, do not really serve the soul. Our culture is full of counterfeits soliciting our assent, and ask-

*As the English theologian William Temple once observed, those who believe nothing can easily be persuaded to believe anything.

ing for pieces of the soul in return. As the poet Hafiz instructed:

> *Learn to recognize the counterfeit coins*
> *That may buy you just a moment of pleasure,*
> *But then drag you for days*
> *Like a broken man*
> *Behind a farting camel.**

DISORDERS OF SELF

There is a range of human suffering that extends beyond the merely neurotic—the so-called "personality disorders." The neurotic personality is aware of his suffering, often blames himself for failing to banish the disquiet of the soul, and yet has the possibility of working through the suffering to an enlarged meaning. The personality disorder is a person who has been significantly traumatized by life. He or she does not merely suffer the wound; they *are* the wound; they are owned by it, and live within its limited imaginal purview at all times. When they act and speak, it is through the window of the wound, with little or no awareness of parallel possibilities.

The Shadow problem manifests itself in personality disorders through the exclusion of alternatives. One is not much threatened by alternatives, as normal neurosis experiences, for one is organized precisely to exclude alternatives. Like Prometheus chained in perpetuity to the rock in the Caucasus, the antisocial personality disorder is chained to the perception that the Other is always here to harm him. This core percept dominates all relationships and drives him through the power complex. As

---

*Hafiz, "Cast All Your Votes for Dancing."
 This poem may be accessed via *www.panhala.net/Archive/Index/html.*

Jung noted, where power prevails, love is not. He or she is doomed to a loveless life. They may be married, or they may be in positions of great influence, but they live in a sterile, self-replicating environment where love and relatedness are banished. All of life is refracted through the lens of power—a Sisyphean reductive and repetitive life—that brings harm to others but forecloses reflection on that harm, and constricts conscience through which it is possible to share another's suffering.

The paranoid personality disorder is owned by the primal fears that beset the child and overwhelmed its resources, creating a sensibility governed by fear. Soon this fear blankets the world, creeps into every crevice, and is accounted for by delusions of persecution or compensatory grandiosity. Discrepant facts are twisted so as to fit the core idea. (As the old joke has it, "The presence of the troubling facts is evidence that the conspiracy is working.") As all personality disorders are also disorders of the imagination, so the person cannot imagine his or her capacities to experience other possibilities than those that threaten; therefore the fears of the past are spread into every corner of his life, and the old terrors are replicated. Thus, the Shadow for him or her is not fear; that is the ego's constant state. The Shadow is the alternative world of compassion and support of both self and others, whose risk seems now too daunting.

The narcissistic personality is devoted to hiding his or her secret, namely, that when they stare into the mirror of life, no one stares back. Thus, they have a constant need to use others in order to elicit positive mirroring, which was sadly deficient when their nascent sense of self was forming. They overcompensate by an inordinate sense of entitlement, without the reciprocity that governs ethically driven relationships. They fail to empathize with the others whom they use, such as their children, to bolster their shaky sense of self. They warp their children into agents of their aggrandizement, perhaps cause them to flee to save their own lives, or they control, bully, and dominate their spouses as the carrier of their archaic, unfinished esteem needs. The Shadow issue for the narcissist is not only the manipulation and misuse of others, but his or her failure to address the deficit within, and to work with it in a more personally responsible way, as in therapy. Sadly, the deficit within robs the ego of the strength necessary to take this task on, and so he or she continues to colonize others in service to the specter of emptiness that haunts their center.

Similarly, the borderline personality disorder is organized around a terror of abandonment. Unable to contain their own fractures, they spill their inner conflict into groups, fractionate them, and blame them for their dysfunctions. They push their friends and partners to extremes by asking too much of them, and then they walk away with a sense of vindication that the other was not enough for them anyway. Fearing loneliness, they drive people away and re-create their loneliness everywhere. The Shadow task here, of course, is to bear one's loneliness so that one can create a more effective relationship to the Self, from which all our healthy choices derive. As Jung put it once, "The patient must be alone if he is to find out what it is that supports him when he can no longer support himself."* This task is intimidating enough for most of us, and seemingly impossible for the borderline personality. At heart they have a rage toward the Other who is always letting them down, derived from an attenuated relationship to their own Self, which is the only reliable source of constancy, direction, and support.

The compulsive personality disorder is driven by archaic anxiety, which expresses itself through him or her with too much work and/or perfectionism, yet also a simmering anger at be-

---

*Jung, "Psychology and Alchemy," *CW 12*, para. 32.

ing so locked into such an agenda. They are often driven to in-sist that the task be done his or her way, lest it have loose ends that occasion even more anxiety. The passive-aggressive per-sonality feels disempowered at heart, and he or she is governed by covert strategies in service to the relational message that the Other is always the more powerful. Accordingly, he or she fo-ments discord behind the scenes, does not carry through on commitments, sabotages agreements, and repeatedly finds ways to surreptitiously control events or others when he or she does not possess the power to do so directly. Again, the common thread in these disorders is that the Shadow task, as with addic-tions, is experiencing what one feels directly, without the pro-tective defense, in order that the task of growth and the agenda of change might be taken on consciously. Sadly, the destructive power of early experience of self and world typically dominates the ego state, leaving the person enmeshed in the archaic wound and its primitive defense.

● ● ●

ALL OF US EXHIBIT "the psychopathology of everyday life" through our organized reflexive responses to our wounds. These responses are virtually institutionalized within us, and therefore exclude so much life, so many other possibilities. All excluded material increases our Shadow. In other words, most of *our Shadow material will be found in what we are avoiding*! And what we are avoiding will not go away; it will show up in our lives somewhere, or be carried by our children as a prob-lem to emulate or to solve. For as Jung observed, what is de-nied inwardly will perforce have a tendency to come to us by fate in the outer world.

As a final example, I recall the work with one of my first analysands while still training in Zurich. Bertha was in her thirties, a survivor of severe, near-fatal bulimia, and still deeply invested in all forms of control. Although brilliant, she had avoided attending the university, lived an abstemious life, binging and purging occasionally, and made her living as a language tutor, whereby she could remain in control of her environment. Bertha's mother had taken her life, perhaps because of the trauma of the war. Her father had fought in the Afrika Korps, returned to Germany broken in spirit, and died in an auto crash. Thus, as a child she was doubly abandoned. She was raised by her reluctant aunt, who denigrated her. As a child Bertha began to steal toys and chocolate, hoping to feed herself emotionally as best she could. As an adolescent she evolved the bulimia that nearly took her life. While economically self-supporting, she lived within an emotionally constricted vision of self and world. She was, she believed, of little value and essentially powerless, and the world outside was generally hostile and uncaring—attitudes that had their genesis in the child's reading of the traumas brought to her by fate.

All of her adult behaviors are "logical" expressions of her personal myth when seen through this lens of deprivation and abandonment. Yet her psyche solicits her attention and continues to seek healing. She dreamt that she was in her room and that a witch entered, stole her doll, and ran down the street. Even in the dream she knew the doll was her "inner child." She ran after the witch, offering to pay whatever ransom the witch asked in order to recover the child. The witch laughed and ran on.

When she caught the witch again, the witch challenged the dreamer to take on three tasks to ransom the child. They were to make love with a fat man; to deliver a lecture at the university; and to go to back to Germany and have a meal with her stepmother. These tasks, symbolically, represent the supreme

Shadow work that Bertha had to undertake in order to ransom her history and recover a more empowered present.

The villain in the piece is of course the "witch," who serves as an archetypal personification of an archetypal wound. Her traumatic visit dramatizes Bertha's relationship to her body—the repository of nature closest to home, and to others—extrapolated from the fact that primal others in childhood "abandoned" or denigrated her. Thus, making love with a fat man asked that she become better friends with her body, risk adult reciprocal relationship, and express her sexuality. (She had had no committed, intimate adult relationship.) Delivering a lecture at the university asked that she overcome her protective sociophobia and bring her talents, and her person, into the world. Returning to Germany to have, of all things, a meal, the source of nurturance, with the evil stepmother, meant to bring her full adult powers to the task of confrontation and to healing the archaic wound. Sadly, both in the dream, and in conscious reflection upon it, Bertha concluded that the witch, the archetypal image of withheld mothering, was asking too much of her, and she felt she was doomed to stay stuck in the present, shackled within her self-imposed defenses against her traumatic, abandoning history.

All of us have stuck places in our contemporary life. We are well aware of some of them, and we mobilize New Year's resolutions to overthrow them, albeit with mixed results. Others are less conscious and reassert themselves through our daily reflexive responses to ordinary life. These stuck places, if tracked, always reveal an invisible filament that leads back to some archaic fear that, overwhelming to the child, still has the residual energy to intimidate, even shut down the adult. Taking on this fear, however real or unreal it may prove to be, is the Shadow task that the psychopathology of everyday life brings to the surface and to challenge each of us. An example of this archaic dilemma might be found in the preoccupation with dieting that forms so many of our resolutions. On the surface, all we have to do is eat less, but we slip into old patterns easily enough and the pounds return. What is the archaic fear that eating is surreptitiously "treating"? Such intimidating fear, if brought into consciousness, would ask: "If I do not eat this, what then will nourish me?" Rather than go unnourished emotionally, we will continue to transfer our psychological needs onto matter, and the pounds persist.

The paradox of healing our sundry pathologies is that only by a continuing attention to them, and a respect for what they are telling us, can we ever be free of them. In the end, we do not wish to believe that our life is governed by the agenda of others, or by fear, or by our defended response to both. We wish to be here, as we are, as *who we really are*. In "the psychopathology of everyday life" we are invited to confront a great deal of personal Shadow material. Even if this summons asks us to revisit wounded places, we are progressively brought to larger life through a more differentiated relationship to our own psychological complexity. When we do not look within, something within is looking at us nonetheless, subtly making decisions for us. We wish to respect our pathos—our suffering—yet not be passive or pathetic.

Chapter Five

HIDDEN AGENDAS
The Shadow in Intimate Relationships

"Sometimes I forget completely
what companionship is.
Unconscious and insane, I spill sad
Energy everywhere."

—RUMI, "SOMETIMES I FORGET COMPLETELY"

The proverbial Tom and Sally engage in daily spats, insult their partner's families of origin, and despair over getting what they want from the other. In how many relationships does this, or some similar dynamic, play out? We all say we value relationships so highly, but why are so many so broken?

Wherever we go, it seems, the Shadow follows. Relationships are minefields—impossible to traverse without hitting triggering levers. Which of us is ever wholly free of a mixed motive? Which of us can ever be in non-manipulative relationship to the other? Which of us can ever be conscious enough to contain our inherent narcissism and its shadowy agendas, strong enough to acknowledge unpleasant truths about ourselves without repressing them anew, and committed enough to work through them in service to an unencumbered relationship with the other?

In any frightened, urgent child we see our profoundly human core—grasping, hungry, needy, insistent, necessarily narcissistic. That child is never left behind. The only question is, to what degree does it play a part in the daily dance of self and other? And who among us could ever escape a profound longing for nurturance, satiety, and security? Poet Tony Hoagland, in a poem titled, "What Narcissism Means to Me," admits that even in our adulthood "deep inside the misery / of daily life / love lies bleeding."* Just how far do we ever really get away from this profoundly vulnerable self, with its narcissistic agenda? Why should we realistically think it would disappear simply because we now occupy bigger bodies in bigger roles in bigger settings? Poet Delmore Schwartz illustrated this paradox in calling his body, with its insistent demands, the "heavy bear" that goes with him always, a shadowy beast that haunts the relationship with the beloved. It:

> . . . stretches to embrace the very dear
> with whom I would walk without him near.†

That lumbering bear follows him, and us, everywhere, and "howls in its sleep for a world of sugar."

THE PROGRAMMING OF THE RELATIONAL IMAGO

As we grow up we progressively learn to contain much of this self-interested agenda—offering restraint for reciprocity, avoiding punishment, receiving conditional rewards, fitting in. As they say, to get along you go along. . . . In time most of us also learn to leave our own limited world to imaginatively partici-

---

*Hoagland, "What Narcissism Means to Me," *What Narcissism Means to Me*, p. 17.
†Delmore Schwartz, "The Heavy Bear Who Goes with Me," in *Modern Poems: An Introduction to Modern Poetry*, p. 320.

pate in the reality of the other, gaining the capacity for empathy, sympathy, compassion—all words whose etymologies imply the capacity to actually share the pain of another.*

Reason and conscious intention can subscribe to a code of behavior, and yet are easily overthrown by the power of the nonrational inner world. The imagination, however, allows one to transcend the limits of our skin, even the limits of our personal or tribal history, and enter the world of the other. We do this every time we read a novel or watch a play or observe a painting. We allow our sensibility to be permeable, plastic, persuadable, and we engage the world of the other, at least for a while. During this act of imaginative enlargement, we participate in a larger world than our own and discover the capacity to share another's experience. An example may also be found at the National Holocaust Museum in Washington, D.C. Each visitor is given a ticket with a person's name on it. At the end of the tour, the visitor learns what happened to that specific, individual soul. What otherwise might be an encounter with history overwhelmed by mind-numbing statistics is brought back to the reminder that, of the six million to nine million murdered, each was an individual, a unique story, a personal brutalization, and a criminally interrupted life.

Those who are limited in their experience by the bounds of their history, their education, their tribe's taboos, their family-of-origin complexes, live in much more emotionally constrictive relationships. Even more, those who are locked into large, traumatic childhood wounding are often defined by hopelessly redundant imagoes whereby they lack the elemental capacity to feel with the other. Thus they can pursue horribly aggressive agendas without compunction and without remorse. Such are "emptied souls," to use Adolph Guggenbuhl-Craig's telling

---

*Recall from the last chapter: Greek: *passio*—suffering. Latin: *pathos*—suffering.

metaphor. While their relationships are invariably conflictual and harmful, their greatest pathos is that they remain locked into such a sterile, monochromatic, repetitious inner world, which can only repeat its same dreary theme and outcome. It is fair to say that *many of our relational difficulties derive from a limited, emotionally bankrupt imagination*, and that we are largely bound to the power of imagoes charged long ago and far away.

So how is this relational dynamic, this energy-charged imago within each of us, programmed, and how susceptible to alteration is it? Why are our relationships so troubled?

Our first relational messages are found in the primal bonding experiences. Is the Other* there, reliably? Uncertain, absent, punitive? Is the Other nurturant, reassuring, meeting us more than halfway? Is the Other withholding, unpredictable, even invasive or abandoning? These earliest relational experiences are powerfully formative, especially in our childhood when we are most malleable, most bound to our subjective reading of the world that tells us: *This is you, and this is the world, and this is how it is, and how it is going to be!*

Of course we receive many different messages, all with the power to modify the programming of this relational imago, but we have to acknowledge that typically the earliest, most powerful, and most sustained messages come from these parent-child encounters, and thereby constitute archaic messages that are always humming beneath the surface of our contemporary engagements with others. The more intimate the relationship, the more the archaic drama with its directives is present,

---

*Here I am capitalizing *Other* in order to underline the inordinate power of our first, primal encounters with others. Our internalized imprint of the generic Other, typically the parent or primary caregiver, is generated from our impressionability in infantile experience, and then is transferred to subsequent relationships. Other forces, including sociopolitical, economic, and environmental influences can also contribute to the programming of the imago of the Other with its accompanying "messages."

whether recognized or not. While we may not be automatons, prisoners of this history, we are naive to ignore its compelling presence.

As relational imagoes are generated by these archaic programs, so lifestyles, personality strategies, and patterned, replicative behaviors are also generated. For example, the two inevitable categories of our common traumatic existential experience are 1) to feel overwhelmed, invaded, harmed, or oppressed by the Other, and/or 2) to be abandoned by the Other. Either one of these experiences has the power to dominate, even replace, the vulnerable child's own capacities for freedom of choice. We have all experienced both categories, but in varying degrees of intensity, and in varying ways they may have also been mediated and moderated by the Other. While no parent can always be there for the child, the general reassurance, consistency, and good intent of the parent can do much to assuage the power of the message of being overwhelmed or abandoned—or, of course, drive its terror deeper.

With regard to the perceived experience of being overwhelmed by the other, the general message the child receives is of powerlessness in the face of the Other. From this compelling message three basic strategies will evolve. First, one learns patterns of *avoidance* to stay out of harm's way. We all have these patterns in our relational lives, both at home and at work. We avoid, we procrastinate, we forget, we divert, we finesse, we dissociate, we suppress, we repress. Perhaps most commonly, we avoid emotionally charged issues, conflicts, and genuine differences with others, which then fester as resentment, depression, or unlived life. Such avoidance leads to a loss of personal integrity. How much resentment or depression in a relationship derives from this abdication of our own selfhood?

Second, feeling disempowered, we are then driven by *the power complex* to seek sovereignty over the environment, become more powerful than the Other, control them instead. Who among us does not fall into such a power complex from time to time? (Underneath this familiar script the heart of the dictator beats, and we all have a small dictator inside of us.) What couple is free of the power motive in any given moment? Power is not evil, but is rather the expression of energy between any two people. The question then is, in any given relationship, what is this hidden agenda? As Jung observed once, where power prevails, love is not; that is, where power replaces relatedness, relationship is then in thrall to a Shadow agenda.

Third, we learn *to comply*, to curry favor, to please the Other in hopes of mollifying them, gaining their necessary approval, and moderating their power over us. Again, complying reflexively with the will of others, without genuine reflectivity, leads to a loss of integrity in our dealings with them. If I am repeatedly nice and compliant, rather than authentic, then I have ceased to be a person with values. (The more extreme form of this compliant behavior is today called codependency.) Where then will one's unexpressed anger at this collusion go? Perhaps it will somatize as illness, perhaps invert as depression, or perhaps leak out in bursts of criticism or harsh retorts. All of us evolve *all three* of these strategies in the course of our early development, and over time they show up repeatedly in our adult relationships.

Concomitantly, the experience of *abandonment* is often internalized as an implicit statement about our worth or value to the other, or lack thereof, quite apart from whether the missing Other is making such a statement or not. Thus, we again evolve three basic patterns, with a thousand variations. First, we *identify with* this apparent rejection and repeat the imago's message by avoiding our talents and desires, sabotaging our efforts, and hiding from the summons that life brings to each of us. Or we get hooked by an overcompensation and are driven to prove to the world how good, how worthy, how valuable we are. Such people often achieve their outer goals but derive no satisfaction from them, for the experience of deficit within is an ever-hungry void that wishes to be fed over and over without respite.

Second, we again fall into the *power complex* and seek to compel the affection, respect, or approval of the other through any means possible, even by making ourselves indispensable to them. (Many parents have disabled their children by doing too much for them. Believing they are helping their children, they are instead sending the message: "You need me, and will always need me to conduct your life, because, of course it is I who needs you.") Or we feed our narcissistic wound by controlling others, constantly seeking their affirmation of our worth. We set them up to feed us. If they do so, they grow resentful over time because they are being used. If they refuse or fail to feed our self-worth, we grow angry and punitive toward them. When the parent lives through the child, or depends upon the partner for self-worth, then the Shadow issue is power, not love.

Third, we find surrogate sources, *addictive habits* to connect with the *Other*—be it a warm body, food, tobacco or alcohol, power, ideologies, creeds, television, the Internet, routinization, shiny objects, and many more—and thereby momentarily assuage the grief and angst of abandonment. How many of us in a materialist society project our emotional needs onto things, yet feel chronically dissatisfied by our possessions, or come to recognize that our compulsion to own things comes in time to own us? Through the thousand subtle variants of which they are capable, these three patterns of relational programming are also at work in all of our lives, whether we recognize their shadowy presence in our relationships or not.

No wonder, then, that these six strategies, arising from the twin categories of universal existential wounding, produce relational patterns. While we believe ourselves free at any moment, how often are we in service to these archaic, primal messages, or better, are we ever free of them?* Their ghostly presence in our social life and in our intimacies constitutes a continuing Shadow dimension whereby *we are not who we are* in the moment, but who we have been, reflexively, historically defined. How can any relationship flourish amid such ghostly presences? And is any relationship ever free of such Shadow agendas?

Additionally, we confront the Shadow in our relational lives whenever we are caught in a *complex* to which we are especially prone in intimate settings, or when we are consciously or unconsciously enlisting the other in our personal agenda. (A *complex* is a historically charged cluster of energy dependent upon the past for its programmed agenda.) Accordingly, the primal imagoes of Self and Other, programmed within from the earliest moments, carrying always the strong imprint of mother and father and other messages obtained in those archaic but formative years, are activated in the presence of the Other. Nowhere are these dynamics more readily enacted than in intimacy, which comes closest to evoking the matrix of the original parent/child imago.

Consider this example. Tom and Sally are well intentioned, yet when Sally peers into Tom's life, offers supportive advice, he withdraws. If she persists, he gets sullen, then angry. When he pulls away from her, she grows anxious, then angry, and then withdraws herself. For some time there is a desert between them, until one of them creeps back into the empty center and the relationship resumes its old comfort and reassurance. What happened there?

---

*For a fuller discussion of these six strategic patterns of life behavior, see my book *Finding Meaning in the Second Half of Life: How to Finally, Really Grow Up*, especially pages 49–64.

Tom grew up with an anxious, invasive parent. When Sally leans in on him, meaning well, his history is activated and Sally is now perceived, through Tom's unconscious filter of history, not as friend but as foe. His withdrawal and his subsequent anger are reactions to his anxiety. He has been here before, or so it seems. He feels threatened by engulfment. Sally, having had an emotionally distant caregiver, interprets his protective withdrawal as a hostile act. Where has she been here before? She experiences the anxiety of abandonment and pulls back into a protective shell. Both will persist in this dance of history until one of them breaks the pattern.

How is it that people who are intentional in their caring for the other can so easily revert to defensive postures, bring harm to their partners, and collude in an abdication of the present moment for the archaic dramas of the past?

In any context of intimacy, the likelihood of such primal activation of complex material is a virtual guarantee. As a historic organ, our psyche metaphorically asks: "Where have I been here before, and what did that experience tell me?" For this reason, our adult relationships have a strong tendency toward repetition of early family-of-origin dynamics. The one who is compliant to the demanding Other, the one who becomes the caretaker of the impaired Other, the one who needs to dominate the Other in service to narcissistic repair, and so on—all are living in the historically charged field of "Self and Other" imagoes. Perhaps perversely, one even seeks out the other with whom to bond in service to this imago. How free ever, then, is such an important choice as marriage, when one is in service to an archaic imago and its attendant strategies?

We do not plan to repeat our lives, at least not consciously, but we have a strong tendency to do so, unconsciously, because of the power of this archaic history. The deeper it lies buried in our psychological formation of Self and Other, the more autonomy it has in our lives. Even when one is trying to break its hold by choosing the opposite, one is still being defined by its demands. Every time one chooses "the opposite" of the relational dynamics of the parental complexes, the more one is bound to them still. Evelyn, the daughter of an alcoholic, naturally rushed out to marry a man with a similar problem. Divorcing him, she swore to seek, find, and marry a teetotaler. She did, and found that he was a good guy, but unable to hold a job. To her dismay, she came to realize that the issue wasn't alcohol, but finding and taking care of "the impaired Other." Who would have thought that the programming of that daughter was such that she was driven to repeat the assigned role of childhood throughout her adult relationships?

Yet avoiding the risk of intimate relationship is even more deleterious to the present, for in defending against the threat of painful repetition, it robs one of the gift of friendship, and the dialectic between two "others" who enlarge each other most by being, profoundly, *Other*. Paradoxically, tolerating "the otherness of the other" is our largest challenge, for choosing only the familiar Other would shackle us to the delimiting values of our archaic imago, and tie us to a dreary repetition of whatever relational messages fate offered us the first time around.

On the other hand, the narcissistic agenda of any individual psyche will have a strong urge to impose itself upon the relationship in service to getting one's needs met, even at the cost of the well-being of the other. (A colleague of mine, Alden Josey, once described this as the shadowy desire to "colonize the other.") The more damaged one's history, or the weaker one's sense of self, the greater is this narcissistic tendency and the more rigid and controlling the dynamics of the relationship. When we see a relationship gone horribly wrong, when the boyfriend shows up to shoot his girlfriend, we are seeing a very weak ego that has succumbed to the archaic message that "I will perish if I do not have the Other at my command."* The independence of the other is experienced as a withdrawal from their unconscious, narcissistically programmed "contract," and therefore sets off all the anxious alarms.

What major city does not have its shelter for abused women? The incidence of violence in intimate relationship is grim testimony to the powers of archaic imagoes with their repetitious, self-serving agendas. The spouse of a former client had bungled four marriages before the age of thirty-five, was violently controlling of her, and naturally blamed all his emotional inflammations on her provocation. Under no circumstances could one use the term *love* to describe such relationships; rather only the word *fear* accurately describes their tenor. The very weak ego of the husband was buttressed by his election of an especially authoritarian career choice, and by bullying his intimidated wife. His capacity to manage his atavistic fear was minimal, and thus he brought harm to others.

So, too, we suffer the worldwide militancy of fundamentalist faithful who are incapable of sustaining even a modicum of ambiguity through their faith, and insist on being validated at the expense of open inquiry and respect for the differing views of others. Not only do they become suicide bombers, but they are the ones who insist on being on the local school boards and committees that select textbooks for the state, for their archaic fear of ambiguity drives them to reject the accumulated findings of scholars and scientists over the last thousand years, preferring the simplistic, archaic world-pictures of their tribal

---

*A parallel example is in the social phenomenon of "stalking," where the weak ego perceives the Other, upon whom its projection has fallen, as necessary to survival. Therefore, he or she must be with that Other, at all costs, lest the child within perish of loneliness. As socially dangerous as this is, an understanding of the pathology leads one to understand the pathos of the abandoned child.

histories. Sadly, it is virtually impossible to get such worthies to genuine dialogue, let alone to examine the Shadow issue of fear, for who wishes to seriously look at what scares them? One simply has to realize that their fear constricts all of us in the name of "religion," and then vote them out of those positions of power.

In all such turbulent relationships, whether in marriage or the tumult of political discord, the unexamined child within is frightened and starving, and reflexively brings the adult powers to bear in service to its infantile agenda. Such a child is in all of us, and most of us struggle, imperfectly, to contain that child's insistent agenda out of our respect and affection for the other. But no relationship is wholly free of such occasional outbreaks of narcissistic self-interest. None of us has reached such a stage of individuation, of virtual Buddhahood, as to transcend our archaic needs. Thus, the Shadow of narcissism haunts all relationships, even the most evolved, and constitutes the ethical challenge of relationship, namely, *"to what degree can I truly love the Other by keeping my own needs from dominating them?"* We repeatedly ask them for what we have not learned to give ourselves, or find for ourselves. As we mature, we learn more and more that we are responsible for meeting our needs, not the Other upon whom we would impose this task. The more we can take on this project, the more we can live with ambiguity— as individuals and as a society—the freer and more worthy of the name of *love* the relationship becomes.

LOVE AS A SHADOW TASK

And how many relationships are governed by the principle of love, by caring for *the otherness of the other*? How many are sabotaged by the reactivation of the archaic imagoes of Self and Other? How many are impaired, not through continuing enlargement and mutual support of their separate journeys, but by dint of habit, fear of change, lack of permission to live one's own journey, and refusal to accept the summons to their own responsibility? As a therapist, I have often been on the horns of a painful dilemma. Having been asked to help a relationship, and having an ethical obligation to do so, at the same time I have sometimes perceived that the relationship was founded on the immaturity of one or both parties. If this immaturity can be brought to consciousness, and responsibility accepted for it, then there is a distinct hope for evolution of the relationship to a more satisfying and developmental agenda. Sadly, the one less developed or less mature is frequently unwilling, or unable, to take on the project. He or she will continue to bring the relationship back to its less mature stage and insist on that stasis, which serves security but not growth, and certainly cannot claim the label of love. Ironically, love becomes a Shadow task for us all when it 1) asks more of us than that which makes us comfortable, 2) asks us to examine our own complexes and regressive imagoes, and 3) asks a greater generosity of spirit than we consider comfortable.

My bias here is clear. *A relationship should serve the growth of each party toward becoming more nearly who he or she is capable of becoming.* I do not see that relationship in which people "take care of each other" as worthy of the name of relationship, at least not a loving, mature relationship. Love is supportive and caring, and therefore we freely offer gifts to each other . . . gifts that sometimes ask considerable sacrifice of ourselves. Kindness, affection, and empathy are part of any healthy relationship, and doing for the other is a gift to both of us, as long as it is not in service to an old codependency, or a sullen compliance.

Love asks independence of both parties, freedom, not control, not guilt, not coercion, not manipulation. Dependency is not love; it is dependency—it is an abrogation of the essential responsibility of each of us to grow up, to assume full responsibility for our lives. Not to take on this challenge is a flight from adulthood, no matter how mature a person may be in other areas of endeavor. This Shadow issue haunts most relationships and constitutes the chief source of unhappiness, blaming, and stuckness. We all find it easier to blame our partners than to grow up, to recognize that we are the only ones present in each scene in that long-running drama we call our life. So it stands to reason that *we* are the ones charged with its outcomes and consequences, not our partners. Acknowledging this responsibility is easy enough in the abstract, but it is fearfully challenging in the context of daily life when our will is fragmented, when we are vulnerable, and when we fall back into our archaic complexes.

Tom and Sally, our prototypical couple, have reached their forties, have the two children and home in the suburbs for which they planned, and find themselves irritable and retaliatory with each other. One will say "something," or not do "something," whatever, and the reaction of the other is immediately inflamed emotion, accusation, and more bad marital karma. What courses beneath the surface of each of them is the haunting fear, albeit essentially unconscious, that, having achieved their outer goals, and having played out their economic and domestic roles, they have no sense of what their life is really about. They are in the second half of life and, while they attend religious and civic organizations dutifully, neither feels a deep engagement with anything. This undiagnosed ennui, drift, and sense of dislocation has not been treated and solved by the solidity of their middle-class life, and certainly not by the marriage itself. Accordingly, their irritation, which is "leaking anger" deriving from "denied depression," reaches the surface in blaming, in picking fights, and in an escalating sense of hopelessness.

Tom and Sally's marriage is so typical because it carries, and suffers, the burden of our chief fantasy, namely, that the magical "other" will fix things for us, render life meaningful, heal our wounds, and help us avoid the task of growing up and facing the huge existential vacuum that all conscious souls must engage.* Because life, with all its possibilities, all its decisions, is so huge, we cling to the small, and hope the Other will spare us the task of growing up. But, since they do not, cannot, and should not, we are angry with them. This is Shadow material, for it feeds on that which lies within us, that which makes us uncomfortable with ourselves, that which intimidates us.

Thus, Tom blames Sally for not understanding him; Sally blames Tom for not supporting her sundry labors. While it is true that each might be more thoughtful about the burdens of the other, each is caught in the shadowy narcissistic preoccupations that are our common heritage. To confess personal confusion, even despair, to confess fear of the future, to confess one's growing sense of inadequacy, is precisely what would invite both to reframe their experience of the other. Sometimes, in marital therapy, I have managed to get people to voice these deepest secrets, but first we had to get beyond the most primitive of our defenses, the ascription of blame to the other. When couples quit marital therapy it is generally because one or both have concluded that the other is not going to make them "happy"—whatever that is—or that, conversely, they are not willing to agree that such a numinous task is theirs to assume. The assumption of this elemental responsibility is what may free each to support the other in a consistent context of care, without expecting the other to solve the convoluted conundrums of one's own life. Yet it often proves too much for

---

*For a more complete discussion of this issue, please see *The Eden Project: In Search of the Magical Other*.

many to accept this Shadow issue as theirs rather than the short-comings of their aggrieved partner. Our most primitive defense is to look outside ourselves for the cause of the problem. Acknowledging that *we* are the only constant in every relationship requires taking on the problem of our Shadow.

How can we ever be free of our narcissistic, self-aggrandizing agendas? The considered answer is that we cannot—to think otherwise is to fantasize an impossible level of individuation. While it is true that we can occasionally reach that high promontory, we are not strong enough to remain there. For example, who among us can consistently address our own emotional needs in a mature way? Who among us can fully assume the task of self-worth and not expect our partners to be an uncritical cheering section? Who among us will not retaliate when the Other lets us down? Who among us can really take responsibility for our emotional well-being and wholly lift it off of our partners? And yet, those are the tasks of maturity, from whence comes the quality of all of our relationships.

And, paradoxically, if we are constantly "the person for others," we risk codependency and the erosion of legitimate self-interest. An autonomous reflex to relinquish self-interest will prove unhealthy over time. We do have a right to be respected, to be treated with caring, concern, and support by everyone in our lives. Our nature does not wish abuse of any kind. Repressing what is natural within us breeds monsters sooner or later. The most common monster will be depression, the sort of depression that comes from our own psyche's protest at our abdication. The next most common monster will be anger, the secondary response to the anxiety begun in the denial of legitimate self-interest. Even with the most careful monitoring, this anger will leak out into the body, into irritability, into acts that have more force and covert aggression to them than we would have consciously granted them. Thus the Shadow is at work, acting surreptitiously because of what we neglected to deal with consciously.

MATURE RELATIONSHIP

So relationship is a continuous paradox, a venue in which legitimate self-interest and the interest of the other are sometimes contending. These separate agendas need not be hostile, nor even antagonistic, for a healthy relationship is one in which each party is devoted to supporting the well-being of the other. A mature relationship is one in which each party assumes responsibility for her or his individuation, and supports the other in hers or his as well. When that intentionality is common to both, even the occasional complex-driven lapses into unbalanced relationship will be quickly righted, or forgiven. When such intentionality is owned by only one party, the relationship will be unbalanced, and is already careening toward conflict and possible dissolution. On paper this definition of a mature relationship sounds reasonable, even easy; in practice, it is very difficult, for the level of maturity it demands asks a great deal of each of us. If I can reasonably assume that the Other is not here to make my life work for me, but intends to support my efforts to do so, then I will have made a huge stride toward cleaning up the debris that hampers and impairs relationships. Sadly, many persons slip into controlling behaviors because they are terrified of not having the child within them taken care of by the Other. Or, they are terrified of the Other growing up, hearing their own drummer, and leaving them. So we who say we value relationships so much are so frequently incapable of rising to the truism that defines all relationships, namely, that the relationship can be no more evolved than the maturity level of each of the parties therein.

When I have seen couples in therapy the first question in my mind is to assess their emotional maturity. Clearly, this maturity is not necessarily a function of age and experience. It is rather a function of personal strength, and, to use an old fashioned word, character. Sadly, by the time most couples come to therapy the blood is drained from the corporate entity, the goodwill exhausted, grievances accumulated, and accusations hurled at the other with no little vehemence. Some couples regress as a result of therapy because these armed assaults bring further, sometimes irreparable, wounds. An old Carly Simon song extolled the virtue of relational communication for several stanzas. In the last stanza she ruefully confesses that, "sometimes I wish I never knew some of those secrets of yours." So even "communication" can be overrated. Yet lest I be accused of condoning secrecy, one suspects that even the material that remains underground leaks into the conduct of daily life and poisons the air that the couple breathes.

In assessing the strength of the relationship, one is really asking the strength of the individual, whether they are mature enough to take on responsibility for their own lives. If asked directly, they readily reply in the affirmative, and point to areas of responsibility and successful management in their outer world, but how often do they take measure of the magnitude of their Edenic hopes that are transferred to the partner? None of us is free of the deep, archaic fantasy that the other will make our life work for us, offer meaning, bring relief to prior wounds, and, if we are lucky, spare us the burden of growing up and taking our life on. The Shadow task here is daunting, for it means that one has to step into the places of doubt and anxiety, one has to accept a larger definition of oneself, and one has to accept finally that we are all alone, radically alone, and never more so than when in relationship with another.

There is an old proverb that says that it is better to be alone than to wish to be alone. Yet when the tenor of popular culture is all about finding the "magical other," or offering a set of diversions from the fact of one's aloneness, we realize that the Shadow of loneliness haunts our crowded lives. (One therapy colleague of mine once said to me, "I do therapy with others to help bear my loneliness.") Another proverb has it that "the proper cure for loneliness is solitude." Solitude is a state of being in which one is present to oneself, present to the various, goodly company within, and therefore never alone. Achieving solitude, paradoxically, is the single best indication for the well-being of a relationship. My capacity to tolerate myself, when I am really present to myself, forecasts my capacity to be in a nonaggressive, non-narcissistic relationship to the other. What a strange paradox this is, then, that *the Shadow summons of tolerating ourselves is directly linked to the Shadow challenge of tolerating the otherness of the Other*. Who'd have thunk?

Thus, the prognosis for any relationship is based on this Shadow dilemma—namely, *can I live with myself as I really am?* If I can't, why should I expect that someone else can, or should? When one party or the other is estranged from selfhood, from truly abiding and containing the fears and aspirations of their existential loneliness, then they will impose this impossible mélange on the Other. No wonder we valorize relationships, yet so many are broken. No wonder we wander amid clamorous crowds but grow more and more lonely.

Possibly it is easier for introverts to develop an inner life, possibly not, but extroverts, whose natural tendency is to value and be energized by engagement with others, are all the more at risk for imposing a flight from themselves on others. Either way, without an inner life, that is, a relationship to a personal, consistent reality, a sense of guidance within, we are going to activate more and more obstructive dynamics that are transferred to our partners, those whom we profess to love. We all know this, but do not wish to hear it. It is much easier to blame the other, or to find a better "Other."

Becoming Psychological

Developing an inner life requires becoming psychological. What does it mean to become psychological? Does it mean that I can more effectively analyze the Other and potentially manipulate that knowledge to my own ends? That is indeed a Shadow temptation! It is probably why folks begin studying psychology in the first place, although this motive may be unconscious. Rather, becoming psychological requires that I ask myself of every impulse, every behavior, every pattern: "Where does this come from within me?" "Where have I been here before?" "What does this feel like?" Although life is forever changing, and each moment truly unique, our intrapsychic history imposes the same old, same old upon those new moments. Being psychological requires so much sustained attentiveness that we all tend to forswear the effort.

Consider our comrades Tom and Sally again. When Sally presses, he withdraws. When Tom withdraws, Sally gets anxious, and retaliatory. What is this pas de deux that so repetitively plays out? These two people, convinced that they love each other and are loved in return, cannot enter the arena of intimacy without some activation of that historic field of energy that constitutes our sense of self and sense of Other. Tom cannot help but project some of his history with women, most notably his invasive, demanding mother, onto his intimate partner. When Sally gets too much in his face, that archaic history is transferred to the present. Because the child's first line of defense was to escape from the threat, this otherwise empowered adult man slips reflexively into an archaic defense and retreats. His behavior activates in Sally her projection of the absent, rejecting parent. In fact, her complex sets her up to expect abandonment. In that moment, she transfers to Tom all the angst, anguish, and anger that that child could never express, and they are both off to the races once again.

Becoming psychological requires that we continuously reflect on the twin dynamics that are forever at work beneath the surface of all relationships, namely, *projection* and *transference*. Any content of the unconscious may be projected onto the Other at any moment. Moreover, the dynamics associated with that content, and its archaic history, will be transferred to the Other as well. This is why our relationships have such recurrent motifs. (Think of Evelyn's marital choices. Why would a very bright woman choose the same pattern over and over?) Again, when described consciously, it sounds obvious, but when we are not conscious, or do not wish to be, we ascribe the genesis of conflicts that arise to the Other. Being psychological requires reflecting continuously on one's own history and one's agenda.

How many of us really want to make that effort? But the alternative of remaining unconscious goes less well, as we all know. I have sometimes cringed within when a couple says, "We want to work on our relationship." Do they know what that means, that such work will require heroic effort on their part, or do they expect that the work will ultimately conform their partner into the template they carry within themselves? What this asks of Tom is not to retreat in the face of Sally's urgency, but to move closer, which will reassure her. What is asked of Sally is not to lambaste the Other for not being there, but learn to take greater responsibility for her own emotional nurturance. To break this wicked cycle of projection and transference, each has to look within and bring great courage to curbing reflexive responses that once saved them but now enslave them. Only then are shackles broken and relationship possible.

What I do not wish to face in myself, what I do not wish to assume responsibility for, is *my* Shadow, not yours. The best I can ask of you is that you try to take your Shadow work seriously, as I seek to do mine. Is that too much to ask? Given the sorry state of so many relationships, the answer seems to be "yes," for such maturational endeavor demands too much of most of us most of the time. Putting it crudely, only grown-ups can have effective relationships, and while there are a lot of people with big bodies and big roles in life, there are not many grown-ups.*

Reluctantly, ineluctably, we are drawn to acknowledge three principles of relational dynamics, principles that are present in all relationships at all times:

I. We have a natural tendency to project onto the Other what we do not know about ourselves (the *unconscious*), or what we do not want to know about ourselves (the *Shadow*), or our reluctance to grow up and assume full responsibility for ourselves (our resistant *immaturity*).

II. Since the other will not, cannot, and should not take on the responsibility for what we have deferred—our unconsciousness, our Shadow, our immaturity—or our hidden agenda is frustrated, and the relationship tends to devolve into the problem of *power*, with its invitation to control or manipulate the other, or to *blame*, with its familiar dyad of victim and villain.

III. The relationship is thereby left with the choices of dissolution, blaming, sustained anger and depression, or growing up. The only way in which we can grow up, and the relationship evolve into a realistic experience worthy of our continuing investment,

---

*In the words of the immortal American philosopher Pearl Bailey, "Thems whats thinks they is, ain't."

is to withdraw the projections and transference over time, own them as our Shadow stuff, and take responsibility for our emotional well-being and spiritual growth, even as we choose to support our partner's efforts to do the same.

To repeat, these three stages of engagement are present in all intimate relationships at all times. What varies is not the dynamics, though they may greatly vary in intensity or form of expression, but whether or to what degree each partner has matured, or is willing to mature. Such a maturing process will oblige facing some tough, Shadow-laden questions. Among them are:

- "Where do my dependencies show up in this relationship, and what must I address to cease being dependent?"
- "What am I asking my partner to do for me that I should be able to do for myself, if I am going to be a self-respecting adult fully charged with the conduct of my life?"
- "How do I repeatedly constrict myself by reimporting my history, with all its charged reflexive responses, into this relationship?"
- "Am I truly supportive of my partner, while not taking on his or her responsibility to grow up and be a free adult?"

These questions require examining our Shadow and being willing to deal with whatever comes onto the screen of consciousness. Hearing the other's experience of us in the face of these specific questions is often a good place to start, if we can bear that. The Other whom we most wish to blame for the shortcomings of the relationship is also the person who knows us the most, or at least knows us from a refracted angle from which we are often unable to see ourselves.

We say we treasure relationships, and yet sabotage them daily. The ghosts that haunt them derive from two sources:

1) the power of history to replicate itself through the mechanisms of complex, projection, and transference, and 2) the inordinate existential angst generated by the summons to grow up. Growing up means owning our vulnerability and learning to function in the face of it. In a poem titled "The Fury of Overshoes," poet Anne Sexton remembers what it was like to be a tiny person, how she necessarily deflected authority onto the big people around her and tried to adapt and adjust as life required, but how, even now, she looks for that guidance from without and wonders how to be a grown-up:

> . . . *where are the big people,*
> *when will I get there?**

Where are the big people who are required to discern what really matters; where are the big people to assume responsibility; when will *we* get there?

*Anne Sexton, "The Fury of Overshoes," in Hunter, *The Norton Introduction to Poetry*, p. 16.

Chapter Six

ONE MULTIPLIED
The Collective Shadow

"That vice pays homage to virtue is notorious,
we call this hypocrisy; there should be a word
found for the homage which virtue not infrequently
pays, or at any rate would be wise in paying,
to vice."
—SAMUEL BUTLER, *THE WAY OF ALL FLESH*

"All humanity is one undivided and indivisible
family, and each one of us is responsible for the
misdeeds of all the others. I cannot detach
myself from the wickedest soul."
—MOHANDAS GANDHI

*W*herever we go, we carry our Shadow with us. In fact, the larger the light, the longer the Shadow will inevitably prove to be. The more "enlightened" we believe ourselves to be, the vaster we discover that which remains unconscious, or must be defended against. (As someone put it to me today, "The more I read, the more I realize I have never read. I wonder if I will live long enough.")* Some of the craziest people I know are graduate analysts. Some are delightfully crazy, and are usually of great help to their patients; others are unable to keep their craziness from harming

*The answer to that rhetorical question is obvious.

those who come to them. No amount of analysis, concerted effort toward consciousness, or willfulness toward virtue proves a sure stay against Shadow irruptions.

Everywhere we move, our Shadow trails us—its hidden agendas, its repressed motives, its imposing history, its unlived life, its fear-driven stratagems. Into relationships, into work life, into the dream I dream tonight, the Shadow elements are dynamically active. And if this is so of any and each of us, only one person, what happens wherever more than one are gathered? Does not the Shadow go with each of them, occasion contrary, or mutual, projections, blend together, provide an even greater sum of darkness? Is not the Shadow of a group more than the sum of individual Shadows, and might it not create a whole new dimension of unconsciousness? Just as two persons can intermingle their Shadows, producing the famous *folie à deux*, so groups can suffer a collective contagion, a group madness, a communal enthusiasm. We have only to look at the sad chronicle of human history to see collective contagions, participatory madness, wars and witch hunts, and the violence that may rise from collective possessions.*

My mother once told me that the most precious Christmas gift she ever received came to her around 1920, when she received an orange, and only an orange, for Christmas, a gift from her mother, who took in washing and sewing for them to survive. This was before refrigerated trucks and trains, so for an orange to even survive the trip north was a small miracle. It was the first orange she had ever seen, and she knew that her mag-

---

*Of the many historic examples possible, see Aldous Huxley's *The Devils of Loudon*, an account of a seventeenth-century outbreak of sexual hysteria in a group of nuns who project their Shadow onto a priest who is burned at the stake as a scapegoat for their unconscious contagion. In 1600, in the heart of Rome, Giordano Bruno is burned by the church for his support of the new astronomy, and Galileo is placed under house arrest by the Inquisition. Why were they all so afraid? What Shadow was afoot in these sacred organizations?

ical gift came through great sacrifice by her mother. I think of this every year when I watch ordinary people pummeling each other to get into a Wal-Mart or Costco at six A.M. on Black Friday, the onset of the celebration of the purported Prince of Peace, the onset of a materialist frenzy that mocks his life and teaching.

Just as the ego of the individual is predisposed to defend itself, prejudice its limited purview of reality, reject those elements that are discordant, disruptive, and threatening, so, too, groups always have a fluid, amorphous, but highly vulnerable "ego." From any region of our psyche excluded from sustained self-examination, much energy may be released, for good or ill, no matter how benign the intent of the group may be. Moreover, that fluid, amorphous ego is always highly susceptible to the manipulation of a charismatic leader. Each individual in the group brings complexes, needs, and hidden agendas waiting to be activated. Dictators, politicians, and televangelists skillfully exploit this group fluidity—comprised both of collective insecurities and the unexamined lives of each individual multiplied.

THE SHADOW OF GOOD

Sometimes we see very dramatic examples of people's beneficent Shadow. In times of national or regional catastrophe, people are often moved to great acts of charity, personal risk, and generosity of feeling. I have been moved to tears by the response of people to their neighbor's plight. Electrical teams travel across state boundaries to restore power, medical resources are mobilized, money and supplies are gathered, and some of my colleagues have flown to these scenes to work with exhausted and traumatized victims and rescuers alike. Many seemingly ordinary folks, who hours before might have proved indifferent to their neighbor, even hostile at times, are strangely, impressively transformed into their neighbor's keeper.* Thus, even our "goodness" may erupt from our Shadow, a hidden, beneficent aspect of our own nature.

A cynic might argue that altruistic behaviors are a deeper form of narcissism, that we secretly defend against our own trauma and isolation by acting in this supportive way. But I am rather persuaded that in these moments of transcendent summons, many are rather lifted out of their conventional isolation into a higher participation with others. Our words that describe this phenomenon are strangely revealing. *Compassion*, which means to share the suffering (*passio*=Latin for suffering) of the other is synonymous with *sympathy* and *empathy* (*pathos*=Greek for suffering) or the German *Mitleid* ("suffering with"). In those moments the person is prised out of his or her narcissistic isolation into a *participation*, or imaginative identification, with our transcendent unity of being. Each perceives, more existentially than consciously, that the spaces between us are delusory, and that we are knit together in a common human identity. In those moments we may be raised above the agendas of self-interest to participate in our common fate, common destiny, and become larger than our ordinary selfish operations.

This transformation from self-isolation into participation with others, this "projective identification," is a deeply energized identification with the other, and from time to time trumps the reflexive defenses of the individual ego. Even this humanitarian impulse is, I submit, a Shadow manifestation. What we have

---

*One may also witness the recrudescence of the vicious, narcissistic Shadow. Within days of the Katrina disaster, some cynics focused on looters, rather than botched governmental operations; some objected to the relocation of minorities in their cities; some complained of minor interruptions of their own life while turning from the devastation brought to their neighbor's lives. One former First Lady opined that the dislocated refugees now in her city must have it pretty good because their life was not so great in New Orleans.

denied inwardly is suddenly active in the outer world and achieves a transcendent hold on our ego. The agenda of impulsive self-interest is momentarily supplanted by those energies that are normally repressed, split off, or operating only at the unconscious level. Where there is so much splitting and animosity in our souls, there may also be *caritas*, which is an expressive form of love.

Working with chronic abusers of children or serial rapists is a most dreary and enervating therapy with very poor prognosis. A corner can only be turned in the treatment of such individuals when he or she is able to experience the pain that he or she has brought on the other. In that moment, their mutually felt pain is a linking bridge to the other, and the possibility of change through identification with the other is possible. In any case, the Shadow dimension that has theretofore been repressed—compassion, sensitivity to the needs of others—has risen to the surface and offers the possibility of mutual healing. As there is no abuser who has not been abused, the capacity to feel empathy for their victim, rare as that may be, is the only hope for their healing. Ironically, such empathy will be experienced as excruciatingly painful, for much of their survival depended on numbing themselves, transferring the pain to another, and learning coping adjustments that bury, desensitize, or dissociate the suffering.*

On the other hand, wherever there are natural disasters, there are also looters, or those who come along with insurance scams, or roofing and siding rip-offs, and are ready to bilk their stricken neighbors. We do not have to look far to see these repulsive

---

*A compelling illustration of this "psychic numbing" is dramatized in the novel and film *The Pawnbroker*, the story of a repulsive merchant who victimizes all who enter his shop. Through a series of flashbacks we learn that he witnessed the brutalization and annihilation of his family in a concentration camp. Only when he is ambushed by his long-buried pain, and feels the suffering of another, can he reenter the world of humanity, which he formerly found necessary to escape.

persons take advantage of someone's vulnerability. Still, as convenient and as easy to label their larcenous, exploitative behavior as Shadow material, it is perhaps even more difficult to account for the behavior of those who rise above the opportunity for self-gain and voluntarily sacrifice on behalf of compassionate support of the other. Both, paradoxically, represent the emergence of what is so clearly possible within each of us, although we may not have called these dual possibilities into consciousness before.

SHADOW ECSTASIES

And how can we forget the old saw, *in vino veritas*? How many shy, repressed young souls, under the influence of "spirits," are surprisingly the life of the party, with lampshades on their heads, suddenly amorous and expressing forbidden desires? How many can suddenly sing, tell jokes, laugh uproariously, be moved to tears and sentimentality? Did not T. S. Eliot suggest in his play *The Cocktail Party* that the bar, or the Dionysian revel, had become the new confessional? How many have discovered their Shadow "under the influence" of some kind, and the next day lived to rue the effects? And yet, how many have discovered genuine aspects of their personality in those expressively free moments, those "hours of the spirits"? Such free spirits live within each of us, but we learned early that their expression proved too costly in one's tribe or one's family, and only the effect of altered chemistry, or group permission, now allows this split-off aspect of the soul to be expressed. When we ask the question, "Why is it that we have to hide so much of who we are from others, even from ourselves?" the answer is found in the cost that was once exacted of us. Thus, we become strangers to ourselves, as well as others, and the Shadow material grows apace.

And still, as we know, the great preponderance of domestic violence, traffic fatalities, sexual indiscretions, and criminal behavior also occurs when people are drunk, experiencing what Pierre Janet, the French psychologist of the nineteenth century, called *l'abaissement du niveau mental*, the lowering of the attention of consciousness, or effective ego filtering. What is the psychological difference between a crowd smoking pot at a rock concert, adrift on the cacophony of sound that numbs ego vigility, and a hundred thousand good burghers at a Nazi rally at Munich raising their arm in frenzied transports to a Führer? Are not individuals in both groups lifted out of their individual consciousness, their ethical limitations, even their conventional fears, and transported into a transcendent realm that is energized, exhilarating, ecstatic?* What leads ordinary kids who the year before might have competed on opposing football teams, and who are now driven by fear, isolation, homesickness, and group numbing, to participate in a massacre, emptying their M-16s into prisoners, or colluding in their torture and humiliation, as we have so recently seen reported on our television screens? Were these possibilities not already latent within us, one would find it difficult to enact these barbarisms, even if it were an expression of national policy. Military authorities were stunned after studies of combat behaviors in World War II and Korea revealed that the preponderant majority of soldiers, even those under fire, did not fire back in anger. It was speculated that most carried a deep prohibition against killing another, even in war. This perplexing resistance was substantially overcome in the training of Vietnam soldiers, and their successors, whereby reluctant instincts are overthrown by more conditioning to reflexively obey orders to fire.

---

*Ecstasy (Greek: *ek-stasis*) means to step outside oneself, to "be beside oneself" with joy or terror.

Who among us does not desire *ek-stasis*, the ecstatic transformation of quotidian life into some great high? What atrocities, pogroms, holocausts, have risen from ordinary folks like you and me when transported by large, seductive ideologies, groupthink, and desperate times into doing what we would not otherwise have done? As Edmund Burke observed in the eighteenth century, all that is necessary for the triumph of evil is the silence of the good people. What happens when "the good people" are themselves the agent of evil, whether through overt acts, looking the other way, or benign indifference?* We know, for example, that the number of people who perpetrated the Holocaust was a distinct minority. We also know that the number who protested was miniscule. The vast number were the bystanders, the trimmers, the indifferent, the intimidated, the ordinary people who took no large interest in such matters beyond their scope or responsibility, like you and like me.

We know that the work of the Holocaust, and other such dreadful visitations to our history, were possible only because of the cooperation of the ordinary folks. There are not that many individual madmen in any age, but great collective lunacy does indeed occur because charismatic madness touches and activates the "mad parts" in otherwise quite sane people. Psychological contagions, Shadow plagues, do occur, and few of us, if any, are exempt. As we will see later, the quite banal Adolf Eichmann was hardly a monster; he was too much the civil servant, the prototypical functionary. Among other things, he solved "transportation problems." What did it matter what cargo of forsaken humanity those trains carried, or where, when

---

*This disturbing paradox is the theme of Goldhagen's book, *Hitler's Willing Executioners*. Hitler did not have to organize the madmen; he had to organize and motivate ordinary people. So, to use a modern phrase, he used distracting "wedge issues" and looked for scapegoats—anything to mobilize the Shadow that waits for such opportunities.

he was secure in the fact that he served "a higher order," was valued for doing so, and was thereby gifted with a transcendent mission for his tawdry life! Even the most terrible things will be inspired by a noble-sounding reason.

Studies of the police battalions, recruited as mobile execution units in Eastern Europe and the Russian steppes, reveal that those who had sworn to uphold the decencies of common law were quite accommodating in committing atrocities. When brought before the bar of justice, their defense was stunningly simple: The law had been changed, and thus they were still upholding the law! Nazi doctors were able to affirm their Hippocratic Oath—the guiding principle of which is to do no harm—visit their families, and then participate in horrific experiments in the name of a pseudoscience. They could live out this Shadow life through numbing with schnapps; through splitting—"Here is my life; here is my work; they exist in separate rooms"—by rationalizing—"This is in service to the New Order"—and by participating in something so large that they could not fathom it or alter it. Contrary to popular assumption, those who did resist such brutalization of themselves and others were often dismissed or marginalized, but seldom if ever killed. One has to wonder if the Holocaust, and similar horrors, would have happened if enough simple citizens had refused the brutalization of their own souls, and thus the brutalization of others.

Lest any of us grow smug, we have to remember the experiments of Stanley Milgram at Yale in the 1960s. He planned to visit Germany and perhaps identify what might constitute the "German character" that would have led this civilized nation to such collective barbarity. Considering that so many ordinary folks succumbed to barbarism under stress, he developed some protocols to explore this possibility. Before going to Germany he decided to test the experiments on ordinary citizens recruited from the streets of New Haven, Connecticut. These ordinary people, like you and me, were told they were part of "scientific research" of a high order. They were asked to slowly interrogate subjects with questions, an unsuccessful answer to which occasioned an electrical shock to that subject. As the subjects progressively missed questions they were increasingly shocked, began to protest, and then to scream when the voltage was increased. When these citizens hesitated to inflict pain on the subjects, they were verbally pressured to continue, to increase the pain and thereby to *serve science,* and to honor the agreement that they had made. In the face of apparent, palpable suffering they were causing, the troubling majority, more than 60 percent, continued the experiment and increased the ostensible pain levels of the subjects to terrible levels.

These were ordinary people, like you and me, and yet most of them continued to increase the pain of their fellow humans because they lacked enough personal integrity, or courage, or ethics, or whatever, to resist and accept whatever costs. What they did not know was that the experiment was rigged, that the subjects were not being shocked but were dramatically acting as though they were. The bottom line of the experiment was that Dr. Milgram had no need to go to Germany to find out about "German character." The Shadow, it seems, knows no international borders.

I have always feared being so tested, whether here today, or there historically, for I do not know how I would have acted under the circumstances. It is easy to judge others, but how would we have acted? How do we act today?*

---

*The question is hardly theoretical, for we all observed the President and the Vice President of the United States oppose the McCain Amendment, which sought to outlaw torture as an official instrument of United States policy.

I recall the doctor who was embarrassed by his son's sexual preference, told anti-gay jokes himself, yet would never countenance anti-Semitic jokes. How many gay jokes, or racist slurs, or ethnic generalizations have you or I perpetuated recently, or failed to challenge? How can we say that the Shadow is *out there* when it is so much a part of our collective culture? Again, just as we have a fragile ego, so does a group. Groups are easily swayed, or manipulative marketers, cynical politicians, and unctuous televangelists would quickly be out of a job. And through them, and chinks in our consciousness, we are led to collude with what we would otherwise repudiate.

In recent years one large Christian denomination chose to affirm the Bible as the normative standard of their faith, rather than the life of Jesus Christ. At first glance, this shift might appear minimal. But in fact what these august leaders were up to was moving away from the troubling paradigm embodied in the lifestyle and the associations of the unmarried Jesus with publicans and prostitutes, and his challenge to love the "other," to an earlier and far harsher set of tribal values. (As Shakespeare observed in *The Merchant of Venice*, even the Devil can find supportive evidence to support any position from the motley biblical admonitions that range over many centuries and many tribes.) These denominational worthies tipped their hands. They were unsettled by their Jesus, and thus moved aggressively so that their personal complexes could be stoutly defended by selective use of biblical citations. While they would never submit their bodies to the medicine of that ancient era, they are perfectly willing to uncritically accept the limited ethnocentric values of a prescientific, culturally isolated, tribal culture. Not long after that, they purged their seminaries and universities of dissenting professors. Is this not the Shadow run amok, under the guise of piety, conventionality, and the defense of neurosis—all in the name of the itinerant rabbi who preached inclusion, and upon whom their faith was once founded?

When we lived in Switzerland, I wanted my children to see the camps, and so we pilgrimaged to Dachau and Bergen-Belsen in Germany and Mauthausen in Austria. Neither child was drawn to ethnic humor or discriminatory behavior thereafter. Both understood that the terminus of the bigotry train lies in such hideous places. Together we counted the steps carved into the quarry at Mauthausen, up which prisoners were forced to run carrying twenty kilo stones; stood and peered over the edge of the "Parachutists' Cliff," so called because inmates were flung bodily over the edge to fall on the quarry floor below; and wondered aloud how such places could exist in our enlightened age. No amount of geopolitical, economic, or cultural analysis can answer such questions. Something dark lurks within our lives, within each of us! I finally concluded that such perplexities will remain unresolved, until at least enough of us can confess, *"Such horrors were committed by my countrymen, or by my coreligionists, or by my fellow human beings, and even I, who was not there, must nonetheless take responsibility."* Only then can any real healing begin.

While we stood at quarry's edge at Konzentrationslager Mauthausen, we peered through the barbed wire at red-cheeked farmers in fields of potatoes and beets, tilling in their timeless ways. Who could ever believe what once happened there? Could we, could they? What did their parents tell them? What did they tell their children? What was that awful smell? What happened to those human cargos that rolled into the village station?

Yet to forget is surely to push such energies, such terrible psychic possibilities into the underworld and insure their recrudescence in the next generation. Between the two great wars Jung reported the appearance of Wotan, the old Nordic storm god, "the Berserker," in the dreams of his German patients. Wotan, it seems, rides upon his eight-legged steed Sleipnir, rides eternally, and reappears whenever we forget his presence. Sleipnir's hooves resound in our dreams, just below the surface of civilization. Such forgetting begets holocausts.

THE SHADOW IN THE WORKPLACE

Still another way in which the collective Shadow manifests is in the workplace. Could we really believe that we leave our Shadows at home in the closet; could we ever believe that groups are not the sum of all of us, and are not burdened by our joint and separate issues? Why is it that groups, perhaps founded to serve a cause, or produce products, are so often dysfunctional, conflictual, ridden with animosities, stuck in low gear, or staffed by troubled souls?

There is a considerable difference between *society* and *community*. A society is formed consciously, deliberately, in service to a commonly perceived goal. We have an amorphous society on an airplane. What we have in common is that we are trying to fly from IAH to DEN or ORD. Should our plane go down, or intimate such to us, we suddenly have community, for each person at that moment is lifted out of his or her individual experience into a transcendent affective engagement which for the moment makes them one—still individuals, yet participants in a common experience. Societies are fragile because they have less binding power, and once the intentional goals are removed or wither in their cogency, the group dissolves.

Communities have staying power to the degree that the affective charge engendered by their primal experience still throbs within them. Societies touch the brain; communities touch the soul. A friend of mine once left a cushy job at a national cookie company because he and his colleagues were spending their free time talking about cookies. He knew his soul was not engaged and he left his economic security for the perilous life of the artist, to the dismay of all and the ridicule of some. He found a society there, but not a community. His community would be found in the paradox of exile, which every artist is obliged to undertake.

Let us recall that the word *psyche* is Greek for *soul*. As we never leave our psyches behind, so the soul is never absent in life. Our minds are directed toward the achievement of discernible goals—more production, conflict resolution, economic success—but the soul is always experienced in the context of meaning, purposiveness, how or in what way the spirit is engaged. A former personnel director of a large multinational told me that he would address his new employees and remind them that *the company did not love them*. The company rented their behaviors as long as they were productive for the company, and would immediately cease doing so once productivity fell off. This stark reminder of the realpolitik of business was quickly coupled with his admonition to find what in their work fed them emotionally, for their paycheck would never do so; and to cultivate relationships at work and at home, for only they would address the needs of the soul. He was a wise man whose real identification was with the worker and not the collective abstraction that every corporation represents.

This personnel director knew that when one loses contact with the soul, something pathologizes—some disturbance shows up in one's health, one's relationships, or one's emotional eruptions. Organizations that do not acknowledge the needs of the soul will be productive only so long; in time they will lose their best employees and spend too much energy trying to solve internal problems. The current penchant for "downsizing," or that obscene euphemism "managed care," or strictly "bottom line" thinking in corporate life leads inevitably to a loss of soul. Thus, the Shadow haunts each corporate entity.

One can divert libido, or psychic energy, only so long toward goals disconnected from the soul without the butcher's bill to pay. Just as individuals suffer neurosis, a split of conscious life from the agenda of the soul, so, too, can corporate entities suffer neuroses. Indeed, a whole new profession called "organizational development"—with degrees, certification programs, and professional standards committees—has grown up seeking to heal the soul of corporate life. OD practitioners are often brought in to help manipulate the bottom line, but find instead that they are having to treat the affective disorders of the company and the people within it. In this gray zone between consulting and one-on-one therapy they try to find their ambiguous way.

Those who work with groups or corporate entities find that just as the individual suffers the interference of *complexes*—energy-charged though buried "ideas" that, consciously or not, direct the person's behaviors—so the group dynamics will prove the sum of the complexes that all have brought to the common labor, and all employees are at the mercy of the dominant complexes of the leadership. It is no accident that the ancients believed that the health of the ruler determined the health of the nation. As the fairy tales express it, when the king is sick, or the queen missing, crops fail, pestilence breeds, children turn to stone in the womb. And people get sick at work.

Among the most common complexes that are expressions of Shadow energy are the parental imagoes. People look to the group entity to meet their emotional needs, and finding that this seldom occurs, they grow depressed, petulant, and unhappy in their work and begin withdrawing in subtle ways. Others, those who experienced parents as invasive, controlling figures, will enact a deep antagonism against their employers, sometimes even sabotaging their projects. The "fight" response that nature provides us manifests as aggression, stealing, sabotage; the "flight" response provides sloth, avoidance, and passive/aggressive behaviors.

Additionally, just as occurs in intimate relationships, the psychological mechanisms of *projection* and *transference* are common to corporate life, as well. People project sibling rivalry onto coworkers, compete for attention and affection, experience dependency or anger toward supervisors, and so on. Transference insures that the power of dynamics past persist into the present. Thus, corporate life often replicates the dramas and disappointments of family life, occasions archaic parent-child dynamics, and produces a familiar pattern in the emotional life of the employee. And, just as the developmental task of the child obliges adaptation to the conditions of its environment, so the employee develops a false self,* a glossy persona, yet plays out its archaic adaptations. In the face of the power of the corporate entity, the employee will avoid wherever possible, or placate, often in ways that are costly to the psychological integrity of the individual. In the face of the insufficient nurturance of the corporate entity, the employee will have a tendency to continuously solicit reassurance, or will be seduced by the power complex into competing for an office with a view, a flashier title, or a special perk. If money solved these emo-

---

*The "false self" is a term popularized by the British psychoanalyst D. W. Winnicott. This is not a hypocritical falsity, but the assumption of an adaptive identity and role instead of one's natural being.

tional needs, we would know it, for money is available, yet people remain troubled, and our corporate life vexed.

What is not faced by the individual in his or her personal psychology will inevitably show up in corporate life and play out its familiar skein of consequences. Any organization, no matter how benign or benevolent its intent, inevitably invokes the primal imagoes that its employees carry within, those charged clusters that derive from and replicate the family-of-origin dynamics. When the contemporary collective invokes reflexive, false-self behaviors and attitudes, any group can prove iatrogenic, infantilizing, and regressive.

When we add to the mix the Shadow agenda of all groups over time, namely, that their original high purpose devolves to preserve the organization at all costs and to protect those who receive privileges from the group, the psychological consequences to the individual can be immense. Among these consequences are the further diminution of personal authority, the evocation of infantilizing reactive patterns, and the replication of personal neuroses. As the psyche is always asking, "Where have I been here before?" what will come up most powerfully in our intimate and our corporate relationships is the programming from our first lessons of self and other—the family of origin. Thus churches, hospitals, and universities* can all serve to oppress the growth and development of the persons whom they are charged to support.

In *The Republic*, Plato asks the question: "Who is fit to govern another?" He answers with "the philosopher King," namely one not only brought to power but one who has gained a measure of wisdom. What we so frequently find in organizations is

---

*We do not call them our *alma mater* for nothing. Historian Arthur Schlessinger once wryly observed that "academic politics is so vicious because its stakes are so trivial."

that what brings a person to office is a driving complex, a powerfully charged script that admits little self-critique, is defensive in the face of criticism from others, and is so often self-serving that groups take on the flavor of the stuckness of its leadership. Therapists and organizational development people see this phenomenon at work all the time. They may have been summoned by leadership to deal with a corporate problem, but that same leadership will also fiercely resist change, genuine dialogue, and the critiques of those who are most affected by the common neurosis.

Thus the Shadow of any organization is constituted by that which threatens the ego in charge, that which carries the unexamined, unconsciousness of leadership. Thus, even the most benign group may covertly be controlled by greed, by immaturity, or by the narcissistic needs of the boss. Whether brought to consciousness or not, all within will suffer and will symptomatically express this conflict in ways that injure the group and the individuals, as well.

Moreover, with few exceptions, most corporate entities are driven by bottom-line values, productivity quotas, and quarterly reports to the board and stockholders. Thus, they ignore the quality-of-life issues. This is not unlike politicians who ignore polluting factories in their city rather than risk losing a tax ratable. They forget that they, too, breathe that same air, as do their children, and that invisible toxins are already working their way into the genetic program of generations. On the other hand, those programs that reward employees in other than fiscal form, those that contribute to the supportive atmosphere in which all are daily involved, or those that pay serious attention to the psychological effects of workplace aesthetics will prove the most stable and profitable companies in the long run. But for those whose eyes can only see the short term, these quality-of-life issues are pushed into the Shadow realm, and, sooner or later, all suffer. No corporate entity, then, can be wiser or more conscious than its leadership. Sadly, corporate leaders are frequently those whose personal psychologies are most resistant to dialectic, change, and dissent.*

The misery brought to both employees and the general public alike by the grandiosity of leadership in such disasters as Enron, Tyco, and others is a reminder of how even the so-called brightest in the room cast a long Shadow. Additionally, how many stock analysts, how many accounting firms, how many law firms sniffed the scent of scandal but were gorging too much from the trough to sound the tocsin? How many circles widened out from those central perpetrators, perhaps with diminishing knowledge of the flimflam, but all driven by lure of easy gain? Again, it is a disquieting thought to ask what *we* would do if, for example, we were in middle management, were profiting from the rise of our stock portfolio, knew that the company's quarterly profits depended upon ever-rosy balance sheets, yet knew that ethical practices were compromised? Would we jeopardize our job? Would we quit? Would we inform the press? Or would we get as much as we could and lay it away? Again, the disturbing parallel to the Holocaust troubles us. Are we perpetrator, witness, bystander, rescuer, victim? In the words of the famous Watergate question: "What did we know, and when did we know it?" To this must be added, "And what did we do about it?"

---

*I recall once hearing a visiting board member praise the president of an institution for which I worked, saying that one could always tell a strong leader because he surrounded himself with other strong personalities. We all, secretly, howled at this idea, for those of us who worked on the inside of the entity knew that the second tier of administration was filled with yes-men and -women, and that the president was notoriously vain and defended. Needless, to say, the turnover in staff was constant.

WHAT DOES THE SOUL WANT?

Just as the healing of the individual requires recovering a connection to soul, so the healing of any group requires a recovery of soul. This means that managers must risk change, personal confrontation, and redirection of energies. An elemental law of psychology confirms that what is not faced in the developmental tasks of the parent will be visited upon the child, so it is true that what is not faced by corporate or collective leadership will be carried as a problem by the employees or members. Whatever we cannot or will nor face in ourselves will, sooner or later, be carried by those around us. A modicum of ethical consideration, then, would oblige each of us to do our personal work, lest we burden those for whom we care or for whom we have a corporate responsibility. Just as much of modern psychology is dominated by a failure of nerve to ask large questions, such as, "What does the soul want?" rather than "What does my ego want?," so each group, to recover its original energy and sense of purpose, must ask how the soul is enlarged or diminished by the current practices and attitudes. This takes either courage on the part of leadership, or desperation, before the large questions can be asked again. As individuals, and as members of corporate bodies, we all need to recover the courage to demand greater meaning, oppose depersonalizing and infantilizing practices, and once again ask the question: What does the soul want?

As a nation, we too have to ask the question of soul. Have we lost ours in the mad rush to profitability, distraction from unpleasant truths, and creature comfort? The scientific evidence is abundantly clear about global warming: We know that we have to act seriously within this generation to slow if not reverse its effects, but how many are willing to give up the SUV, reduce carbon emissions, and take the thousand other steps that are so clearly within our reach, if it means compromising a smidgen of our creature comforts? We have plundered and we are depleting the finite resources of a finite planet, and we *all* know it. Where is the national leadership on this matter? Where is the outrage at this collective suicide? And what have we done about it? This Shadow is upon us and our children, and we are collectively guilty of passivity.

We are so easily seduced by our own constructs, mesmerized by our institutions, our scientific expertise, our ability to distract ourselves from the world's suffering—and the Shadow grows apace. We have seemingly lost the capacity to critique ourselves and are quite charmed by our own delusions of progress and rapidity of change. Were someone to visit us from afar, what would he or she think of this house we have constructed, this spiritual house in which we live out our brief transit on the planet?

We got ready and showed our home.
The visitor thought: you live well.
*The slum must be inside you.**

*Tomas Tranströmer, "The Scattered Congregation," *The Soul Is Here for Its Own Joy*, p. 12.

Chapter Seven

Lowest Common Denominator
Institutional Shadows

"Anyone who can get you to believe absurdities,
can get you to commit atrocities."
—Voltaire

"You see, in this world, there is one awful thing,
and that is everyone has his reasons."
—Jean Renoir

"The most savage controversies are those about matters as to
which there is no good evidence either way."
—Bertrand Russell

*J*ust as there is a personal Shadow, so the Shadow is distributed among us, infiltrated into collective expression, through our social interactions with each other. This Shadowy infiltration grows especially ratified whenever it is institutionalized.

One day a discussion with a distressed analysand revealed that she no longer understood what was happening to her world, the world in which she had grown up, in which she believed, and whose values she presumed both noble and envied by the world. The acrimonious divisions within her church mirrored the bitterness, animosity, and vitriol of the culture wars in her nation. This was no longer the America she once knew and believed held the high ground. When I mentioned the darker fringe of our history—that such divisions were not new, that we had once slaughtered 600,000 of each other, with a million others wounded, that we had destroyed indigenous civilizations and forcefully placed them in concentration camps called reservations,* that we had sanctified by law that most hideous of human practices, "the peculiar institution" of slavery, and that even now, awash in affluence as we are, nearly 20 percent of our population are going to bed hungry every night, that the state in which she resides is first in executions but a bottom-feeder in health care, education, and vision for all its people—she acknowledged that she never really knew her country at all. That America in which she, and I, believed—with the brooding presence of the Great Emancipator, the Marshall Plan, the land of opportunity for all—is also the country that has repeatedly waged aggressive wars, invading Mexico (1846–48), Hawaii (1893), Cuba (1898), the Philippines (1898), Iran (1953), Guatemala (1954), Iraq (2003–), multiple indigenous nations, and many others, subverting legal governments in Iran, Argentina, Nicaragua, Vietnam, and many others, and that this champion of human rights and the rule of law also created de facto concentration camps for our citizens, the Nisei, and the blatant human rights violations of Abu Ghraib and Guantanamo.† She acknowledged that the administration for which she voted had jimmied the evidence to jus-

---

*An inscription at the U. S. Department of Agriculture once read, "To the ancient races of America, for whom the New World was the Old, that their love of freedom and of nature, their hardy courage, their monuments, arts, legends, and strange songs may not perish from the earth." Never mind that these same people who brought these potsherds and artifacts to Washington had destroyed those "ancient races" through virulent disease, gunfire, and invasive, coercive assimilation.

† Do these contemporary examples not recall Mark Twain's denunciation of our treatment of captured Filipino nationalists a century ago, which "debauched America's honor and blackened her face before the world"?

tify settling old grudges and a new imperialism, undermined scientific evidence about reproduction, global warming, noxious emissions, and sex education, cynically reduced protection of natural resources, eroded the protective boundaries between church and state, privileged by alteration of law the wealthy at the expense of the poor and middle class, abandoned broad-based consensus for coercive imposition of minority moral dogma, deliberately divided its citizens with so-called wedge issues, reduced health-care assistance to the less advantaged, created extralegal rationalizations for the erosion of privacy, politicized classified intelligence data leaks, used the red rag of war on terrorism to exceed executive powers and to obey laws selectively (as judged by the Supreme Court and the American Bar Association), alienated our friends and created new enemies, and dared to label anyone who differed, or called them to account, unpatriotic or soft on terrorism—all this from an administration that advertised itself as devoted to family values and strict moral standards.

Are these examples not a corporate Shadow, the darker hue of a self-congratulatory people who quickly extol their virtues and good intentions? Are we not reminded of Emerson's observation that what we do speaks so much louder than what we say? Is it not true that corporate life, no matter how noble its intention, is forever being brought back to the lowest common denominator?

Former Illinois governor and United Nations ambassador Adlai Stevenson once said that the moral measure of a nation is how it treats its least advantaged citizens. This healing agenda was paramount in the hopes of this analysand, yet the government she voted into office proved bent on foreign adventure and domestic constriction through narrow ideologies. How much Shadow is involved in sending someone else's son or daughter off to war? As the children who do go are so often drawn from the poor and from minorities, what would be the foreign policy endorsed by the middle and upper classes whose children were drafted to implement the next foreign adventure?* So much for homeland security and family values.

The light from the statue in New York Harbor remains truly a beacon to the world, yet it has also cast a very long, very dark Shadow. As is true for all other nations, as well! The collective, aggregate, institutional Shadow always contains the unexamined Shadow of each of us. That of which we are unconscious, or unwilling to face, will contribute to our collective, institutional Shadow. For years the favorite whipping boy for moralists and social critics has been Nazi Germany, which provided a critical laboratory for the preservation of Western humane values and civilizing institutions. But there, clearly, the moral, educational, religious, scientific institutions failed to prevent domination by the Shadow. How, we legitimately ask, can the culture that produced Goethe and Beethoven have also produced such swine as Goebbels and Himmler? How could it have elected an Austrian corporal, a sociopathic know-nothing, and given him its soul? How could it have murderously turned on its ethnic minorities and its handicapped? How could its engineering skills be devoted to solving the problem of mass transportation and efficient extermination in the camps? How could the surviving tree, the Goethe Oak, under which the Sage of Weimar once sat to write, stand in the literal center of Buchenwald? How could the enlightened culture that produced *Faust*—echoed in the location of a murder factory named the "Wood of Books"†—provide the setting for such

---

*Or, in the first large test of the mega agency called "Homeland Security," the privileged escaped while the poor were left to perish in the fetid bowl of New Orleans. A new circle in Dante's *Inferno* must be set aside for the institutional incompetent and the spin doctors who first fumbled and then rationalized such appalling suffering.
† *vis.* Buchenwald, literally "beech forest."

descent into dark degradation of the human spirit? How could the culture of Dichter and Denker also become the culture of Richter and Henker?*

At the same time, most Americans are appallingly ignorant of the Shadow of their own history. A nation that prides itself on being a citadel of freedom but that formerly institutionalized slavery and the deliberate destruction of indigenous civilizations, only outlawed segregation and sexual discrimination in recent decades, and still maintains laws that discriminate against sexual identities and preferences, has much for which to account. Moreover, whoever our schoolteachers are who fail to present the darker hues of this history are especially accountable, lest we perpetuate this sanitized, self-congratulatory fantasy. Whoever our national leaders are who trade the highest principles of the American experiment for reelection are especially accountable. And whoever sent them to office is especially accountable.

Underneath the civilizing fantasies of any institution lie the archaic issues of anxiety management and self-interest. When these two threats are activated, institutions, like individuals, tend to regress and abandon their founding vision. Such regression leads to our multiform fundamentalisms, because all fundamentalisms are driven by fear, and each is captive to some ideology that is worshiped without doubt, for it promises to deliver them from what they fear. No fundamentalism serves evil consciously, but in its inability to critique itself, fundamentalists create the monsters of history—the pogroms, the inquisitions, the persecutions, and the violence that is the silent companion of faithful fervor. After walking through the Dachau concentration camp, Gregory Curtis concluded:

*The culture of poets and thinkers became the culture of judges and hangmen.

What contaminates one's spirit at Dachau is the knowledge that this immense engine for evil could not have been constructed and operated in the name of evil. Such energy could only come at the service of some ideal. How could this have happened, one asks? And the answer is, they believed.*

We may hope that we may perhaps be spared the fanaticisms of "true believers" and be allowed to admit who we all really are in the unconscious—members of the tribe of honest doubters.

But institutions, like the individuals who comprise them, are subject to regression, and thence to a fortress mentality. In the marketplace of ideas, let the best ideas, the ones that work, win. Yet any slippage in our moral or intellectual certainty sets off compensatory swings toward rigid, unswerving conviction; any erosion of assumptions and presumptions ignites a fervor for reactionary revival. This defensive move is in all of us, for there is a fundamentalist in all of us. As a result, an openness in searching for truth, and a willingness to admit the subtlety and complexity of all great mysteries, are finessed into a certain hysterical bravado and the desire to eliminate contrary voices. When this uncertainty prevails, people will swallow anything. Jung puts it very dramatically:

> Once metaphysical ideas have lost their capacity to recall and evoke the original experience they have not only become useless but prove to be actual impediments on the road to wider development. One clings to possessions that once meant wealth, and the more ineffective, incomprehensible, and lifeless they become, the more obstinately people cling to them. . . . The result is . . . a false spirit of arrogance, hysteria, woolly-mindedness, criminal amorality, and

*Curtis, "Why Evil Attracts Us," *Facing Evil*, p. 96.

doctrinaire fanaticism, a purveyor of shoddy spiritual goods, spurious art, philosophical stutterings, and Utopian humbug fit only to be fed wholesale to the mass man of today.*

Naturally, each country has its Shadow, its dark history of bigotry, racism, and oppression of indigenous populations or minorities. As one example of the many that could be cited, my Brazilian colleague, Roberto Gambini, has written a courageous and telling book about his nation's history called *Indian Mirror: The Making of the Brazilian Soul*. The Jesuit missionaries brought their Christianity to the Indian civilization and destroyed it in the name of the Prince of Peace. Armed with the pieties of realpolitik, they projected their own Shadow onto the simpler culture that theretofore had lived in harmony with its natural environment. As Gambini notes, "Europeans transformed the spirits of the forest into the Devil of Christendom and chose the Indians as their exclusive victims."† Citing not only secular historic records, but the letters of the Jesuit missionaries written back to Portugal, Gambini writes, "For the Jesuits in the 16th Century, as for white men in Brazil ever since, the Indians have never been touched by light: their nature, their culture, their bodies and souls have always been regarded as belonging to the dark fringes of the human condition."‡ Still another illustration of the unconscious life and its destructive projections is found in the hesitancy of the Jesuits to mingle with the natives whom they have enslaved: "The problem is to visit their villages, because one cannot go alone; the pathways are full of women and we all go under a holy fear."§ (Imagine how scary those women must have been! Who

*Jung, *"Aion,"* CW 9ii*, paras. 65, 67.
†Gambini, *Indian Mirror: The Making of the Brazilian Soul*, p. 125.
‡*Ibid.*, p. 120.
§*Ibid.*, p. 136.

are we talking about, then—the native women, or the mother-ridden priests who were afraid of their own nature?)

Where is this fearsome darkness coming from—the native soul, or the Shadow of European hubris, imperialism, arrogance, misogyny, and unconsciousness? How can the "civilized nations" repeatedly rationalize the invasions of another's land and culture by bringing their own unacknowledged heart of darkness to them? The simple truth is: *It is easy.* All one has to do is find a "reason," because a "reason," a putative "just cause," can justify anything. This sad chronicle of base motives and inflated complexes that befuddle consciousness is found everywhere, and is the secret, shadowy shame of our Western fantasy of progress. Gambini's operative metaphor is that the Indians were a mirror of the European soul, seen through a glass darkly, for what these apostles of faith, salvation, and progress would not see of themselves in the mirror they projected upon the native peoples. (It was not until 1537 that Pope Paul III declared that the Indians had human souls. Until then, it was as legitimate to kill them as a beast of prey would another beast.) Every nation, every corporate entity has employed the Other, be it a rival faith or a minority or ethnic group, to avoid seeing itself "through the glass darkly," to avoid seeing the beast that haunts the jungle within.

Is not this discrepancy between professed, enlightened institutional values and historic behavior a summons to the Shadow task? Where the light is greatest, the Shadow is longest. The same intelligence that creates can be turned to destruction when seized by a complex, special interest, or driven by fear. Not to brood on this ongoing dilemma is an abdication of consciousness, and an assurance that it will happen again. Jung wrote a series of essays on the phenomenon of Germany, essays from which we all might continue to learn. He noted that the historic and socioeconomic conditions in the Weimar Republic produced both economic collapse and a cultural depression. In the face of this depression an overcompensatory superiority arose. (Thus, when I feel so bad about myself, perhaps I can at least feel superior to you. And in my despondency, I may be able to justify almost anything.) Moreover, Jung noted, beneath the institutional values of the Judeo-Christian tradition, the pagan energies still course. Beneath the instruments of scientific achievement, the Shadow agendas of fear, control, and domination persist. What is denied inwardly will soon break forth into the world. As the nineteenth-century poet Heinrich Heine presciently observed, a nation that burns its books will some day be burning its people.*

Still another example of the many that might be cited will be found in post–World War II France. In the Toronto *Globe and Mail*, Doug Saunders recounts the story of more than 200,000 children born of German soldiers and French mothers during the war. France's quick surrender, defeat, and occupation traumatically shamed the nation, along with the fact that only a tiny percent had joined the Resistance, leading to self-protective denial and persecution of the innocent children born during those desolate times. Only now are these children able to come forth, in the waning decades of their own lives. Many report lives of degradation, exile, and physical and psychological abuse—all for the crime of having been children. Their crime was not that they were "illegitimate," but that they were reminders to Gaullist France of how much collaboration occurred. Called *les enfants maudits*, or "the wretched children," they were wretched indeed, and very much living testimony to how unsettling it is to confront national Shadows.

Søren Kierkegaard observed that "the crowd is untruth."

Das war ein Vorspiel nur, dort, wo man Bücher verbrennt, verbrennt man auch am Ende Menschen. ("That was only a prelude, for where they burn books, they will also, in the end, burn people.")

Our fondest hope for democracies is that from time to time the crowd gets it right. Nonetheless, once one moves beyond the conscience and the consciousness of the individual, other forces come into play. The mutuality of complexes, the collective contamination of psychic toxins, projective identification—all can lead to the psychiatric condition called folie à deux, or "joint madness."

We need to create institutions whenever we need to affirm, preserve, and transmit values, perceptions, agendas, causes, and revelations. An institution is a formal structure for the purpose of maintaining and transmitting values. As history bears witness, however, institutions over time gain their own identity, their own momentum, and often ironically outlive their founder's vision and values, even as they continue to grow and complexify from generation to generation. All of us have been victimized by bureaucracies; all of us have felt depersonalized by institutions. Institutions tend to become bloated and top-heavy with administration, and they ultimately evolve their own structured, self-serving values, even if they contradict their original vision. Specifically, in time, institutions devolve to serve two abstract principles more than their founding values:

1. The survival of the institution, even after it has lost its raison d'être, even in contradiction of its founding values.*
2. The maintenance, preservation, and privileging of its priesthood, whether professors, priests, politicians, or corporate presidents.

Thus, institutions can carry a very large Shadow. Those who work within its walls are often caught in tautological justifications—"we do this because this is what we do"—rather

---

*For example, how could the church create the Inquisition, with its horrible euphemism, *auto-da-fé* (act of faith), breaking the bodies of dissenters, or the merely different, in the name of a man whose life radiated love and inclusion?

than questioning the premises of the institution. Institutions can depersonalize, crush dissenters and reformers, and roll over those whom they were founded to serve. Whether the institution is a corporation, a religious, academic, or charitable body, or a government, it has its own limited vision and always begets a Shadow agenda and a Shadow cost. How many institutions have proved so enlightened, or their leadership so visionary, as to vote themselves out of existence once their purpose has been achieved or ceased to be relevant?

No one better depicted this recurrent institutional nightmare than Franz Kafka in his novels *The Trial* and *The Castle*. By day he worked in a workman's insurance corporation, and by night he went home to write his lonely parables of the desouling of the modern individual. "In the Penal Colony," describes one victim upon whose back is inscribed by a vicious harrow, HONOR THY SUPERIORS. What better portrait of the fascist mentality that can so often lie at the heart of collective social agencies? When he was alive, Kafka might have seemed a fantasist, even a diseased imagination. Who could have guessed that only a few years later his three sisters, and his lover, Milena Jasenka, would be transported to Auschwitz, where they were murdered by the state, an institution whose elemental raison d'être is the protection of its citizens? In "The Metamorphosis," he dramatizes a man who is transformed into a gigantic insect, a metaphor for radical depersonalization. How outlandish, this image! Yet shortly thereafter, his coreligionists were called *Ungeziefer*, or vermin, by state institutional authorities, in order to depersonalize them so that the conscience of those who grew up in Christian institutions could murder those who had become "only insects." How anxious, uncertain must a people be to try to annihilate another people?

It is the very erosion of the old "certainties" that has given rise to fundamentalism around the world. Whether Muslim or

Jewish or Christian, fundamentalism flourishes in a context of fear and uncertainty.* Such fundamentalist camps have seen the enormous seductive drugs of affluence and secular diversions, and sincerely believe that "down that path lies the abyss." With the erosion of their tribal mythologies, distortions and diversions quickly fill the gap. But such uncertainty does not grant one person the right to impose his or her beliefs on another, especially as such beliefs are so often fear-driven, even bigoted. At the heart of their fear lies the Shadow of violence, whether that of overt terrorism or the compulsion to dominate others and drive out dissent. It is this shadowy violence, whether they employ the "thought police" or the ones with truncheons, that brings greatest harm to others.†

One of the most elemental of all psychological observations is rather crudely expressed as, "What you sees is a compensation for what you don't sees." In other words, the militant certainties, the evangelical fervor, the scarcely disguised animosity, are all sure evidence of secret doubt and dismay. What I cannot admit within, which by definition is a Shadow issue, I can militantly deny without. This is why I become the fanatic and must get you to agree with me, through coercion if need be. If we agree, then, I must be right, and therefore, I will be secure. How many individuals are capable of acknowledging the historic fortuities of their faith, the accident of the time and place into which they were born, or their nervous desire to belong to a consensus? The Shadow of coercion is seldom if ever brought to consciousness in the mind of the true believer, who seeks

---

*Is it not interesting that this fundamentalism rises most stridently from the Western monotheisms? Those Eastern religions that affirm the relativity and impermanence of things seem to afford a more flexible psychology to their adherents as well. Perhaps having accepted the impermanence that lies at the core of "nature naturing," they are less dogmatic, less spooked by change.

† John Stuart Mill observed that the only reason that most people do not impose their will on others is because they lack the power to do so. Some will seek that power and, unchecked, produce the tyranny of the few over the many.

consensual validation from others, defense against the terrors of ambiguity, and as little thinking as possible.

As Arthur Mizener once noted, "Doubt is what gets you an education." But when we are insecure we ill tolerate doubt, and we therefore think nothing of ignoring the nuanced achievement of centuries of scholarship and scientific evidence. In both the Middle East and the United States, a minority of hard-core believers have, through organizational fervor and divisive politics, seized control of national governments to impose their values on the majority. My grandson came home weeping and frightened because some religious worthy told him that he was going to hell since he did not believe in Jesus Christ. Nicholas is seven years old. Another self-appointed worthy appeared at my daughter's door and informed her that she, the neighbor, and a schoolteacher in their public school would see to the children's religious instruction. What arrogance, what Shadow! Why should a child, or anyone, have to be governed by someone else's emotional immaturity, someone else's inability to tolerate the ambiguities of life? Just as domestic abusers are always weak, insecure individuals, so ecclesiastical bullies belie the core precepts and lived paradigms of their prophetic founders through their own agitated psychopathology and need to dominate others.

Still another current example of the institutional Shadow at work is the interference in the classrooms of trained teachers of science by special interest groups who promote pseudoscience. By taking over local school boards, by pressuring administrators and those who write textbooks, those ignorant of centuries of accumulated knowledge, or apprehensive about its theological implications, impose their values on trained professionals. It is not a question of whether one is to choose between so-called "intelligent design"—that delightful word spin, for who could be against "intelligence" or "design"—or "evolution."

One is sexy, with plenty of pizzazz, and the other is boring, taking millennia to unfold. Rather, shadowy is the complex-driven ignorance that confuses the metaphors of theology with the metaphors of science. It is not only possible to "believe" both metaphors, or reject either or both of them, but it is obligatory that an informed public understand metaphor, and understand the difference between theological speculation and the patient construction of theory, its rigorous testing, and its modification when conflicting data arrives. It is hard to believe that in the twenty-first century we are still lagging behind the knowledge of the nineteenth, or retrying the debacle of Dayton, Tennessee, in the twentieth. (How embarrassing is it that even the President of the United States, the one who is to lead the free world into the twenty-first century, throws his unlettered weight into these debates.) One thinks of the arrogance of Bishop Wilberforce, who, in the debates of the nineteenth century, argued for the imposition of a literal reading of the old texts, versus the humility of scientist Thomas Huxley. After the benighted bishop sneered at the idea of having an ape for an ancestor, Huxley famously replied:

> . . . a man has no reason to be ashamed of having an ape for his grandfather. If there were an ancestor whom I should feel ashamed in recalling it would rather be a man . . . who, not content with an equivocal success in his own sphere of activity, plunges into scientific questions with which he has no real acquaintance, only to obscure them by an aimless rhetoric, and distract the attention of his hearers from the real point at issue by eloquent digressions and skilled appeals to religious prejudice.*

---

*Cited by Roger Shattuck, *Forbidden Knowledge: from Prometheus to Pornography*, p. 36. Remember that the average person at the time took as fact Bishop Ussher's assertion that the world was created on Sunday, October 23, 4004 B.C., notwithstanding the presence of vast fossil and geologic evidence pointing toward millions of years earlier.

The philosophy, and in most cases, the practice of science is the presumption that truth is not yet fully found, for whatever truth we have discovered is soon antiquated by discovering a more sophisticated question. Living with doubt, being willing to dump one's hypothesis, being open to contradiction, lies at the heart of both science *and* mature religious faith. Fundamentalism's incapacity to critique itself, examine the gap between intentions and outcomes, is based on a great deal of unexamined hubris, and a largely unconscious defense against doubt. Nonetheless, as Jung has indicated:

> People who merely believe and don't think always forget that they continually expose themselves to their own worst enemy: doubt. Wherever belief reigns, doubt lurks in the background. But thinking people welcome doubt: it serves them as a valuable stepping-stone to better knowledge. . . . The believer ought not to project his habitual enemy, doubt, upon the thinker, thereby suspecting him of destructive designs.*

Three and a half centuries ago the lens grinder of Amsterdam, Baruch Spinoza, was excommunicated in perpetuity from his synagogue. His crime? He observed that his co-communicants, themselves refugees from Spanish bigotry, were themselves bigoted and insistent on their version of the truth. He sadly but presciently concluded that "no group or religion could rightly claim infallible knowledge of the Creator's partiality to its beliefs and ways. . . . He understood the powerful tendency in each of us toward developing a view of the truth that favors the circumstances into which we happened to be born. Self-aggrandizing can be the invisible scaffolding of religion, poli-

---

*Carl Jung, "*Psychology and Religion: West and East*," *CW 11*, p. 170.

tics or ideology."* For pointing his figure at the Shadow that haunts our society still, Spinoza was thanked with exile.

Most therapists spend a great deal of time repairing the damage done by even the most benevolent of institutions. One of them, of course, is that indispensable institution we call the "family," necessary for the nurturance and security of the child, but often a most iatrogenic alembic in which the child's soul is permanently wounded. Sometimes the institution is called "marriage," where two people swear they love each other and then bring great hurt to each other. (One recalls the old joke: "Marriage is a great institution, but, hey, who wants to be institutionalized?") Yes, institutions are composed of ordinary folks like you and me, and therefore grace, understanding, and forgiveness are necessary to foster healing. But saddest to me has been the damage done by religious institutions that, professing to serve both God and the individual soul, so often infantilize and intimidate those for whom they are responsible. Just this day I received a series of dreams from a seventy-one-year-old man who, to his embarrassment, was obliged in a dream to defecate in public and yet hide this fact from others. When we inquired as to what old stuff, now no longer useful, he was having to discard but that he felt exposed him to criticism and ridicule, he immediately associated with the religious indoctrination that had governed his life through guilt and fear. Such is a long, dark Shadow that has wounded at least as many as it has brought comfort.

On the other hand, it is certainly true that institutions are necessary to provide the maintenance of values and to serve their continuing implementation, and that we would deteriorate into isolated, ineffectual groups without institutions. We

---

*Goldstein, "Reasonable Doubt," *The New York Times*, July 29, 2006.

have seen too many moments in history when civilization broke down and the Shadow reigned. St. Augustine had to write a treatise against suicide among the faithful because so many sought to flee the discords of this world for the presumptive peace of the next. His more famous *De Civitas Dei** endeavored to reframe the perspective of the community in the face of institutional collapse, namely the Pax Romana. When "things fall apart" and "the center cannot hold," the Shadow comes quickly to the surface. Another notable occasion is witnessed in the years after 1348–49 when Europe and the Middle East were wracked by the Black Death. So ineffectual were the professed divinely sanctioned institutional powers of mace and miter that the forces of secularism gained a momentum that has never since been reversed. As John Kelly cites contemporary witness Matteo Villani, "It was thought that people whom God by his grace in life had preserved . . . would become better, humble, virtuous, and catholic, avoiding inequities and sins and overflowing with love and charity for one another. But . . . the opposite happened. Men . . . gave themselves over to the most disordered and sordid behavior. . . . As they wallowed in idleness, their dissolution led them into the sin of gluttony, into banquets, taverns, delicate foods and gambling. They rushed headlong into lust." Added the Siennese Agnolo di Tura, "No one could restrain himself from doing anything."† When institutions lose their credibility and their power to sanction behavior, the Shadow rushes to fill the vacuum.

As necessary as the ego is to the individual psyche, so institutions are to our culture. Yet as we have seen, the ego is so easily

---

*The work sought to contrast The City of Man, which is evanescent, with The City of God, which is eternal. Thus one is to serve this transient city first, in order to inherit the enduring city later.
† Kelly, *The Great Mortality,* pp. 276–77.

supplanted by the split-off parts of the psyche that great harm may be brought to self and others. So, too, both the promise and the price of institutions must be weighed, and a certain vigilance obliged. Thomas Jefferson, primary author of the Declaration of Independence, asserted that every twenty years or so the Tree of Liberty should be watered by the blood of its patriots, as well as that of tyrants. Inflammatory words, to be sure, but he was acutely aware of what oppression institutions and their adherents can foster. When we acknowledge such tasks as foreign relations, national defense, economic coordination, preservation of the rule of law over special interests, we see that institutions are necessary. Still, with each corporate entity the Shadow remains. Corporate whistle-blowers are so at risk that we have recently had to enact laws to protect them. Socrates was martyred for his role as gadfly to Athens, his corporate city-state. Institutions, like individuals, do not like their shortcomings pointed out to them.

Just how much wisdom can an institution really possess, embody, renew, transmit? Surely institutional wisdom will never prove greater than the wisdom of those who lead, we think. Yet the founding vision of institutions may also call into question the actions and beliefs of those who follow. How institutions interpret the intent of the founders, whether religious, political, or charitable, is legitimately open to considerable debate. Most nations have supreme courts to wrestle with these questions, religious entities have curia, and nonprofits have boards of directors. Who determines, and how it is determined, that wisdom and vision will guide the institution is problematic at best, and unlikely at worst. As Yeats prophesied in 1917, when things fall apart, the best lack all conviction, while the worst are full of passionate intensity.

One thing is clear: Institutions seldom tolerate or welcome the dialectic of criticism, whether from without or within, if their leaders are themselves insecure. Those who work as organizational development agents frequently find that the leadership does not wish to hear the reality, that "telling truth to power" is not welcome. When it comes to collective wisdom, it would seem that we are still far from finding the Philosopher Kings for which Plato hoped so long ago. If, as Lord Acton suggested in the nineteenth century, power corrupts, and absolute power corrupts absolutely, then we can expect our leaders to attempt to manage the news, attack dissenters and impugn their motives, and use the resources of the government to manipulate public policy to serve special interests. Even in a democracy, the will of the people can and will be manipulated, deceived, and subverted by special interests, both through the neuroses of its leadership and by the immense power of the unconscious of each of us.

Only vigilance, awakened conscience, and aroused consciousness, allied with a civic commitment and healthy skepticism, can challenge the Shadow of institutional life. Skepticism is not cynicism, not disloyalty. Skepticism is based on the very sound premise that even in the most well-intentioned the Shadow is present, active, and on the move. Skepticism is critically necessary for the health of any institution, especially those purporting to democratic governance. No matter whether it is government, big business, or a benevolent institution of any size, the Shadow agenda is always present, and always at work. The health of any institutional entity depends, as does the conduct of personal life, on the willingness of the individual to come to consciousness. But institutions do not have an individual consciousness, do not think, do not have a conscience, and are not capable of moral choice, for they, as institutions, are abstractions. They depend on us. Our capacity to identify and confront the Shadow in institutional life obviously begins with and forever depends on our capacity to identify the Shadow in our personal life.

Chapter Eight

PROGRESS'S DARK EDGE
The Shadow of Modernism

*"Our hearts have overbrimmed with new agonies, with new
luster and silence. The mystery has grown savage, and
God has grown greater. The dark powers ascend, for they
have also grown greater, and the entire human island quakes."*
—NIKOS KAZANTZAKIS

*A*rguably, the last time the Western world made much
collective "sense" was somewhere around the fourteenth century, during the so-called High Middle
Ages, when so much of the modern world was forming. Not
that the world then was all that comprehensible. As English
philosopher Thomas Hobbes noted of the lot of our predeces-
sors, life was "nasty, brutish, and short." As we observed earlier,
in the years 1348–49 the Black Death annihilated 40 percent
of all of Europe. Entire villages disappeared. The "best," those
who tended the sick, often perished first; the "worst," those
who fled, had a chance at living a few more fugitive years. The
soteriological claims of the church, and the divine order of
kings, proved powerless in the face of general hysteria, and of
course the tiny fleas on the backs of the rats that carried the
plague bacillus. All institutions, especially those of church and
state, were shaken and, in the Western world, have never been
the same since. As sacred order erodes, occasioning a general
spiritual and psychological disquietude, it is slowly replaced by
the uncertain claims of the secular. As Harriet Rubin notes of

one such tipping point, "The death of Boniface on October 11, 1303, marks the beginning of the victory of national-
ism over supernaturalism. Politics will overtake the spiritual in
its power over men and women and social institutions."* In
other words, the old world ended, the "middle ages" between
the classical era and the present lost their mythic underpin-
nings, and the rudiments of what we now call "modernism"
emerged.

Still, in the early 1300s Dante published his *Il Comedia* (*The
Comedy*) because it had a happy ending—namely, salvation
(later called *divine* for its aesthetic excellence by some of his
ardent readers). His vision of the universe—a cosmic order
above, a moral law sanctioned by sacred institution, a three-
storied universe—represents the last coherent picture of the
world that both king and commoner alike might endorse.
Dante's highly structured vision depicted a vast network of
cause and effect, of choice and consequence, and of divine/
human interaction within a comprehensible model. Both king
and commoner could still look in one direction and see the medieval castle as a visible embodiment of the secular/sacred order, since the divine right of kings claimed both. And they
could look in the other direction toward the medieval cathedral for an embodiment of the sacred/secular order, since
priests wielded a far larger dominion over the conduct of daily
life and social institutions than their otherworldly savior ever
imagined.† Together, these two institutions incarnated the lon-
gitudes and latitudes of the medieval soul. When one has lon-
gitudes and latitudes, those "tangibly invisible," usefully fictive
lines, one can know where one is, no matter how turbulent the

---

*Rubin, *Dante in Love*, p. 49.
† Their savior, in his admonition to render unto Caesar what is Caesar's, and to God
what is God's, seemed to make a clearer distinction between the often competing
claims of secular and sacred than his successors.

sea. Yet since Dante's death in 1321, that troubled, only barely integrated sacred/secular synthesis, and its intimation of cosmic order, has been unraveling. We have their images still in our mind's eye, but their compelling power is lost forever. As Shakespeare noted in *Troilus and Cressida*, "untune that string, / and hark what discord follows."

Our modern experience derives from those moments of spiritual and psychological dislocation, and the subtle shift from institutions grounded in divine will to those grounded in popular consensus. Our modern world is first fully intimated in the psychological anguish of that Everyman Shakespeare named "Hamlet." This precious Dane knows full well what he wishes, what tradition requires of him, and yet he is strangely undermined from within. His resolution is "sicklied over with the pale cast of thought and lose[s] the name of action." He is the first truly realized psychological portrait, a portrait of deep internal conflict caught between myths. He is what we all would become. Bereft of divine certainty, undermined from within, he is our neurotic brother.

The modern tendencies and attitudes are clearly launched in the seventeenth century, not only with Shakespeare's depiction of neurosis and existential angst, but with Bacon's articulation of the scientific theory and methodology that so successfully triumphed over the world of antique authority.* The separation of observer and observed, and the dispassionate exploration of theories that are to be demonstrably tested, moves us from the realm of subjective fantasy to putative objective verification. Who could imagine that this separation of human sensibility

---

*Most would not look through Galileo's telescope because they "knew" from classical authority that Jupiter had no moons. Those few who did risk a look were disquieted. But, having looked, and realizing that the old geocentric system, with its crystalline shells revolving in divine harmony, was no longer tenable, they began to understand that the theology attached to this ordered, comforting picture of the cosmos was now also suspect.

from external phenomena could lead to the wonders of the lightbulb, or the light of a thousand suns above Hiroshima? And who would ever guess that from such brilliant light a very deep Shadow would emerge?

We who inhabit the modern Western era have an enormous investment in the fantasy of "progress." As a child I heard General Electric's repeated mantra: "Progress is our most important product." We are convinced that we have progressed, for we have attained hitherto unimagined control of nature. We live in climate-controlled containers, vault vast distances in pressurized cylinders of steel, and participate in an instantaneous global community wired to events occurring around the world. However, having abolished slavery in most parts of the world, we yet enslave billions to economic strictures and structures. We provide the miracles of advanced health care, and yet have new diseases and sundry collateral costs that are the by-products of our cultural expansion. And we have learned the powers of destruction at least as fast, if not faster, than the powers of creation. So how are we supposed to measure progress, then?

A few paragraphs ago I suggested that the old-world picture began decaying in the fourteenth century, though its remnants are with us still. While the first whiff of modernist disaffection and alienation may be found on the Elizabethan stage by the early seventeenth century, a more complete annunciation of modernist sensibility, with the widening gulf between the fantasy of progress and our descent into the abyss, is announced at the beginning of the nineteenth century when the so-called "Sage of Weimar" refashioned the medieval tale of *Faust*. Let us follow this track, which leads to the divided soul of "modernism" and the Shadow that haunts our time.

WHEN FAUST BECAME FAUSTIAN

The story of Faust is an old story, first appearing in the Middle Ages, reappearing in the Elizabethan theater through the work of Christopher Marlowe's *The Tragical History of Dr. Faustus*, then showing up in moralizing puppet shows on the Continent—all trying to depict a dire warning that any deal with the Devil will result in damnation in one form or another. As Marlowe put it in the final pronouncement of the chorus:

Faustus is gone; regard his hellish fall,
Whose fiendful torture may exhort the wise
Only to wonder at unlawful things,
Whose deepness doth entice such forward wits
To practice more than heavenly power permits.*

Johann Wolfgang von Goethe took this moral parable and turned it to another end, however. Though Goethe still sets the work in the Middle Ages, he depicts Faust as a scholar in a midlife crisis, so to speak. Faust—and here he begins to sound suspiciously like many of us—has achieved all his goals, and yet feels empty. There is no horizon, nothing further for which to yearn. He suffers a classic midlife depression that occurs when our projections either fail *or* are fulfilled, and we are left only with our own selves. But although Faust, like Hamlet, is our comrade, deeply conflicted within, he nonetheless embodies a heroic impulse, perhaps best summarized in Tennyson's "Ulysses": "to strive, to seek, to find, and not to yield." Faust has a reckless passion to know all, to step out into the space left by the departed gods, and to build his world there. Though both God and the Devil show up in stereotypical ways in this

*Cited by Walter Kaufman, translator of Goethe's *Faust*, p. 16.

version, one senses their antique irrelevance to Faust's desire to live on his own terms and by his own rules. If salvation was the pronounced hope of Dante, then self-realization is the secret hope of Faust. Here again he is "the modern," more desirous of fulfillment in this life than investing in the fantasy of another, celestial realm.*

In the midst of the mélange of depression and desire, Mephistopheles appears to Faust. He is not the familiar guy in the red underwear with the tail and horns. In fact, he is a traveling scholar. (If the Devil is going to come to us, so to speak, he will come in the guise of that which is most acceptable to us—familiar, comforting, reinforcing, soporific, consensual, and mouthing what we most want to believe.) Mephistopheles rather cryptically informs Faust that he is: "part of the force which would / do evil evermore, and yet creates the good." He is, moreover, "part of the darkness which gave birth to light."†

Mephistopheles clearly is the carrier of the Shadow, the necessary "Other" that we carry always. Our proclivity to routinely presume our purity of motive, certainty of outcome, and high-minded agenda is often undercut by a later recognition of hidden causes and unexpected outcomes. Thus, Goethe depicts Faust as an essentially noble soul, a well-intentioned guy who nonetheless manages to destroy the life of another and bring the roof down upon his own head. Who would think such consequences could come from such admirable intent? Who among us has not set off with nobility of intent, whether it was to guide our child rightly, to intervene in the life of another, or to contribute to a noble cause, and later came to humbling

---

*Faust proclaims, "*Dasein ist Pflicht, und wars ein Augenblick,*" which might be translated, "Self-realization is a duty, if only for a moment." *Faust,* line 1552.
† *Ibid.,* lines 1336–7, 1350.

astonishment over the outcome of these motives? As Mephistopheles implies in his conundrum, whenever we fail to factor in the presence of a Shadow agenda, we ignore the vital dynamics of the whole and live to see those disregarded energies play out in troubling ways. For example, my presumption that I always act with virtuous intent is reframed by the fact that every choice I make has hidden costs, some of which prove harmful to me and to those whom I love, and some of which will never be accounted for. Or, as another example, we who live with so many comforts in the Western world are so often the beneficiaries of the exploitation of others elsewhere.*

For this writer, a clear expression of the shift to a modernist sensibility occurs when Mephistopheles takes Faust to the witch's kitchen. The head witch, mired in her antique sensibility, believes she is meeting the old guy in the red underwear. "Squire Satan," she says in salutation. And Mephistopheles corrects her, "That name is out, hag!" Why?

> It's dated, called a fable; men are clever,
> but they are just as badly off as ever:
> the Evil One is gone, the evil ones remain.†

There it is: the clear demarcation of the modern sensibility, our begrudging recognition of the Shadow. The guy in the red underwear is gone, and with him the old metaphysical machinery that carried our projections of evil onto the "Other" and facilitated a convenient dissociation of evil from ourselves. Nonetheless, for "the modern," the Evil One may be gone, but we are left with our many expressions of evil nonetheless. Put an-

---

*In *Candide*, one of Voltaire's characters remarks, after he has seen the horrific conditions of a sugar plantation in the Caribbean, that he now knows "the price" of a lump of sugar in a Parisian cup of tea.
† *Faust*, lines 2504–9.

other way, evil is dethroned, but evil is democratized. Evil is not "out there" on some metaphysical plane; it is in us, in our daily acts, in the history we beget.

A notable example of the democratization of evil is found in the book that Hannah Arendt wrote after she attended the trial of SS Lieutenant Colonel Adolf Eichmann in Jerusalem. Here was the man who had joked that he would joyfully jump into his grave knowing that millions of Jews had gone there before him. She journeyed to Jerusalem expecting to find a monster— if not the guy with red underwear and horns, at least a clear embodiment of evil. What she encountered was a balding, bespectacled civil servant who had passed unnoticed in the streets of Buenos Aires for decades. In other words, someone so much like us that he passes among us, anonymous.

Eichmann presented the same tired defense that he only followed orders, but went on to add that he was a devoted civil servant whose administrative burden was to solve pressing problems of transportation. The fact that his skillful routing of rolling stock carried millions of human souls to the crematoriums seemed irrelevant to his plebian sensibility. David Cesarani writes, "He managed genocide in the way the CEO of any corporation would run a multinational company."* Shocked by his ordinary appearance and demeanor, Arendt coined the phrase, "the banality of evil." While her phrase angered some who thought she was diminishing the monstrous catalog of atrocity that Eichmann had facilitated, her deeper point was precisely to recognize the ordinariness of this man, a man like us who performed inordinate evil, and to call him not evil, but banal, like us.

---

*Cesarani, *Becoming Eichmann,* p. 12. Cesarani differs from Arendt's perspective as he describes a more sinister Eichmann with a long history of racial hatred and full knowledge of the suffering he helped foster.

Her phrase, "the banality of evil" haunts us. Surely I wish to distance *myself* from this murderer. Surely I, who consider myself rational, humane, and sensitive, cannot see myself as passively compliant in systems, philosophies, and institutions that bring harm to others. Yet Eichmann, along with Hamlet and Faust, is also our Everyman. He is a disquieting residue of Faust's witch's kitchen, a reminder that the Evil One is gone, but that evil persists in the things we do, the things we do not do, and all that we do not bring to consciousness and own as ours.

How much easier it is to demonize our neighbor than to see the darkness within ourselves. We have learned from history's repeated atrocities that for a murderous regime to prevail, one need not gather psychopaths, one has only to mobilize ordinary citizens, frighten them, co-opt them, seduce them, or lull them to sleep. That is all it takes! Sober citizens all, we learn to our dismay that our professed intentions, and our venerable institutions, do not serve to protect us from ourselves and the thousand small compromises of our values. How disappointing it is to learn that our great religions do not spare us ourselves. Our achievements in science, art, and humanities do not exempt us. Our "progress" does not save us. George Steiner reminds us that in the testing laboratory of Modernism we failed the summons: "We know that some of the men who devised and administered Auschwitz had been taught to read Shakespeare and Goethe, and continued to do so."*

Let us further remember that the word *Faust* has been adjectivally transformed into *Faustian*. Our age is Faustian. What does that mean? Goethe took the old moralistic legend and transformed it into a modern parable. His Faust is not caught in a deadly contract. He and Mephistopheles enact a wager!

*Steiner, *Language and Silence*, p. 5.

Mephistopheles bets Faust that he can so provide him with pleasure and distraction that Faust will call a halt and voluntarily consign his soul. Faust wagers that the nature of his soul is so given to yearning for the life-giving mystery, for the absolutes, that he will never be satiated.

But Mephistopheles knows us too well. He is like a game-show impresario, a suave host of a reality show, who says to us, "Who here would not like to work for Mr. Trump; who would not like to win the prince or princess to their bed; who would not like to add a million dollars to their account? All you have to do is shelve your conscience, or jettison your dignity, or relinquish your values, for a while. . . ." Millions line up to volunteer, or consign their spiritual life as vicarious witnesses of these seductive morality masques on television. Mephistopheles knows us well. He has thoroughly won the battle for our soul, for the modern spends his or her life mostly by killing time, hanging out, and trying to make money, get laid, or both. As T. S. Eliot asked already in the 1920s, will not *our* banal monument be concrete highways and a thousand lost golf balls?

And yet, Faust is a noble soul in his aspiration. He wishes to know all; he shuns the seductions of the witches and the seductions of power. He is also our best representative, our hero complex. He is the person who inquires into the quantum mysteries: the genome project, the subatomic universe, the imaginative landscape of the arts, the desire to finally feed the hungry and clothe the naked. Yet inadvertently, he is the same who, conquering the insect, pollutes the environment; who, bringing the jet age, imports AIDS into all regions of the world; who, splitting the atom, brings nuclear horror to blind the people of Hiroshima, Nagasaki, and Chernobyl, and distributes strontium through the air, across boundaries, to abide in the bones of all of us, to perpetually abide in the marrow of our bones. Where there is light, so there also is Shadow.

Faust is our best, most representative, self. He is heroic, unconscious, well-intended, and dangerous. He is the light of aspiration, achievement, the heroic challenge to limits, *and* he is the bringer of so much of our suffering. Like brother Hamlet, torn and paralyzed within, riddled with doubt, Faust, lacking doubt but full of desire, is also the one who brings us the world we presently inhabit, for good or ill. Never in history has so much been possible, and never before has there been so much attendant neurotic misery. Never before so much light; never before so much Shadow.

THE UNDERGROUND MAN AND THE BIRTH OF THE PSYCHOLOGICAL

In 1851 Queen Victoria and her consort Prince Albert opened the first international exhibition of trade and technology in a large glass and girder structure popularly called "The Crystal Palace." Announced both as a celebration of progress in technology and social amelioration, the Crystal Palace also served as a symbol of humanity's "moral" improvement. From this hubris came two fantasies, the cult of *progress,* with its conflation of increased material sophistication with moral progress, and *meliorism*, the doctrine that with concerted social effort the ancient scourges of humankind—war, poverty, disease, ignorance—could be eradicated. Who among those celebratory worthies could imagine that a few decades later, those same nations, those apostles of progress, would be tearing at each other's throats with those same technologies? Of the many examples of this discrepancy between naive fantasy and Shadowy enactments, consider the following. Who would have imagined that the British would sustain 60,000 casualties in one day, that the Germans would lose a million men in the first five months of 1914, that the French would lose more than 300,000 men in two weeks, that one brigade would lose 9,000 men in eighteen days?* Who would have imagined that the ruined hulk of that Crystal Palace would be used as a navigational aid by the Luftwaffe in their approach patterns to bomb London in the Battle of Britain during their grandchildren's generation? Who could have imagined that less than a century after the gates of the Crystal Palace swung open to self-congratulation, that the gates to Dachau, Bergen-Belsen, Mauthausen, Auschwitz, Sobibor, Treblinka, Maijdanek, Sachsenhausen, Terezinstadt, and Ravensbruck would swing open to reveal horror? Who could imagine such?

Yet, both progress and meliorism are noble fantasies. Earlier in life I invested a great deal of psychic energy in believing both, and they have a continuing appeal for many, despite the testimonies of recent history.† I have devoted my life to the practice of learning, education, communication, and therapy—all in service to human need, and in service to the idea of improvement. But such fantasy too often ignores the human Shadow, the capacity to fill any newly created space with our manifold forms of darkness. I recall when the Internet was first becoming a reality for ordinary folks. One person said to me that this breakthrough would ensure world peace and the spread of democracy because now individuals could operate outside the walls of their governments and promote brotherhood and concord. I predicted that if a new instrument was

---

*Ecksteins, *Rites of Spring*, pp. 100–1.

† As I write these words, the nations of the Middle East are bombarding each other still again, children are wheeled into hospitals with missing limbs, and hundreds of thousands of refugees are on the roads. How often have we seen this same sad spectacle in the "Holy Land"?

available, new darkness would follow. I am sure I was accused of perverse cynicism behind my back, rather than sober realism. So today we know the Internet is used by terrorists to communicate, that the virtual ether is full of pornography, seductions of innocents, political vitriol, and that phlegm in the body of capitalism called "spam." So much for enlightened progress.

Hindsight is always easy. Who in Victoria's time would have seen that beneath the panoply of progress, multiple dark selves congregate? At least one person did. In 1863 the great Russian novelist Fyodor Dostoevsky wrote a strange piece, a sort of perverse novella titled *The Underground Man*. In this work he presents the most unflattering literary portrait ever, and spawns the epithet "antihero," which came to be such a force in modernist fiction. This "antihero" is very much the hero, if we define the hero as one who expands our imagination, who enlarges our sense of what it means to be human. We readily thank an artist who depicts some sublimity for us, or a composer who brings new sounds to the delight of the soul, or a chemist who brings a new vaccine to heal the ravaged body, but who would celebrate this hero of perversity?

Dostoevsky's gift to us in *The Underground Man* is dual: the "invention of the psychological," decades before Janet, Charcot, Freud, Breuer, and Jung, and a compelling portrait of the Shadow that extends behind the gigantic swath cut by an heroic age of materialism. His "antihero" is mean, dyspeptic, cynical, and most of all, narcissistic, like us—that is, when we can face ourselves. He speaks aloud his selfish agendas, his fears, his defeats, his sense of being ridiculous—everything we would be obliged to confess if we were strong enough to be honest. Dostoevsky's vision is not tragic, for it neither ennobles nor transfigures with redeeming and healing knowledge. His knowledge rather leaves the modern skewered on the point of his own ego. His vision, probing and profound as it is, is ironic, and as such cannot rescue, but brings with it a caustic recognition of our divided consciousness and our divided souls.

Even today, we pride ourselves on our modernity, believing we have transcended the idiocies of the past and stand poised on the brink of ever-new advances in the cause of enlightened progress. Of this popular fantasy Dostoevsky observed:

> Men love abstract reasoning and neat systemization so much that they think nothing of distorting the truth, closing their eyes and ears to contrary evidence to preserve their logical constructions. . . . What is it in us that is mellowed by civilization? All it does, I'd say, is to develop in man a capacity to feel a greater variety of sensations. And nothing, absolutely nothing else. And through this development, man will yet learn how to enjoy bloodshed.*

When Dostoevsky was writing these seemingly cynical words, he hyperbolically claimed that as far away as St. Petersburg he could hear the rattle of musketry and the rumble of cannon from a small Pennsylvania crossroads called Gettysburg, where 51,000 fell in three days. Looking at the decades that follow, with all their spurious clamors for bloodshed and dubious rationales for empire from Sarajevo to Iraq, who is being cynical, who being honest? And on what does our popular culture thrive more than an incessant drumbeat of sensations, including the perverse invention of compensatory "reality" shows while we live our days amid such abstractions as economics, information technology, 401(k)s, and the diversions of sensate culture?

The Underground Man is of course a metaphor for our inner world, which is so profoundly neglected in the modern era,

* *Notes from Underground*, pp. 107–8.

yet is an autogenous world that seethes, disrupts, and defines our outer life. His portrait of this inner world with its drives, its agendas, its self-delusions is unsparing. "Now, then, what does a decent man like to talk about most? Himself of course. So I'll talk about myself."* He is, as we so often are, irredeemably self-absorbed. Just how welcome was Freud when, at the end of the nineteenth century and beginning of the twentieth, he described the narcissistic, infantile agendas that inform so much institutional and relational life? He was vilified for telling us what we do not wish to know about ourselves. He described a daily soap opera wherein a pulsing Id, condemned and rebuked by a Super Ego, left the harried Ego to produce makeshift compromises, jury-rigged repressions, rationalizations, projections onto others, and incessant distracting displacements in order to live unvexed in his shaky house of conscious life.

Dostoevsky's perverse, troubling confessant challenges us: "After all, how can a man with my lucidity of perception respect himself?"† How can we in the postmodern era continue to lie to ourselves about the rich mixture of drives and agendas within, when both our cultural and our personal history bear bloody witness each day? Who among us does not smile with familiar recognition when hearing Mark Twain's observation that man is the only animal that blushes, and has reason to? Strangely, this underground man in each of us embodies a summons to a different kind of heroism. It may be that our capacity to know this "Other" that dwells within each of us will bring us a new venture: the task of integrating this energy and this knowledge into conscious life, lest it continue to play out through unconscious venues to the injury of the self and others.

* *Notes from Underground*, p. 93.
† *Ibid.*, p. 101.

Robert Louis Stevenson,* exploring the same territory as Dostoevsky, demonstrated the cost when the gentle Dr. Jekyll autonomously evolved into the demonic Mr. Hyde. How troubling it must have been for our Victorian ancestors, so deeply vested in the idea of correct behavior, to glimpse this wild one within! And how troubling it remains to find that we still, unconsciously, glory in our Shadow. The underground man, having observed a cavalry man boasting and strutting with his saber muses,

> This kind of showing off is just as much in poor taste as the saber rattling of that officer I mentioned. But I ask you, who on earth goes around showing off his sickness, and even glorying in it? On second thought though, I'd say that everyone does. People do pride themselves on their infirmities and I, probably, more than anyone else.†

And how shamelessly does our culture flaunt its Shadow on game shows, local newscasts, and in the daily papers?

How is it, then, that we can bring such darker selves to the surface so easily? The underground man has a thought about that; one can, he says, "wish upon himself . . . something harmful, stupid, and even completely idiotic. He will do it in order to establish his right to wish for the most idiotic things and not be obliged to have only sensible wishes."‡ So, now, curiously, we begin to see where this antihero is in fact becoming heroic. When we define the hero as someone who expands and extends our imaginative sense of the possibilities of being human, then we realize that this strange perverse creature is not

---

*Stevenson also wrote a poem called "My Shadow," whose opening lines are: "I have a little shadow that goes in and out with me, / And what can be the use of him is more than I can see. / He is very, very like me from the heels up to the head; / And I see him jump before me, when I jump into my bed."

† *Notes from Underground*, p. 93.

‡ *Ibid.*, p. 112.

so alien after all. He is, in all fact and fractuosity, also our personal claim to individual identity. In our perversity we are more fully human; no longer humanity manqué, but more fully filling out the range of possibilities. In the end, we architects of the modern are less the builders of girder and glass and much more the common perverse selves we are, and always have been. In our Shadow life, we are more fully human—that is, embodying more fully whatever the gods intended by our diverse possibilities. Only the conventional ego thinks it is supposed to be rational, predictable, manageable.

DARK SELVES, WITH DARK HEARTS

In 1898 Joseph Conrad published *Heart of Darkness*. If there was ever any doubt about the dark fringes of progress in the glorious century to follow the Crystal Palace, it was definitively ended on the Somme in 1916 during the great "War to End All Wars." But any prescient reader would have heard the death knell of meliorism in this novella by a Polish immigrant writing in English about the European investment and usurpation of Africa, the so-called "Dark Continent." In 1876, King Leopold of Belgium convened a conference of European nations to find a high-minded rationale to carve up someone else's land, someone else's religion, someone else's identity, someone else's wealth. But such a nefarious project could hardly be countenanced in its naked brutality by such illuminati, so they proclaimed that the goal of their project was "to open to civilization the only part of our globe where Christianity has not penetrated and to pierce the darkness which envelopes the entire population."* Ah, that is so much better, so much more palatable. It seems that these bemedaled worthies, perfecters

*Conrad, *Heart of Darkness*, p. 87.

of pogroms, artists of autos-da-fé and soon the creators of the concentration camp,* were eager to bring their civilization to their lesser brethren, especially those living near great natural resources, such as precious metals.

Conrad's protagonist, Marlow, visiting some of the same colonies where Conrad himself had once worked, now travels to the interior to meet up with one Kurtz, a stationmaster who had mysteriously gone off the radar. On his quest, Marlow reaches his own conclusions about the new order:

> The conquest of the earth, which mostly means the taking it away from those who have a different complexion or slightly flatter noses than ourselves, is not a pretty thing when you look into it too much. What redeems it is the idea only. An idea at the back of it . . . something you can set up, and bow down before, and offer a sacrifice to.†

Notice that an *idea*, a rationalization like *progress*, a justification like bringing Christianity to others, improving their lot so that they can live like us, helps one live with one's own Shadow. Just as the Japanese launched the Pacific war with its high-minded Greater East Asia Co-Prosperity Sphere, which led to the rape of Nanking and Manila and so many other butcheries, so America launched its invasion of the Middle East to bring democracy to those who had not asked for it. (Reportedly, the CIA had smuggled caches of small American flags to distribute when the U.S. Army rolled into Baghdad so that the joyous population could celebrate its transportation to the new democratic order.) Nothing is as powerful as a seductive idea. Nothing is as

---

*The particularly odious euphemism *concentration camp* was coined by the British in the Boer War in South Africa.
† *Heart of Darkness*, p. 7.

powerful as an idea that allows us to justify our complexes, our hidden agendas, our self-interest. Privileging our special interests, wrapping them in a flag or a justification, will allow us to swallow our Shadow without choking on it.

When Marlow finds Kurtz he has "gone native." He is quite mad and can only repeat the dark mantra, "The horror . . . the horror. . . ." Kurtz has seen atrocities committed against the indigenous populations in service to that most popular religion—the religion of commercial gain. He served those rationalizations, those slogans himself, but, underneath he discovered the seductive sibilance of *ivory*: "The word *ivory* rang in the air, was whispered, was sighed. You would think they were praying to it."*

Kurtz was, like other moderns before him, and many to come, seduced and corrupted by such ideas and the dark agenda that they serve. Like others who have no strong relationship to the soul, he believed that the powerful, collective voice of his culture was the voice of the soul, and he obeyed. But such unconscious fealty to the idea led Kurtz to a very dark night of the soul. As Nietzsche once observed, we need to beware when staring into the abyss, lest the abyss stare into us. Kurtz entered the abyss, and did not return.

> The wilderness had found him out early, and had taken a terrible vengeance . . . it had whispered to him things about himself which he did not know, things of which he had no conception till he took council with the great solitude. . . . It echoed loudly within him because he was hollow at the core.†

One is inevitably reminded of T. S. Eliot's indictment of the hollow men, headpieces filled with straw. All that is necessary

---

Heart of Darkness, p. 23.
†Ibid., p. 59.

for the seduction and compliance of the good folk is the power of a collective idea in service to whatever tawdry ends. Such a repeated consequence must surely cause us all pause to reflect on what moves us, our culture, and our time. Marlow, Conrad's persona, struggles with this issue, disdains the fatuous twaddle of "the white man's burden," and concludes, "The most you can hope from it is some knowledge of yourself."*

This humbling, private recognition may not seem much after such an arduous journey into the heart of darkness, but it is surely a better alternative than that elected by enthusiastic nationalists who only sixteen years later sent their youth to be butchered "in Flanders's fields, [where] poppies blow, / Between the crosses, row on row." With a modicum of insight into their own Shadow, they might have kept their precious children home, and proved themselves less nuisance to the world.

A sensitized reading of the prophetic voices of modernist culture, the Goethes, the Dostoevskys, the Conrads, and too many more to mention here, invites—rather, demands—that we become psychological. It is no longer sufficient to view our time through political or economic lenses alone. We are obliged to look into the deeper designs of the soul, to track the truculent engines of our darker selves. Artists, who live there, and depth psychologists, who venture there, are instructive guides to the places we must go if we are ever to heal ourselves or heal our age. Never before in history have there been greater freedoms, and never before has the Shadow possessed so many instruments for healing or for destruction. What changes is history, social structure, popular attitudes, and the vagaries of popular will. What is constant is human nature, with its tendencies toward self-delusion, inflation, and a readiness to act unconsciously.

* *Heart of Darkness*, p. 71.

Chapter Nine

DARK DIVINITY
The Shadow Side of God

T he ancient Xenophanes once wrote that if horses had hands, the gods they would draw would take the form of horses. Throughout history our theologies *and* psychologies, which generally claim to be objective readings of tribal experience of the transcendent metaphysical or personal experience, are in fact subjective confessions. Our gods look very much like us, do they not? Is not the most common analogous image of a god that of a parent: variously wise, stern, loving, compassionate, just; in short, someone like us? Do we not expect that our gods esteem the same values as we, perhaps share the same prejudices, perhaps even agree with our tastes, as well? What does this say of "the gods," who, by definition, are wholly participant of a transcendent realm and therefore quite beyond our fractal consciousness and limited cognitive apparatus? And how much does it reveal of us?

From the standpoint of a divinity, or from the perspective of nature, there is no good, no evil. The cancer eating us, the shark pursuing us, the grim specter of our approaching annihilation is not "evil." It simply is. Even social evil is relative to the context. What is permissible in one cultural setting is heinous in another. One culture sees matter as evil, another venerates earthly things. One culture constricts sexuality, another finds it a path to God. One culture establishes moral strictures, while another finds religious justification for their violation. But the human ego, which in its fragility splits so frequently, bifurcating what is supportive from that which is threatening to its own survival, creates the problem of good and evil. While it is true that the transcendent injunction of the great Western religions is to relinquish this divided ego posture—to fear God, to let go—or to "let God," as AA suggests—and the great Eastern religions counter that it is the deluded ego itself that is the problem, it is nonetheless the human ego, not the gods, that creates "theologies." Theologies are thus secondary or epiphenomenal responses to primary phenomena, and they say more about the limited functioning of our ego and the complexes through which experience is processed than reveal very much about the mystery we call *the gods*.

The virtue of the polytheisms that have prevailed throughout most of recorded history is that they have a greater tolerance for ambiguity. A particular deity, amid the polytheistic many, may embody numerous contradictions, as seen from the limited position of the human ego, and many gods can more adequately express the complexity of the universe and the opposites that are so much a part of our experience. But the Western world—Judaism, Christianity, Islam—in desperate competition with dualisms and polytheisms, threw in its chips on the idea of the single, preeminent God. For better or worse, most Westerners subscribe to "theism," the notion of a single God, omnipotent, omniscient, omnipresent, and moral to the core.

Placing one's theo-psychological bet on the theistic horse leads, however, to considerable tension, both within the *imago Dei* and within one's personal psychology. Putting it bluntly, how can a God whose nature is posited as good, loving, just, and involved—the typical attributes of the theistic understanding—permit the existence of both natural evil and moral evil? If God is omnipotent, then It is not powerless to act, powerless to prevent evil. If omniscient, then It is not ignorant of evil. If omnipresent, then It is the ready witness of, if not participant in, the ongoing saga of evil. Such is the agonizing dilemma of the true theist.

So painfully perplexing has this apparent contradiction been that theistic theology has evolved a whole sub-enterprise called *theodicy*, a word whose etymology embodies the question of how, and in what fashion, God may be called just, loving, involved, and moral, given the world we experience.

Some tribes finessed this dilemma by embracing those contradictions that trouble the more timorous ego. Polytheisms embody the complex disparities of natural energies as multiplicitous gods. Dualisms, such as Zoroastrianism, posited the idea of a good god of spirit at war with an evil god of matter, with the presumption that the god of spirit triumphs at the end of history.

But the modern ego has not generally proved satisfied by these polyvalent, protean godheads. With the development of the ego through an accretion of consciousness through the centuries, our existential angst has also increased, and our demand for unity, for consistency, and for predictable order rises apace. We even tell ourselves that monotheisms are superior to polytheisms, that dualisms are only contradictions. But the contradictions of most theistic positions are then driven underground, only to surface later as troubling paradox, or unacceptable ambiguity.*

---

*In the nineteenth century, Huxley coined the term *agnostic*, meaning, "without knowledge," to create an in-between position in which the question of God, and the attendant problem of good and evil are acknowledged, but the individual feels him- or herself insufficiently possessed of convincing information to reach a final conclusion on the matter.

GOOD BOY MEETS GOD

The seeds of discord are deeply buried in the Western psyche and its *imago Dei*. A *locus classicus* for this tension in our hearts is found in the testimony of an unknown Hebrew poet who, some 2,600 years ago, borrowed an earlier Sumerian story of a righteous man who, despite obeying the presumptive rules of his tribe and his god, ran terribly afoul of life and was stunned into a radical reconsideration of all he believed true. He believed that he, and his people, had an understanding with God; namely, right belief, followed by right conduct, would eventuate in divine reciprocity. The story of his *nekyia*, or dark descent of the soul, reveals the large Shadow issue for Western theology, and haunts us to this day. Job is that man, and *Job* remains our story.

Who among us has not presumed such invisible contracts with the universe? When I was a child and fell ill, I concluded that since my experience was bad I had somehow offended something or someone, that the flu was punitive, the croup tent purgatory, and that I had to mend my ways. This sort of magical thinking causes all of us to project a *quid pro quo* onto the universe: "If I do this, You will do that; or, if I fail to do this, You may do that!" Such "sacred contracts" are presumptive, hubristic, and delusory, but we all have signed onto them at some point in our lives. They are our archaic parental imagoes, or our security complexes, projected onto the blank screen of the inscrutable universe. Thus, Job dramatizes our prototypical, besieged consciousness, our chief object lesson from which is to be prized back into an encounter with the radical mystery of the gods.

Job finds his wealth eroded, his family destroyed, and his assumptions violated. Quite apart from his trauma, he is also morally enraged. He has, after all, been "a good boy," obeyed the rules, and now he expects the payoff. Three so-called comforters visit him, each one still invested in the magical thinking of his tribe. Accordingly, they upbraid him for his transgressions, which he denies, for his disregard of the rules, which he denies, and for his unconscious complicity with evil, which he denies. Finally, as so much of this text employs legal metaphor, he summons Yahweh to be the chief witness for the defense that he has not transgressed the moral code and thereby the presumptive contract. But, as one quickly learns from history, chief executives seldom respond to subpoenas from prosecutors.

When Yahweh does finally manifest before Job, as a metaphoric voice out of the whirlwind, he confronts Job's unconscious arrogance—namely, the presumptive fantasy that one can control the universe, manipulate the gods, and thereby secure one's ego comforts. Job, abashed, observes that heretofore he had heard of this god with his ears, but now he sees him with his eyes.* That is, he had lived in the sweet comforts of venerable tradition, received presumption, and hitherto had not experienced the radical contradictions of life, nor swum in the unfathomable depths of divinity. *Job is the story not of the Shadow of God, but of our Shadow problem with that mystery we call God.*

After this encounter God chastises the three comforters with their conventional pieties, and blesses Job. What has happened here? When I initially encountered the story of Job in high school, and later in college, I was deeply offended at what I took to be the high-handed acts of a celestial bully with brass knuckles who merited no respect. Upon more mature reflection, I came to realize that what Yahweh is communicating to

---

*We need to read this sentence metaphorically, for the Near Eastern tradition avers that one may not speak the name of God directly, nor picture it, nor depict it without blasphemy. Hence most Islamic art leaves a deliberate flaw in each tapestry or carpet, reserving perfection for Allah alone.

Job is that the universe is infinitely more complex, more nuanced than the human ego will ever comprehend. Our hubris is not our fear or our awe in the face of the brutal majesty of the universe, both of which are honest emotions in the face of the numinous *Other*; our folly is our presumption, our hubristic efforts to control this great mystery, to strike deals, to ensure our ego preservation in the face of the inexplicable powers of the cosmos. It is the oldest of crimes in the human catalog— the crime of arrogant self-delusion. Job, the pious good boy, seeking to curry favor by compliant behaviors, gets to meet the real god. Those who casually say they seek religious experience should beware of hubris—they may come upon religious experience, or it may come upon them, as Job found.

What we discover in the work of this unknown poet who wrote *Job* is a nuanced critique of his tribal presumption of a contract, a covenant that, while promised to the patriarch Abraham, had been presumed upon since. That covenant is now revised, not as securing the tribe the gratuitous blessings of their god, but as summoning them to a higher, more responsible mindfulness before the almighty Other. The ego, with its hubristic tendency to privilege its own agenda, had finally run into the Shadow of God, that is, the shadow side of the theologies we manufacture to serve our needs.

Notice that *the problem of evil is a problem of the human ego, and the imago Dei it constructs.* The supreme deities are not, apparently, concerned with good or evil. They simply *Are*, in all their inscrutable mystery. So-called "natural evil" is simply nature naturing. And so-called "moral evil" is very slippery in its definitions, so often a function of variable cultural contexts. The problem of evil is rather a problem of that part of us that splits life into opposites—like good and evil, life and death, you and me—when clearly nature, or divinity, makes no such split at all. Nature does not seem to think that our mortality is evil, nor an enemy to be opposed. Nature does not "think"; it is energy expressing itself. But we do, and our thinking splits us off from nature naturing. For example, our medical armamentarium is arrayed against death, *the enemy*, rather than the natural outcome of a natural process. Accordingly, our stratagems are described as "heroic measures." The fragility of our ego seems to make it cling all the more to its tenuous hold on things, even as the core message of all of the great religions has been to trust in the gods and accept their will. As Dante expressed it, "*In la Sua voluntade e nostra pace*": "In Thy Will Is Our Peace." Easier said than done.

Yahweh's communication to Job is not what it appears to be: a brute summons to acquiesce before a superior power. What is required of Job's awakened consciousness is that the ego open to a more differentiated *imago Dei*. Job's *imago Dei*, and that of his tribe, says a lot about them, as our images say a lot about us, and very little about the ultimate mystery. Whether consciously or not, our ego wishes an *imago Dei* consonant with its own agenda, but the gods refuse to comply with our reductive expectations. Our god-image is *our* image, and has rather little to do with the complexity and transcendent reality we call divinity. So the Shadow problem rears its head again, the ego is rebuffed, and Job acquires a larger vision of self and cosmos. He is transformed from compliant child to respectful adult in an enlarged psychology and theology. Most theological growth, and all psychological growth, comes from the greater defeating the lesser, often to our dismay.

THE HEALING OF GOD

The healing—or better, the enlargement—of the Western *imago Dei* has haunted our history. The goal of Greek tragedy was not to destroy the protagonist but rather to restore him or her to a proper relationship with the gods. Out of hubris and hamartia, arrogance and limited vision, the protagonist chooses wrongly, begets consequences, and through suffering is brought to a humbled relationship before transcendent powers. Such a transformation occurs in the example of Oedipus as wise ruler—who knows neither himself, his true parents, nor the consequences of his choices—to the blinded Oedipus, in disgrace and shame and exile, to the Oedipus who comes to Colonus after years of penitent wandering and is blessed with a healing apotheosis, a healing of his *imago Dei*, and his restoration to right relationship to the mystery we call God.

Augustine wrestling with the same dilemma borrows from Platonic metaphysics and articulates a *privatio boni* theory of evil. His faith position, and that of most of Judeo-Christian theism, is that since God is good, loving, wise, just, omniscient, and omnipresent, evil cannot be allowed to contaminate the godhead. At the same time, while there is a tacit acknowledgement of evil as an autonomous energy in our history—dramatized as *Satan* ("adversary,") or *Devil* ("one who casts over against")—evil cannot be accorded an equal place as in older dualisms. Thus, the theodicy of *privatio boni* asserts that evil is the *privation* of the good, and is not produced *by* the good. Evil is a distancing from the good. (This theory may seduce the brain for a moment, but it seldom captures the heart. Still, it has persisted and is the chief straw man against which Jung inveighs in the twentieth century in his *Answer to Job*.)

In 1710 Gottfried Leibniz published *Theodicy*. In this tome he argues that the truths of rational philosophy and theology will not contradict each other. Thus, evil exists because every structure will have a flaw, and will be less perfect than its Creator. The presence of evil helps make the presence of good possible, and more noticeable when it appears. This world, monstrous as it sometimes is, is "the best of all possible worlds," he argues, because it preserves the freedom of God, and does not limit the Creator; we, too, are invested with freedom and so bear responsibility for choices and for those consequences we consider evil. To create a world without human freedom would be to rob us of our moral capacity, so this world, as it is, serves us best through our summons to right knowledge and right choice. This is the theodicy of the philosophers, and the emerging scientists, who place the premium upon education and rational self-examination to understand better the complexities of choice and consequence, and scientific knowledge to interact more harmoniously with the ineluctable laws of nature.

François-Marie Arouet, better known as Voltaire, challenges Leibniz's benign view. On All Souls' Day, November 1, 1755, while the faithful are at mass in Lisbon, an earthquake levels the churches, killing some 30,000 souls at their worship. Aroused by this catastrophe, Voltaire writes *Candide*, whose eponymous simpleton has the honesty to speak truthfully and see through cant and persiflage. He is accompanied on a world tour of human suffering by a Dr. Pangloss, who represents the optimism of Leibniz and who sophistically announces amid disaster after disaster, that "this is the best of all possible worlds." Candide returns at story's end to the simple life, a candid respect for the mystery of both moral and natural evil, and the resolve to till his own garden and thus avoid being a nuisance to his neighbors.

Three further, modern texts on the subject of dark divinity are worth our summary view here: Archibald MacLeish's play, *J.B.*, Jung's *Answer to Job*, and Ron Rosenbaum's "Degrees of Evil."

In response to the question of whether there is someone playing Job today, a character in MacLeish's verse drama *J. B.* replies:

> Millions and millions of mankind
> Burned, crushed, broken, mutilated,
> Slaughtered, and for what? For thinking,
> For walking around the world in the wrong
> Skin, the wrong-shaped noses, eyelids:
> Sleeping the wrong night in the wrong city—
> London, Dresden, Hiroshima. . . .*

J. B. is a modern business man for whom life has been sweet—a spouse, car, kids, life in the burbs, and then . . . all gone. He takes his place in a long line of querulous humanity, stretching back earlier than Job in his lament: "If God is God He is not good, / If God is good, He is not God."[†]

His wife, Sarah, reinforces the presumptive contract.

> God doesn't give all this for nothing:
> A good home, good food,
> Father, mother, brothers, sisters.
> We too have our part to play.
> If we do our part He does His.[‡]

Bingo. There it is—the *quid pro quo*, the "contract," and we have God in our pocket! J. B., having also bought into the contract, must thereby affirm his guilt if things go south. "We have no choice but to be guilty. God is unthinkable if we are innocent."[§]

This modern author also provides contemporary "comforters." They are in turn a fundamentalist, a Freudian, and a Marxist. The first sees the problem in the old way: a sinner in

*MacLeish, *J.B.*, p. 12.
[†]*Ibid.*, p. 14.
[‡]*Ibid.*, p. 30.
[§]*Ibid.*, p. 111.

the face of an inscrutable, tyrannic god, and salvation through abject repentance alone. The second sees evil as a neurosis— surely cured by multiple hours upon the couch. The third sees the fault in an unjust society with revolution as the only eschatological hope.

But MacLeish the humanist finds satisfaction in none of these partial views. To meet the terrible dark side of God, he concludes, we can only bring the balm of human compassion, human love. As Sarah says, "You wanted justice and there was none— / Only love."* When J. B. replies, "He does not love. He is." Sarah rejoins, "But we do. That's the wonder."† MacLeish, perhaps summarizing his own theodicy, wrote, "the poet, as Yeats put it, has only his blind, stupefied heart."

The heart of this humanist theodicy is most eloquent indeed, for what we do have to bring to the table is compassion, witness, and love—perhaps impotent powers in the face of a dark divinity, but redemptive and ennobling ministries nonetheless.

After many years of stewing over the issue, the deeply religious Jung, son of a parson, delivered his cri de coeur in 1952 in the book *Answer to Job*. He puts Yahweh before the bar of justice, so to speak, and finds Him unjust, selfish, and incapable of self-reflection. In short, he is less moral than Job! When Job asks God to witness his piety on his behalf, Job invokes both sides of God—protector and persecutor. While the Christian dogma of Christ as the *agnus Dei*, the Lamb of God, offers propitiatory relief, in fact the old contract is being reinforced. Then Jung voyages into risky territory. He suggests that humanity, with its profound awareness of antimony, the interplay of opposites, is more evolved than the consciousness of Yahweh, as presented in the Bible. Humanity, with its awakened

*J. B., p. 151.
†Ibid., p. 152.

awareness of opposites—not only the good, but the Shadow side of God—has as its chief mission to be the witness, the conscience, and the enlarger of the sensibility of God. God is thus to be humanized, and enlightened!

As with MacLeish, Jung writes with a sense of personal outrage but with a sound grasp of biblical text. Yet his seeming hubris is audacious, even preposterous, if taken literally. What Jung means by this critique of the long history of theodicy is quite compelling. *What is to be healed is not Yahweh, who, after all, is only a metaphor for a particular tribal experience of transcendence, but rather the Western imago Dei.* While an image of God is inherent to the species, what is singular is the unique way in which the image is recast from tribe to tribe, from individual sensibility to individual neurosis. What is to be healed is the ego's understanding of the Shadow, which places Jung in the same corrective tradition as the unknown poet of *Job* twenty-six centuries earlier. It is our theology that needs healing. It is our magical thinking, our sentimentality, that is to be healed. The quiddities of the ego, its agenda of security and satiety, are overthrown by the demands of transcendent reality and the summons to a more capacious consciousness.

It is human consciousness, not God, that is summoned to enlargement. We are challenged to embrace the idea that the transcendent energies of the universe, which we experience as contradictions, are somehow one, somehow purposive, somehow explicable, albeit not to us. Our personal *imago Dei* is a product not of the transcendent powers, the inscrutable gods, but our ego formulation with all its limitations. The healing, then, is not of the gods, but of our ego's enlarging relationship to the inexplicable cosmos, to the unfathomable soul, to the inscrutable gods. There is no contradiction in nature—nature is merely *naturing*; no contradiction in the gods—the gods *god*; but with so much contradiction besetting the ego, we have historically sought to resolve the problem by splitting into opposites rather than by embracing the mystery.

A more recent example of this ego splitting is described by Ron Rosenbaum in his article "Degrees of Evil," where he observes that huge evil has been done, repeatedly, by people convinced of their righteous motives, convinced that their God approved their programs. All nations have claimed divine guidance as they marched on their neighbor. But Rosenbaum argues that there is a special category of evil retained for those who perform their evil with "artistry." In other words, it is not the magnitude of the suffering alone that they beget. Napoleon, after all the suffering he produced, abides in an honored tomb in the heart of Paris. General Grant became President of the United States and is entombed on Riverside Drive in New York. Both of them were butchers who served national interest and are therefore venerated to this day. Rather, this special category of evil is a form of self-consciousness—a sly wink, a knowing that one is performing gratuitous evil, Rosenbaum suggests—that moves one to this rarefied tier of malignity.

Rosenbaum cites, as an example, one moment among many when Hitler and his henchmen savor their joke, that they are simply deporting people to "the marshy parts of Russia" rather than murdering them. Their "artistry" extended to the slogans that adorned the death camps, not least of which was, "Work Sets You Free." When Osama bin Laden chuckles that thousands were incinerated by the gas from the wing tanks of the planes, he turns sordid slaughter into private comedy. "It is in that shared laughter that Hitler and bin Laden shake hands."*

In this form of gratuitous evil Hitler and various thugs of other times and places move beyond the simple splitting of the ego to a place where the separation is celebrated. Yet we know

*Rosenbaum, "Degrees of Evil," *Atlantic Monthly*, p. 68.

that many good people, raised in the tenets of their compassionate faith, also survived by splitting. "On this side is my
family and my value system—both intact; on this side is this
brutal work that I must do to serve a national emergency."
This split caused some to go mad; many to anneal the split with
drugs of various kinds; but allowed most others to function
perfectly normally in an abnormal universe of aesthetically calibrated murder.

What Shadow remains when one embraces it so fully, as
many ordinary people have? What Shadow may be acknowledged when well-educated, conventionally decent chaps, as
George Steiner observed, could read Goethe and Rilke in the
evening and go to their jobs at the concentration camps in the
morning? What aesthetically calibrated evil moves contemporary politicians and radio commentators to exploit fear, using
wedge issues to promote splitting, for the advance of their
party or as a rationale for eroding our freedoms?

What surely must make all of us shudder is the recognition
that not all of our institutional religion, not all of our human-
istic and scientific training, not all of our collective mores could
keep perfectly civilized, highly educated souls from murderous
possession by the Shadow. There is no day when I do not find
this paradox troubling, when it does not thrust me even more
fully into my vocation of education and to renewal of the
Greek admonition to "Know Thyself," even as I am simultaneously depressed to recognize that our cultural stays against barbarism are so fragile. Surely Goethe was right two centuries
ago that "the Evil One is gone, but the evil ones remain."

A final thought must be spoken here. Again, we recall that
the problem of evil is an ego problem. The very title "Dark Divinity" is an ego problem. Do the gods consider themselves a
problem, an untenable contradiction? The question is absurd.
The problem of theodicy is primarily a Western problem where

the collective ego has been developed to such a high degree, and now, of course, by those cultures, such as Japan, China, and India, that suffer the fever of ego-driven materialism and emulate us. Historically, the Western religions—Judaism, Christianity, Islam—posited a fall from grace, an archetypal disconnect that they attributed to a flaw of the ego, a choice badly made, an apple rashly eaten. Their hope for reconciliation is vested in the idea of submission (which is what the word *Islam* means) to the will of God. In the Eastern tradition, the problem of separation, of alienation, is also an ego problem, a problem of attitude. The East has seen that the splitting of the ego begets only alienation. Hence the great Eastern religions, Buddhism and Hinduism, treat our sundered condition by seeking the transcendence of the ego (Buddhism) or its relocation in the great wheel of *Samsara* (redundant fate) where karma, or consequences, are relieved through progressive generations made possible through metempsychosis or rebirth. Accordingly, salvation, or healing, in the collective Eastern tradition requires "changing one's mind" by releasing the ego from its bondage to anxiety and desire. The German word for serenity is *Gelassenheit*, which could literally be translated "the condition of having let go." Having let go, one experiences harmony, reconciliation, serenity. The serenity prayer of twelve-step groups asks the most difficult thing of the ego, that it acknowledge its limited powers and give way to being itself; in other words to stop the driven, compulsive, angst-ridden splitting.

That great soul traveler, novelist Nikos Kazantzakis, placed the following inscription on his tombstone:

"I want nothing; I fear nothing; I am free."

His is the final, existential revolt against powerlessness in the face of an implacable nature, a nature in which one eats the other, and, inevitably, is eaten by the other.* His is the elective freedom of the doctor in Albert Camus's novel *The Plague* who knows he is powerless, that the plague will win, but who creates his meaning by affirming his vocation, by ministering to those suffering. Ending suffering is not an option; but bringing compassion to those who suffer is redemptive of their common condition. So, too, is the work of a lawyer I recently met who defends those about to be executed, telling his clients from the first that he cannot save them, that the appellate laws are stacked against them, that no rich person is on death row, but that he will fight for them to the last. The enemy in these instances is not the dark gods, but despair, nihilism. As Camus once argued, we are free precisely because the world is absurd. If it were "meaningful," it would be someone else's package. Since it is inherently inscrutable, we find our freedom in the character of the choices we make, the values for which we wish to stand.

In the end, the issue of dark divinity is *our* problem, not that of the gods. The Shadow problem is ours, not that of divinity. In the end, ego consciousness is obliged to face its greatest nightmare, that it is so profoundly limited; but we are also invited to acknowledge and embrace our greatest paradoxical freedom—in the midst of our greatest defeat—that we are not in charge after all.

---

*The reader should visit Annie Dillard's novel, *Pilgrim at Tinker's Creek*, to be reminded of the daily drama of life and death, of life engorging itself on other life, right in our backyards, right in our bodies.

Chapter Ten

LUMINOUS DARKNESS
The Positive Shadow

*"The Shadow is the landfill of the self. Yet it is also
a sort of vault: it holds great, unrealized potentialities
within you."*

—JOSEPH CAMPBELL, *PATHWAYS TO BLISS*

How could the Shadow be positive when it is defined, and so often experienced, as troublemaker,
rejected Other, interrupter of ethical life, enemy,
usurper, Devil, demon, antagonist, opposer of our interests, wiz-
ard of subversive legerdemain against our conscious intentions,
and, most of all, a slippery, ubiquitous confounder of how we
wish to think of ourselves? And just how do we wish to think of
ourselves? Righteous? Moral? Consistent? High-minded? Caring? How could we admit our Shadow to this goodly company?

Do we not recall "Young Goodman Brown," the eponymous
hero of Nathaniel Hawthorne's tale, a young Puritan worthy
who wandered one day into a dark wood and found his pious
neighbors, even his fastidious wife, Faith, worshipping at a
black mass in honor of the Dark One? Do we not recall that he
was so shattered by this encounter with darkness so close to
home that he lost his Faith, withdrew from humanity, and died
a lonely, bitter, cynical, unlamented death? What good, then,
might come from this Shadow world? Who would ever wish to
traverse that dark wood? But is there really a choice; does not
this dark wood accompany us all the time, anyway?

In asking this question we might begin by asking why a writer like Hawthorne devoted so much energy to exploring this darkness we carry. So many of his short stories and novels dramatize Shadow eruptions, perhaps because he and his lineage were haunted by the memory of one of their progenitors having presided as an examining magistrate at the Salem witch trials. But when we read Hawthorne, whether it be *The Scarlet Letter*, or "Ethan Brand," or "Rappaccini's Daughter," or "My Kinsman, Major Molineaux," we sense what captivated Hawthorne—the tremendous power of the Shadow.

Literary critic Harry Levin once wrote a study of Hawthorne, Melville, and Poe titled *The Power of Blackness*, wherein he explored the strange fascination of nineteenth-century American authors with the darker powers. Add Twain to this list and what we sense in these authors is their intuitive awareness that collective consciousness had grown one-sided, that the inflationary powers of nineteenth-century Americana, an age of imperialistic expansion, slavery, extirpation of indigenous civilizations, and hubristic triumphalism had begotten its own dark consequences.

So what is good about the Shadow, and how might one gain access to this alleged good? First of all, we have to consider how the ego functions. The human ego is itself a complex, that is, an historically charged energy system that serves as a centrum, a point of focus that provides consciousness, intentionality, consistency, and continuity—all important tools of learning, social functioning, even survival. Yet that same ego is easily overwhelmed by other charged clusters of energy, aka complexes, that usurp the ego and make us do things that upon reflection we sometimes regret. ("Write the letter but don't send it. . . ." The energy recedes and we feel differently, less intense, having been restored to the central complex of consciousness we call the ego.)

As a complex amid other complexes, the ego is easily frightened, easily nudged off its center, and learns from the earliest days that adaptation serves survival. So we learn to adapt to the demands around us, real or perceived. In time we even tend to identify with our adaptations rather than our intrinsic nature.

The story of our first half of life is an implicit saga of progressively sophisticated adaptation to environmental messages, our unwitting identification of who we are with those internalized messages, and how they compel us to be in the world. Thus, we all get off course, estranged from our nature, separated from the Self. Yet that Self expresses itself through the language of insurgent symptomatology, whether in the venue of body as chronic pain or gastric distress, or forbidden behavior that nonetheless leaks into the world, or compensatory dream image, or affective disorder, such as depression, that rises from suppression of our psychic reality. It is this experience of contradiction between our ego's program and our psyche's agenda that brings conflict between outer and inner, producing such suffering that we often begin to question the premises by which we are living our lives. Thus, through this conflict, we begin to see how the recrudescence of the Shadow can have a compensatory, even healing effect upon us. When we remember that the simplest, most functional definition of the Shadow is *that which renders us uncomfortable with ourselves*, then we realize that authentic, less adapted parts of us may challenge and even threaten the ego but remain who we really are, and insist on coming into expression through us into the world. In this way we see that the Shadow can play a positive role in our individuation process. It is less adapted and therefore more honest; it is less acclimated and therefore more original; it is less conventional and consensual and therefore more nearly expressive of the whole person we are meant to share with others.

In Chapter Three we examined two *loci classicus* of Shadow

sensitivity: anger and sexuality. We saw how interruptive these emotions could be to the well-governed life we believe we desire. But let us return to them a moment, to see more clearly the positive agenda their Shadow insurgence might serve.

Surely anger often is disruptive to the fabric of the family, to the social contract that binds a society and prevents it from being ripped apart. On the other hand, we have ample clinical evidence that anger suppressed can produce higher blood pressure with the threat of strokes and infarcts as well as depression. How, then, can it be that the expression of anger is healing to us, and yet to be creatively channeled?

Let us recall that the etymological root in the Indo-Germanic language for the words *anger, angst, anxiety,* and *angina* is the same, *angh*. And *angh* means "constriction." Thus, when the organism experiences constriction, it automatically, instinctively, responds first with anxiety and then anger toward any threat to its well-being, or it may somaticize as a constricted heart. In other words, anger is one of the resources provided by our instinctual life to protect us, to defend us. How then can anger be inherently wrong? Yes, anger can be disruptive, as we have acknowledged, but anger itself is an instinctual, protective energy. Respect for others asks that anger be channeled in some constructive way to address grievances, but anger is not wrong, as we have so frequently been taught.

It required some decades before I learned this elemental lesson, that anger was a part of our natural energy in service to life itself. Through the years I gradually learned to channel the energy that anger provides in service to resolve, to determination, and to mobilize the will to bring matters to a resolution. This good, necessary, life energy had, because of the complexes of family and culture, too often been diverted from addressing causes directly to the underworld, where it cannot help but breed monsters. Years later, as a therapist, I treated a man who was so dominated by his version of religious instruction that he was profoundly depressed. Though he lived with a harridan amid impossible domestic circumstances, he felt that his reactive emotions were forbidden, and their tumultuous presence demonstrated the magnitude of his sins. I would like to report that I was able to communicate out of personal experience and reframe the natural role of anger in his life. I failed. He quit therapy, and shortly thereafter he quit his life. His suicide was the final expression of his full, authentic feeling, an act of violence against the only person whom he had permission to aggress.*

Sexuality is of course the other major area of Shadow material. Sex, too, can be anarchic. When the hormones, or the God Eros, take possession, people can be driven to madness. In service to this energy they have betrayed their vows, committed violence, and made rash decisions with long-term consequences that they lived to regret. Yet again, sexuality is part of our nature and cannot help but be a transcendent form of how life expresses itself. The famous Kinsey Reports of the late fifties alerted America to the lie that it was so easily telling itself, that we were a passive, gentle folk with little sexual activity, variety, or enthusiasm. When America spoke under the guise of confidentiality, the lid blew off. People who were shamed because of their sexual energy and its multiplicitous forms of expression began to learn that they were not alone, not abnormal, and that they were part of nature naturing. When I was in college during this time, the "Marriage and Family" course textbook, which featured one chapter on sexual intercourse, and a mild one at that, was wrapped in a brown paper wrapper and sold only to those students who could prove they were members of that

---

*My father, the kindest man I ever met, suffered blinding headaches during a large part of his life. I actually saw him pound his head sometimes when he hurt so much. Trying to drive that pain out of his head, I often wonder if he, too, was striking the only person he had permission to hit.

class. That an institution of higher learning was governed not by the ideal of disinterested pursuit of truth, nor even an honest spirit of inquiry, says much about the power of the Shadow. What is so powerful in us, in this case Eros, rightly called a god by the ancients, must be rigidly controlled if not forbidden. Again, what monsters rise from such denial of nature?

The spread of information, allied with the discovery of the birth-control pill, fostered the so-called sexual revolution of the sixties. On the one hand the abundance of information and permission to be what one is, a sexual being, led to greater freedom, and on the other hand it provoked enormous fear of the powers of nature. The opening of greater freedom, greater permission, not only in the field of sexual mores but other value systems as well, catalyzed the fundamentalist assault on accurate sex education that continues to this day. These anxious souls have no problem repressing reality, and scientific information about it, in service to their fear of its power in their own Shadow lives. As a result, they have successfully influenced national governmental policy through cutting funds for sex education, AIDS research, and open discussion of lifestyle choices. By inculcating guilt, shame, and anxiety, such religionists foster more and more ignorance, and more and more neurosis. The magnitude of their repression is of course a subjective confession to the power of Eros in their lives. The greater the forces of repression, the greater that which is repressed grows, and the truth will out—whether naturally, spontaneously, or pathologically.

OTHER ENGAGEMENTS WITH THE POSITIVE SHADOW

A client became an ob-gyn because she knew this was the only way she could obtain the approval of her medical parents. As a physician she was competent, caring, and devoted to her work. What brought her into therapy was her anxiety in confronting her patients, or telling them what they did not want to hear. While not a particularly pleasant task, this face-to-face dialogue is as necessary in therapy as it is in any marriage. She was so close to this issue that she did not initially see that she was caught in a negative countertransference to her patients, namely, that her unconscious set her up to experience the sometimes needy, sometimes narcissistic, sometimes demanding patient as replicating the insistent, invasive power of her parental complexes. A parent is a giant authority, for good or ill, to every child. Hers gave her no break, no latitude to be herself. So when the patient demanded that she step forth with her opinion, she felt paralyzing anxiety. Her core complex, the negative parent, was replicated over and over, even though the piece of paper on the wall said that she was the authority in that room.

Yet as difficult as this conflict within was, it was not the worst she suffered. Her real talent and calling was music. She had an opera-level voice and a fine composition capacity. When she neared her real love, music, she also froze, saying, "What if I did write and the critics destroyed it?" Getting a negative critical review is hardly a pleasant experience, but can it ever be enough to keep one away from the summons to create? For twenty years she remained depressed as the piano stood gathering dust in the other room. In her mind the devouring voice of her mother persisted. As a college-age woman, she had played her composition for her parents and her mother said, "You're no Mozart." Who is Mozart?* But that is not the point. The critical, invasive voice merely added to the denial of personhood that had been there since childhood. As problematic as

---

*Reportedly, Cary Grant once said of his screen image, and all that strangers projected upon him, "Even I am not Cary Grant."

her countertransference with her patients was, a far greater suffering was occasioned by turning her back on her genuine love. Her Shadow healing required that she claim the considerable talent that had been given her.

I am pleased to report that as a result of her therapy, this person, while continuing a flourishing medical practice, finally confronted her parents and her own parental complexes, began composing, and is presently in the final phase of an entire musical comedy that she plans to record. Her Shadow apprehension rose from her parent's constant criticism, but her task was to grow up, leave home psychologically, and to honor the talent given her by the gods. What parent should ever stand in the way of the gods? But this generic issue is common to us all, namely, the recovery of personal authority in the second half of life. The recovery of such authority is critical to the examined life, critical to the recovery of one's proper journey, and is only possible by the reclamation of whatever has been consigned to our Shadow.

Consider another example, that of a man in his seventies who had led a distinguished professional life and yet had never quite felt it was fully his life. He had the suspicion that all the while he was following someone else's instructions. Clearly, the dominant presence in his psychological formation had been his controlling mother whose wishes he learned to read, as most children do, by tone of voice or lifted eyebrow, when not overtly directed by her. Finding one's own truth, one's own authority, is a task that is never too late to take on. In one dream of many that tracked the development of a new relationship to masculine identity that had been so suppressed in his life, he relates:

> The area around my cabin [his occasional retreat from the world in the Texas hill country] was flooded. The whole countryside was under water. Water came right up to the cabin, but there was no water inside. Then I saw something under the water in the flooded

yard. At first I thought it was a big fish swimming near the surface. But then I saw a light coming from the object and realized the animal was not a fish but a scuba diver. He came out of the water and onto the porch, and we began to talk.

This dreamer had never read Joseph Conrad's "The Secret Sharer," but his dream replicates a psychodynamic phenomenon that Conrad had described and published a century earlier.

In "The Secret Sharer," a young sea captain, just graduated from mariner's school, begins a journey through the South China Sea. His crew is overtly disdainful of his inexperience and chafes under his command. One night, while he is brooding on the deck, a form emerges from a phosphorescent sea. He pulls the man aboard, and instantly feels a kinship. He hides this man in his captain's quarters, and learns that the man, in order to save his ship in a gale, had to kill a seaman who froze at a critical moment. Knowing he will be hanged, he jumps into the sea and swims to the young captain's vessel. The next day, a ship pulls alongside and the captain asks if anyone had seen this fugitive. The younger captain protects his charge, even though, as a captain, he is entrusted with upholding the laws of the sea.

After a series of conversations between the two in which the youth gains a deepened understanding of the secret of authority, that it does not come from a piece of paper on the wall, the young captain enables his charge to escape. The last paragraph of the story is virtually identical to the opening paragraph, with a major exception, for now the crew looks on their captain, standing alone on the bridge, with admiration, since he has demonstrated skill, knowledge, and, most of all, authority. He has learned from his shadowy visitor that the secret of command is to attain his own authority, by whatever means, whether approved by others or not.

Though Freud was just beginning his publishing, and Jung was still in medical school, Conrad the artist intuited the dynamics of deepened conversation with the Shadow. How could we imagine that Conrad's story, and this twenty-first-century dreamer, would produce the same images if they were not collaborators? But these images come from deep within the unconscious that seeks to guide us all, if we would but begin to pay attention. That we are so hesitant to do so, and that so many contemporary schools of psychology and psychiatry dismiss the power of the unconscious and abandon the dialogue with that which courses so deeply within us, is a failure of nerve, a failure of imagination, and a consignment to the trivial.

What Conrad intuited, and my analysand dreamt, is that our Shadow courses deeply within and seeks to connect with consciousness. In both cases the swimmer emerges from an aura of light—a numinosity that occasions awe—and seeks to engage the protagonist in developmental dialogue. Can the reader imagine that something inside you wishes to "talk" to us? As a result of this conversation, consciousness is strengthened, new energies are available, and each person lives a richer life, one that is more authentically one's own. The conversation that this man has begun in his seventies has already produced a more conscious grasp of his journey and broadened the choices he now has before him. It is a conversation that persists in all of our lives and invites our attention and respect.

These stories of the Shadow's presence in our lives are so common, but they feature a million variations. A daughter becomes the carrier of her father's anima. She is charged with making him happy when his own life so clearly depresses him. Or the son is charged with being the instrument of his mother's unlived life. He is not even to bother asking what he wants for his life. He gets his marching orders: please her in arenas that she will acknowledge as safe, and convenient, and that bring reflected glory to her. Jung's reminder that the greatest burden the child must bear is the unlived life of the parent is cautionary to us all. The Shadow their parents did not address has a tendency to become a Shadow issue for their children as well, for they will unwittingly repeat those patterns, or overcompensate for the unlived life, or slip into a neurosis arising from the great conflict of life models contending within them.

Personal authority, which is distanced from all of us through the powerlessness of childhood and the necessity of adapting to the messages and demands of whatever environment is provided by fate, requires that we continue discerning what is true for us and then mobilize the courage to live it in the world.

Finding and expressing a personal authority is thus a huge Shadow task in the second half of life, for we have grown allied against our natural, best selves. For the ob-gyn, the acquisition of personal authority means that she risks both telling the truth as she sees it to her patients *and* answering the summons of the muse as she experiences it. She has a twin call, then, as we often do: the personal call to individuation, and the societal call to bring the gift of our unique selves to others. Not answering the call is not only a personal Shadow issue, but an abrogation of our obligation to others.

For the seventy-year-old-man, personal authority means a radical revisioning of the relationship to the Self, the linkage to which was repeatedly interdicted by the demands of the controlling mother. Consider how healing the following dream is, and how, after all these years, the soul seeks to reconnect, and to invite consciousness to bear witness to its personal truth:

Joe S. (a friend whom he respected from childhood) and other old friends from high school sat in a circle. Joe pointed to a chimney above a cabin roof, as though there was an owl there. I looked but saw no owl, but around the chimney there was a narrow metal strip that reflected our images back to us . . . ! Then Joe said the owl's message could be understood because its sounds made an impression in our ears that could be removed and read.

Although his life has been enveloped in the demands of the mother, nonetheless producing distinguished service to his community, his hitherto unknown authority is intimated through this circle of masculine energies. What the dreamer needs to know from this owl of archetypal wisdom he can discern through engaging with the Self, the image in the mirror, and by learning to "read" the wisdom that is imprinted within. Who would make these images up? Who among us is so ingenious? These dreams emanate from the Self, the deepest layer of being, which seeks to bring us not to goodness, his mother's ideal, but to wholeness, the soul's agenda. After all these years the dreamer is invited to deal at last with the positive Shadow, and to recover a personal authority so long ago abducted by the unconscious parent who lived out her anxieties and imposed her unlived life upon her malleable child.

What was true for us in childhood remains true throughout life. How sad, indeed, how tragic it is that one becomes allied against one's own nature. But most of us are thus divided against ourselves. So who we are, what we are summoned to incarnate in this world, in service to the gods, falls into the Shadow. Shadow work thus requires discerning what wishes to be expressed through us and mobilizing the energy, courage, and commitment to sustain it, even amid conditions unfavorable to its expression. Our positive Shadow, like the dark Shadow, is *who we really are*. The Shadow is always an expression of the will of the gods, however uncomfortable that may prove to our nervous consciousness. As with the problem of theodicy, we have to remember that even splitting the Shadow into positive and negative aspects is the problem of our ego, not the problem of our nature.

ACCEPTING OURSELVES, ACCEPTING OUR SHADOW

Another Shadow issue that haunts anyone in the second half of life—that is, anyone who has a modicum of consciousness, who is not a narcissist, not a sociopath, is the problem of self-acceptance, self-forgiveness. In *Notes from Underground*, Dostoevsky asks how a person of any consciousness can stand himself. He is right, at one level. When we become conscious that our values and our choices and their unforeseen consequences are often quite divergent, we are face to face with an unintended hypocrisy. When we realize that our behaviors hurt others, especially those whom we love, we are crushed. When we realize that our unconscious choices produce lasting harm in the world, or that we who live in privileged societies do so through the exploitation of the wretched and the powerless, how can one profess one's religious and ethical values with clear conscience? This is a Shadow dilemma that each of us who claims some moral sensitivity surely suffers.

The weight of this divided consciousness poses a difficult task of self-acceptance, self-forgiveness. While the capacity to accept responsibility for the consequences of one's choices, even to acknowledge guilt for them, is the measure of a moral being, to still be consumed by one's guilt is a form of hubris, of moral inflation. No one wakes in the morning, per se, and says, "Today I shall bring harm to myself and others," but by day's end we often have, one way or another.

To be in this fallen, fractured, compromised world, with our own sundered selves, is to be an accomplice. For a person not to acknowledge moral complicity in the world's woe is itself a Shadow issue. Albert Camus, an agnostic, nonetheless chose the theological motif of "the Fall" as the title of his most compelling work. In *The Fall* the central character, Jean-Baptiste Clamence, a voice in the wilderness who is also a soul seeking clemency, acknowledges that his indifference to the suffering of others, and his cowardice, are what he has to live with the rest of his days. His story is ours as well. As T. S. Eliot ruefully queries in his poem "Gerontion," "after such knowledge, what foregiveness"?

Yet, is not the Shadow task here precisely self-forgiveness, not denial, but self-acceptance? How can I accept you if I cannot accept myself? How could I ever love you when I despise myself? When I do despise myself is that not an inflation as well? Where is it written that I am to be perfect, that more of me is demanded than my human limitations allow? The delusion of perfection is not unlike the paradox that the moment I think I am virtuous I am guilty of inordinate pride. So, conversely, when I am utterly wretched, I am also guilty of moral inflation, for I am expecting more from myself than a human is capable. Are we not all, in Nietzsche's phrase, "human, all-too-human"?

Self-acceptance, then, can be one of the most powerful Shadow issues. To affirm this wretched soul that I am is a positive redemption from the Shadow world of self-estrangement. From this self-estrangement rises irritability with others, self-punishing behaviors, depression, and further division within. Just as the recovery of personal authority is a critical task in the second half of life, so too the engagement with the positive Shadow requires that we come to accept ourselves as we are. We are creatures more unconscious than conscious. While responsible for all our choices, we are still riddled with complexes and hidden agendas, narcissistic motives, driven by fear, and always frail, frangible, and finite. Who should not muster some compassion for such a tragic soul? *Tout comprendre, tout pardoner*, as the French proverb has it. Yet who among us can mobilize compassion for that most wretched soul we know—ourselves? Who among us can undertake such redemptive work in the positive Shadow world? (The twelve-step programs wisely build in the honest inventory of one's history, including the making of amends to those harmed, as long as it will not do further damage.)

Accessing the positive Shadow will necessarily require that we enter forbidden territory, at least territory hitherto forbidden to us. We will have to hear unpleasant feedback from others, not only their criticism but, far worse, their compliments. Their compliments may be suggesting that they see something in us that we were conditioned to deny in the face of our adaptive sense of self. We will have to examine our projections, especially those that esteem and value others, and ask where they come from in us, what we might be denying in ourselves. We will also have to attend to our dreams and fantasy life to see what agenda the unconscious is bringing to the fore, and, even more, to interpret that material symbolically, lest we be caught in its literalization, which would only divert our possible growth. One analysand recently was stunned when I said that her negative view of herself meant that she was repeatedly denying others the gift of herself. She found this idea so hard to comprehend because she was so invested in her long-running fantasy of essential unworthiness.

My kindly analyst in Zurich once suggested of training in a foreign country—"To get through here, you will need to access your Shadow." He meant that reminder in several ways, not the least of which had to do with economic survival, since I was far from a trust-fund baby or a rich divorcee. Accordingly, I learned to go underground, to clean houses, teach English, and similar occupations in the world of *Schwarzarbeit*, or "black work." Entering the underground economy was necessary to gain the Swiss Francs necessary for bread and soup, and, more importantly, for analysis. I learned a lot about myself during those days, all of which has been helpful in later years. We do not know who we are until we are obliged to reach deep within to draw upon the resources nature has given us. As Rilke wrote to a troubled young poet, "We are set down in life as in the element to which we best correspond, and over and above this we have through thousands of years of accommodation become so like this life. . . . We have no reason to mistrust our world, for it is not against us. . . . And if only we arrange our life according to that principle which counsels us that we must always hold to the difficult, then that which now still seems to us the most alien will become what we most trust and find most faithful."* In these moments of recognition, *and* self-acceptance, we integrate some richer aspect of the Shadow and gain some small, further purchase on the immensity of the soul.

SHADOW AS WHAT DO YOU WANT?

To gain the positive values rising from that "landfill" we call the Shadow, we have to wrestle with Jung's suggestion that to be a full adult, we have to *know what we want*, and to *do it*. Knowing what we want, really, takes a lot of sorting. And living what we find, really, takes a lot of courage and endurance. In reflecting on the task of therapy, Jung once noted that it can only bring us *insight*. Then, he said, come the moral qualities of our character—*courage* to face what must be faced, and then to take the leap, and the *endurance* to stick it out until we ar-

*Rilke, *Letters to a Young Poet*, p. 69.

rive at the place intended for us from the beginning. So much of our lives have been lived through reflexive adaptations, so knowing what we really want is difficult, and then scary, but it feels right when we live it, as we were meant to do.

> *"America has the one true faith—dozens of 'em."*
> —MARK TWAIN

I feel obliged to add a sort of coda to this chapter about the positive Shadow. At the present we are swamped with feel-good theologies and psychologies. The minister of the largest church in America repeatedly tells his flock that God wants them to feel good, to be happy, successful. His wife speaks of once desiring a certain house, and by dint of the beneficence of God, she now lives in that house. So, too, is their flock to live righteously, and presumably receive similar beneficence. One wonders if either has seriously studied the Book of Job, which twenty-six centuries ago critiqued this casual equation of grace with right conduct and right intentions. What will happen to all these good souls when a ton of grief falls on their heads? Will they curse God for His betrayal of "the contract"? Or will they lacerate themselves for proving unworthy? The former is magical thinking, and the latter is the parental complex of a fourth grader. And where is the cross of suffering in all this? But who can argue with "success"—the aisles and the coffers are overflowing. (Mark Twain talked about the calm confidence of a Christian with four aces, so apparently this phenomenon of ideological inflation is not limited to our shallow time.)

This happy-talk theology has an immense Shadow, the Shadow of infantility, of wishful thinking, of denial, of simplification of the complex, and most of all, of the absence of *gravitas* that comes to us when authentically in the presence of the mystery. Such popular theologies and psychologies tempt most by offering transformation without suffering, magic without maturation, and not only infantilize the believer but betray him in the end, for, as most adults know, there is no magic, only real life with all its complexities and tenebrous gradations.

Recently I walked through a large bookstore and found that the "Psychology" aisle had disappeared altogether and been replaced by something called the "Self-Help" section. Now there is nothing wrong with self-help, but the titles there all promised rapid solutions to lifelong problems. These books are what I would call "Soul Lite." Amid the books collectively called *Thinner Thighs in Thirty Days* and *Finding Boomer Happiness in Love* and *Tax-free Shelters While Shedding Pounds,* I could not help but think that they would betray their readers in the end, leaving them with the taste of cotton candy—initially sweet, but nothing there that really nourishes, or even worse, nothing that summons the hero archetype that lies within each of us. In addition, the reader would feel even further inadequate since some guru had advised him or her how easy it would be, and here he or she was still stuck in life.

In her brilliant biography of the Buddha, Karen Armstrong zeros in on this finessing of the Shadow:

> There is a creeping new orthodoxy in modern society that is sometimes called "positive thinking." At its worst, this habit of optimism allows us to bury our heads in the sand, deny the ubiquity of pain in ourselves and others, and to immure ourselves in a state of deliberate heartlessness to ensure our emotional survival. The Buddha would have had little time for this. In his view, the spiritual life cannot begin until people allow themselves to be invaded by the reality of suffering, realize how fully it permeates our whole experience, and feel the pain of all other beings, even those we do not find congenial. . . . A good deal of what passes for religion is

often designed to prop up and endorse the ego that the founders of the faith told us to abandon.*

Not only do these theologies, and today's pop psychologies, reinforce the ego, but they sanctify and legitimize our complexes, as well.† So much of our popular theology, and our consumer-pandering psychology, is fear driven, for their greatest appeal is the implicit promise to dispel those fears. It is my belief that the psychological and spiritual maturity of an individual, of a group, even of a nation, is found precisely in its capacity to tolerate ambiguity and ambivalence, and the anxiety generated by both of them. It is the psychologically immature, the spiritually jejune that lusts for certainty, even at the expense of truth, rigorous investigation, and consideration of alternatives.

Nothing really important will prove simple. Denial and shallowness never prove worthy of what Socrates called "the examined life." The examined life will oblige us to consider that all issues, *all* issues, have more than one facet to consider, that our capacity for self-delusion is very strong, that *we* are always at least part of the problem, and that we will ultimately walk right into what we have fled, sooner or later. What is wrong with saying, "I do not know; I do not possess certainty; I think this is a fascinating journey and I am open to discovery?" Why should this simple confession require so much courage?

---

*Armstrong, *Buddha*, p. xxvii.
†If the will, or ego assertion, were so easy and so efficacious, why would we have so much trouble simply willing the life we wish? Even Freud once asserted, "Where Id was, there Ego shall be"—an imperialistic fantasy if there ever was one. As we all learn, to our dismay, the power of the unconscious, the Shadow government, is infinitely more resilient and resourceful than mere ego consciousness.

Chapter Eleven

SHADOW/WORK
Encountering Our Darker Selves

*"Life can be compared to a piece of embroidered
material of which, everyone in the first half of his
time, comes to see the top side, but in the second
half, the reverse side. The latter is not so beautiful,
but it is more instructive because it
enables one to see how the threads are connected together."*
—ARTHUR SCHOPENHAUER

*"Consciousness is the last and latest developed of
the organism, and consequently also the most
unfinished and weakest part of it."*
—FRIEDRICH NIETZSCHE

*"In a dark time, the eye begins to see,
I meet my shadow in the deepening shade . . ."*
—"IN A DARK TIME," THEODORE ROETHKE

As we near the end of this discussion of the Shadow, the reader may quite appropriately say, "Well, that is all very interesting . . . it helps me understand the world around me a bit better. But what is the practical use of this Shadow work? How does it apply to me? *What is my Shadow, and how may I begin to access it?*"

We first begin to learn more about our personal Shadow in the many avenues of feedback that come to us. We hear the criticism of our presumptive enemies, which we reject as being about them, not about us. (It is, after all, hard to remember the wisdom of Tibetan Buddhism, which averred that we bless those who curse and revile us, for they will become our greatest teachers.) Our loved ones tell us how they experience us in painful ways, and that hurts to hear. We begin to acknowledge, however ruefully, that our excessive reaction to small events reveals not only a complex hiding beneath, but quite often a Shadow issue, as well.

As we mature, we are more likely to become able to discern the patterns of our history—the repetitions, the reactivation of old wounds, familiar stuck places—and acknowledge how we are the ones who made those choices, created those familiar outcomes. We find our dreams disturbing as they present aspects of ourselves that are inconsistent with how we wish to view ourselves. Knowing that we did not consciously create those dream dramas is a reminder that something inside us, some separate agency of awareness is observing and reporting in. Slowly, if we are courageous, or simply driven by events to an accounting, we are asked to come to terms with our Shadow. A person who has any level of consciousness in the second half of life will also be a person with a history contaminated by Shadow issues, and may even feel crushed by their cumulative weight.

It is understandable why so few attempt Shadow work. It is much easier to scapegoat others, blame, and feel superior to them. What Shadow work requires is growing up, maturity, and who wants to do that? Italian analyst Aldo Carotenuto put it very bluntly:

> The ultimate purpose of psychotherapy is not so much the archeological exploration of infantile sentiments as it is learning gradually and with much effort to accept our own limits and to carry the

weight of suffering on our own shoulders for the rest of our lives. Psychological work, instead of providing liberation from the cause of serious discomfort, increases it, teaching the patient to become adult and, for the first time in his life, actively face the feeling of being alone with his pain and abandoned by the world.*

Who welcomes this inescapable fact that the complexity of the world in which we live, both outer and inner, increases as we mature? But therein is the moral task—to grow up and to lift this burden that we bring to the collective, to free our children, our partners, our tribe. And yes, as the bumper sticker of the Jacksonville, Florida Jung Society puts it: "So Much Shadow Work . . . So Little Time."

Though I thought I knew the good, I did not always do the good, apparently . . . no, clearly did not. And sometimes I have to admit that even my deliberated moral positioning produced consequences harmful to myself or to others. As analyst Liliane Frey-Rohn observed of this paradox, " 'Too much morality' strengthens evil in the inner world, and 'too little morality' promotes a dissociation between good and evil."† Thus, the rigid fundamentalist idealist in me, nervously running back and forth, begat as much misery as the less noble me. The damage done by our personal fundamentalisms, with their one-sided pursuit of moral consistency at the expense of the other values that life demands, is as grievous as it is so seldom acknowledged.

As we examine the personal Shadow, let us remember that its contents are composed of many elemental energies from many different regions of our personality. It is not simply that we have repressed those parts of our personality that are inconsistent with our ego ideal, but that many times we have had no

*Carotenuto, *The Difficult Art*, p. 54.
†Frey-Rohn, "Evil from a Psychological Point of View," *Spring*, 1965.

choice but to repress vital aspects of ourselves as a necessary response to the demands of the world around us. Thus, were I given a certain talent or a calling that is disregarded by my family, or my culture, and I depend on that social environment for my emotional well-being, then it is quite likely that I will collude with self-estrangement in the face of my much greater need for acceptance and approval. As children, we learn to "read" the world around us to find what is acceptable, what dangerous. Many learned that matters of sexual character were not permissible in their family or religion, and so they associated their own natural impulses and desires as something evil, or at best furtive and contaminated. So, too, our genuine spiritual aspirations, our honest questions, curiosities, and intimations of the soul, grow suspect. The by-product of our necessary collusion with the realpolitik of childhood vulnerability is guilt, shame, inhibition, and most of all, self-alienation. We all, still today, reenact these collusions, suffer this shame, and retreat from our wholeness.

Ultimately, the price of obligatory collusion is neurosis, an experience of suffering occasioned by the split between our nature and our cultural imperatives. These collusions, whether conscious or not, seek to control our nature but end by separating us further from our nature. Water, under suppressive pressure, does not go away; it seeks its outlet and will attack the weakest point in the container. All violations of our nature ultimately go underground and reappear as symptoms—behavioral, somatic, intrapsychic, relational—for what is denied consciously will only hide for a while and then break through again into our world.

Often what is shadowy in our psychic life is projected onto others, whomever we can blame, denigrate, attack, or accuse of precisely those motives that we have denied. It is a stunning revelation to come to the recognition that what I find wrong in the Other may also be found in me, and that I may even have chosen this "Other" in order to enact a Shadowy pas de deux. How often do we ask ourselves the confrontative question: "Of what am I unconscious, here?" As we know, the problem with the unconscious is that it is unconscious. Moreover, as we have seen, there is a self-aggrandizing tendency of our ego to dissociate those contents that are Shadow material, hence such self-knowledge usually comes to us the hard way. In the meantime, it is much easier to blame someone else. As Jung noted in his 1937 Terry Lectures at Yale University:

> We are still certain we know what other people think or what their true character is. We are convinced that certain people have all the bad qualities we do not know in ourselves. We must be exceedingly careful not to project our own shadows shamelessly. If you can imagine someone brave enough to withdraw these projections, then you get an individual conscious of a pretty thick shadow. . . . He has become a serious problem to himself, as he is now unable to say that *they* do this or that, *they* are wrong and *they* must be fought. . . . Such a person knows that whatever is wrong in the world is in himself, and if he only learns to deal with his own shadow, then he has done something real for the world. He has succeeded in removing an infinitesimal part of the unsolved gigantic problems of our day.*

Toward the possible prospect of ceasing to blame others and owning our part in this general messiness we call our life, I offer to the reader the following questions designed to stir the archaic materials within each of us,† invite reflection for those

---

*Jung, "Psychology and Religion," *CW 11*, para. 140.
†Interestingly, the etymology of the word *analysis* intimates a stirring up from below, as in stirring a riverbed to see what contents lie on the bottom.

brave enough to withdraw projections, and occasion the expansion of consciousness that makes true freedom, and true choice, more possible.

Before we begin, we must recall an old Near Eastern story of a man looking frantically under the arc of light cast by a lamppost. When he was asked by a passerby what he was looking for, he replied, "I am looking for the keys to my house." When the passerby asked in return, "Well, is this where you dropped them?" The man replied, "No, I lost them in the dark, but this is the only place where the light is." We will not find the keys to our psychic house by looking where the light is, that is, where the ego can survey its familiar territory. We can only find our personal keys in the darkest places, just where we lost them some time ago.

QUESTIONS FOR SHADOW WORK REFLECTION

1. Since we all aspire to virtue, or aspire at least to consider ourselves virtuous, *what do you consider to be your virtues? Can you imagine the opposite of your virtues? Can you imagine that they could lurk in your unconscious? Can you see some place in the present, or in your history, where those opposites may in fact be manifest in your life?*

Let us say that one aspires to be honest. That is a virtue, we agree. Is there a place where our honesty is harmful to another? Is there a possible place in one's psyche where dishonesty, even mendacity lurks? It there a place in one's life story where our dishonesty casts the decisive lot? Of course there is, if we are honest for just this moment.

Let us say that one is always caring and thoughtful of others. Do not our own unaddressed needs lurk in the underworld? Do not those needs, so often reflexively ignored, show up in leaks of anger, in depression, or in unacknowledged narcissistic manipulation? If I am so kind and thoughtful, can I even recognize these symptoms of repressed anger for what they are? Given how identified one may be with caring for others, is there a price paid for neglecting one's own agenda? If professional caregivers are so devoted to their good work, shouldering the pain of others, how is it that they so often suffer depression, substance abuse, chronic back and shoulder pain? Why is it that their own Shadow is found in the demanding inner tyrant that grants them no release from the injunction to take care of others?

Joanna was the third child of a troubled family. She learned early that daughter number one was the golden child, the one upon whom her parent's hopes for their own validation rested, that child number two was the rebel, the miscreant who had to carve a place for herself outside the territory occupied so fully by her elder sister, and that Joanna's role was to be the servant, the fixer, the go-between, the bringer of balance between the warring parents. As an adult she "chose" to be a marriage and family therapist, spending her days serving others, throwing herself between the conflictual opposites, daily revisiting the place of her own archaic wound, and daily suffering the displacement of her own needs. So where did the affective overflow of her unaddressed needs to go? Joanna grew chronically depressed, chronically angry, and suffered a host of somatic disorders. The one thing for which she lacked permission—the possibility of *challenging the "virtue" of her consuming virtue*—denied her respite. In giving care to so many others, she neglected herself, and so brought a large personal Shadow into the field of undeniable works of light.

Sometimes a virtue is not a virtue. Even our *virtues become demonic when not balanced by their opposite*. Virtues become sins when measured not by our ego, not by our complexes, but by our souls, which encompass a much wider range of possibility than that which offers comfort to an uneasy consciousness. One man dreamt of stealing from his corporation. In waking light he was scrupulously honest, but when we explored the theme of "theft," he admitted that his whole life had been a theft of sorts. He had had a quite easy road, always smoothed by the sacrifice of others. Privately, he despised himself, for he thought nothing he had achieved really came from his own gifts. When asked what he planned to do about this, he said he should give away his wealth and live as a mendicant, but this fantasy would only flip to the opposite without holding the tension of opposites. In time he came to see that in his life of privileged self-loathing, he had stolen from himself repeatedly. He realized that he was not a bad person at all, but rather an unrealized person. In the years that followed, he came to give the most he had to offer: his natural, spontaneous self, with all the richness each of us brings. When we discover our richness, remember that nature or divinity brought us here to be who we really are, then there is no need to look over one's shoulder at another. We are enough, and this man's discovery was that who he was, apart from all his history of wealth and privilege, was a person eminently worth knowing. It is good that he discovered that person, and came to appreciate him, before he died.

What gave rise to the cliché that the road to hell is paved with good intentions if not a general recognition that our virtues often beget consequences that ego consciousness did not foresee? For those of us who live in the so-called First World, how virtuous are we when children are enslaved to make our sneakers, or our sweaters, or the many gewgaws that entertain and distract us? How comfortable should we be amid our self-congratulatory virtue when others are sweating and suffering for our comforts? In a culture that brays about "family values," what other families are suffering because life-saving pharmaceuticals are withheld from them in service to the profit motive of shareholders? Who among us has not learned to turn away, to distract and divert such unpleasant thoughts? Who among us does not have to look away when the homeless offer to wash the windows of our car while we wait for the light to turn? Who among us is truly ignorant that many of our fellow citizens live in appalling circumstances, suffer physical and emotional exploitation, and live with hopelessness amid the comforts we take for granted?* Who among us can bear looking at such matters very long, lest we find sleep difficult that same night? So we, the virtuous, learn to divert, anesthetize, and rationalize. Virtue as intent without act, then, is hardly virtuous.

One might even consider the possibility that the very idea of *virtue* simultaneously creates a Shadow field. As Nietzsche noted, when we insist on the maintenance of virtue—our virtues, of course—we also necessitate the thought police with their truncheons so that we may impose our idea of virtue on others, in service to our own psychological security. How virtuous is that? Moreover, those who claim they are on virtue's side will sooner rather than later solicit, then claim, then co-opt the reward of God's blessing for their efforts—hardly an inherent, disinterested love of the good! How virtuous is that? And how often does the claim for one's virtue camouflage the will to power underneath? And how virtuous is that? For this reason the Danish contemporary of Nietzsche, Søren Kierkegaard, argued that the spiritual development of the person requires that a person sometimes must, in "fear and trembling," transcend the merely ethical, even as he or she once transcended the merely narcissistic to achieve an ethical sensitivity. What is done

---

*One consequence of Hurricane Katrina was that the facade of The Big Easy was ripped away to reveal the hard-core subsistence of the chronically impoverished who live beneath the radar of modern affluence. One fatuous politician said that in future people who ignored orders to evacuate should be punished. He thought for a while . . . and then added, "if they have cars."

out of love may not be virtuous, and yet it serves a spiritual value. What is done out of fidelity to the highest may well transcend "the good." As the old proverb has it, "The good may prove to be the enemy of the best." From the tree of virtue, much good may come, yet no good fruit, no truly virtuous fruit, ever drops from the trees of denial, resentment, guilt, or self-hatred. This latter forest of trees, with their multiple bitter fruits, always comes from virtue, which is unaware of its opposite. The opposite of virtue, then, is unconsciousness, which sooner or later begets what we least intended.

2. What are the key patterns of your relationships? That is to say, where do Shadow issues manifest in patterns of avoidance, aggression, or repetition?

None of us deliberately sets out to repeat our history, but its redundant themes are replicated in subtle, variegated patterns every day. Those repetitions, as we have seen, rise as expressions of the "core ideas" or complexes we have. Jordan, a forty-year-old man, compulsively sabotages his relationships. He draws close to the partner, begins to feel threatened, and breaks it off. Why? Are all his partners in fact threats to his well-being, or is he not suffering the replay of an earlier drama? His psychologically invasive parent programmed his primal imago of "Self and Other." Whenever he gets to the point of trust and commitment, the complex says, figuratively, "What do we know about intimate relationship? Oh yes, run before it takes you over." He is not conscious of this message, of course, but it nevertheless retains the power to move him to find fault, to sabotage, to bail out. The Shadow task here is not what happened in that distant past, but in his collusive servitude to its archaic admonitions. What was fearful and destructive to the child still powerfully floods his adult connections. Never mind his larger capacity as an adult to manage his own boundaries, protect himself if necessary, and choose freely out of a consciousness and a resilience that was unavailable to the child. The Shadow work here is found in differentiating the threat, in separating the person with whom he has a relational possibility and the insistent message of his archaic imago. His partner is not the enemy; the power of history is.

Locked within each of us is not only a history of wounding, but an understandable narcissistic agenda. Every child says "I want, I want, and I want it now." Yes, we learn to manage this insistent demand, sometimes even take responsibility for it, but it is never absent. Can uncontaminated love even exist? We all wish to think so. We wish to believe that we can have a "disinterested" caring for the other, but are we really ever free of our own narcissistic history? "Disinterested caring" is perhaps a contradiction, certainly an oxymoron. Can we love another without self-interest prevailing or at least infiltrating our motives? Probably not, but we can surely make the effort to sacrifice, or contain at least, our selfish needs on behalf of the well-being of the other. Can I rise above my own needs to recognize the wounded Other, and support him or her? I can certainly try, and that is the best love can ask of us. Philo of Alexandria recommended many centuries ago, "Be kind. Everyone you meet has a very large problem." When we remember this, the heart softens our complexes and relationship is opened to healing.

Sometimes, surely, we transcend our narcissism, but we are never free of it, and it will pop up in some minor argument, some sharp-edged response, some moment of withdrawal. When we ask too much of the other, are manipulative or aggressive toward them, or reject them for failing us, then we are in the grip of this Shadow. The problem is not the narcissistic need, for that is universal; the problem is our failure to take responsibility for it so that it does not burden our partners.

Where we found others most deficient and most neglectful in our history is where we will prove most needy, most demanding, or most manipulative of the one we profess to love. Such needs do not go away simply because we occupy big bodies and big roles in life. As Jung noted, "Where love reigns, there is no will to power; and where the will to power is paramount, love is lacking."* The key word here is *paramount,* for the subtext of power is never wholly absent. Power itself is neutral. It is the exchange of energy between people. When, however, that energy is directed by a complex, rather than the mere performance of a task, then the power complex prevails. When the power motive prevails, our knowledge of Shadow tells us, it is in those moments when we feel least powerful and therefore need to assert ourselves in compensatory ways.

The long catalog of love and love's disorders fills our literature and inflames our popular culture. For any relationship to survive, or even more, to provide a growth platform for each party, some luck, a good deal of grace, and a capacity for maturity is demanded. And who of us is lucky, full of grace, or mature all the time? No wonder, then, how obsessed we are with relationships, yet repeatedly ask too much of them, and wind up so disappointed in them as a result.

Romance is the chief delusion, elixir, and magical potion of our popular culture. It is itself a Shadow fantasy, for in this blissful state, one's wounds are healed, one's needs met. But because the seductive power of romance is so powerful, it distracts from the accountability of consciousness. Who really wants to examine relational dynamics with a critical eye? Who

*Jung, "Two Essays in Analytical Psychology," *CW 7*, para. 78.

wishes to look within when it is so much easier to look for rescue without? Yet without a knowledge of our history—the programming fate inscribed on the intrapsychic imago of Self and Other, and the relational dynamics that accompany—who could really expect any current relationship to be better than its archaic paradigm? Even with such knowledge as comes from troubling experience and a mature willingness to look, who can expect to be wholly free of this ancient traffic? Thus we are driven to repetitions or overcompensations in opposite directions, and either way, remain enthralled by the power of the unexamined life.

Only through a humbling reflection upon those patterns brought about by whatever messages we internalized, as well as our own areas of immaturity, are we likely to come to consciousness. Only by such consciousness, and the courage required to confront our Shadowy history, can we pretend to enter into any relationship with love. Romance promises relief, but love demands only new hardship—the hardship demanded by owning our Shadow issues and removing them from the Other. Life is difficult enough, and relationship very fragile, so this personal Shadow work may in fact be our best way of loving the Other. The fact that our relationships never prove more evolved than the relationship we have with ourselves obliges Shadow work, for what we do not know, or will not face, is bound to show up and impair the relationship with the Other.

Doing Shadow work within the context of relationship is especially difficult, for it may require us to relinquish our chief, perhaps unconscious, desire—namely, to be taken care of by an Other. We do care for the Other, and experience care from the Other, but failing to recognize that urgent desire, that heavily charged complex to be taken care of, means that relationship sooner or later breaks under the burden of expectation, for no one can, or should, or will, take care of us. Let us change that sentence . . . we *have* met the person who is charged with taking care of us, and that is the one person with whom we have lived since the moment of birth, and with whom we alone journey toward death.

3. What annoys you most about your partner, or others in general?

My sagacious wife defines a committed relationship as the act of "finding someone whom you can annoy for a very long time." I want to believe she is joking, but I am not too sure about that. Rubbing shoulders with anyone means that sooner or later they will annoy us, or we them, no matter how conscious, how intentional the relationship aspires. Perhaps we need to look at this question of "annoyance" a bit deeper.

Is it not possible, indeed, is it not the case that we chose that person, or something within us chose that person, precisely because of that annoyance? The very thought is preposterous to the ego that, remember, thinks it knows enough to know enough. I recently attended a wedding where the devoted couple swore to enduring love, lifelong commitment, and to sustain those feelings for eternity. Not only did their vows feign an unknown future, but they ignored the simple fact we have all known since childhood, that feelings are autonomous and fickle. We do not choose them; they choose us, and they have a will of their own. Who in his or her right mind could predict a feeling state years from now? But then, couples in love are not in their right mind. And perhaps it must be so or no one would be willing to make a commitment of such magnitude.

But why, in heaven's name, would we ever imagine that we might choose a person for their power to annoy us, unless we were full-blown masochists? There are several speculative answers to offer to this point. Freud noted the strange phenomenon of what he called "the repetition compulsion," namely, the compelling urgency toward repetition within each of us. So we repeat our patterns, even self-injurious patterns, in service to the power of historic conditioning. One may even take a strange comfort in the familiar pain—one knows who one is, who the Other is, what this familiar pas de deux is about and how it is programmed to produce the same old, same old. Freud noted that this "familiar suffering" is often preferred to the unknown suffering of the unfamiliar, the risky abyss of alternative choice.

Of the many examples possible, I recall the expression on the face of the man who finally recognized that his "inner script," derived from his "reading" of the messages of his family of origin, demanded that he "choose" an angry spouse who felt betrayed by everyone. He continuously sacrificed his own desires to take care of her, manage her, and try to keep her anger toward others, and her paranoia regarding their motives, contained. He had watched his father and learned that managing the stress level of his mother was his chief role and ongoing identity. Could we ever imagine that something in him set out to find such an angry person, to slip into the familiar role, to be forever on guard against his own strong feelings, and to replay his father's life? When he saw that the pattern of his childhood, and the pattern of his marriage, coincided, he knew that his annoyances were chosen for precisely the reason that they were familiar.

Others have suggested that we choose the annoying, even painful, Other as an effort to solve the issue the second time around. This choice, they argue, is the way in which the psyche heals by working through the old wound in a more mature, more empowered way. This theory may be true, but I have seen enough anguish in relationships to suspect that most people still do not get it, and are not working it through. They may stay married, for example, but they know somewhere in their heart that they are chained to their constrictive history.

Our psychological history of relationship, deriving from the intrapsychic imago, is powerfully programmed toward such repetition. Sometimes, intuiting the familiar path, we deliberately choose the opposite and are trapped in a new way. Still others, unwittingly, elect a third path that seeks to treat the problem, without knowing what they are really treating. These are the folks who anesthetize their pain through work, drugs, or diversion. Or, if they are especially troubled, they might become couples therapists and try to get it right within themselves by fixing other relationships.

Given the fact that one will find familiar annoyances in one's face sooner or later, and given the fact that every human being does in fact have a narcissistic agenda that may prove injurious to the other, we can expect that the problem of power, the temptation of controlling the other, will soon make its appearance.

Who among us is prescient or strong enough to see the invisible energies flowing back and forth between any couple? Who could see which energy is flowing from the heart, which is flowing from the intrapsychic factory of history, and which is flowing from the complexes that seek to recapitulate themselves at any cost? Since we cannot see such energy, or only see it rarely, most relationships are a mess. Who would dare tell this to the couple at the altar? Who wants an ancient mariner to show up at the wedding feast with the shadowy albatross of psychological wisdom about his neck?

Shadow work on relationship obviously and once again begins at home, with ourselves. But who wants to do that when it is so much easier and more gratifying to blame our partner or friend? Those who have experienced early relationships as invasive will suffer a schizoid split in their psyche and, fearing intimacy, will find ways to distance themselves through diversions and emotional reserve. Those who suffered the insufficiency of the nurturant other will have a tendency to ask too much of the other, be clingy, demanding, controlling, obsessional. Both will get what they expect, and what they secretly want. It requires Shadow work to bring this to the surface and to find that the annoying antagonist is within after all.

How many of the pop books on relationships—*How to Find Your Soul Mate, Making Love Last, Finding Mr. Right*—have anything interesting to say about our Shadows? How many of us wish to mine our histories for the rich ore of discernment? How much easier it is to conjure up a "Magical Other" who will spare us all sorts of work? Regrinding the lens through which we see proves to be a lifelong employment. We continue to view the world, to perceive the Other out of our historic lens, but we can also learn to broaden the scope and range of that lens and spare ourselves, and those whom we profess to love, the burden of our unconsciousness.

Lifting our history and our narcissistic agenda off of others contributes to ethical relationships, more developmental friendships, and proves to be the best way we love others. We claim we wish intimacy, but do we really? Can we bear intimacy? Can we evolve a relationship while we grow individually, or will that violate the subterranean contract both partners signed years ago? What happens when one person grows and the other refuses to do so? (I hear this question perhaps once a week, and certainly once every time I give a public lecture. The speaker, presumably, is always the one who is willing to grow, and their partner is stuck. Perhaps . . .)

Shadow work requires a heroic willingness to take responsibility for oneself, to grow up, and therefore be less demanding and expectant of our partners. This allows them the freedom we wish for ourselves—the freedom to have different tastes, different development agendas, different friends, and so forth. How many relationships are up to this task of mature differentiation? Most of all, Shadow work in the context of relationship asks that we see that what is wrong in the world is wrong in us, as well. We are less likely to wound our partner, despise our neighbor, or hate our enemy when we recognize that we share a common condition, a common set of aspirations, and a common fallibility. A whole subgenre of literature has dramatized the *Doppelgänger*, or the Double, the Other whom we see as other and come to recognize as ourselves.* What we hate in the Other is what we hate in ourselves.

While sitting in a waiting room of a hospital while my wife was in surgery, I sat across from a young man who was waiting to be treated for what appeared to be a broken hand. His nervous wife, with a bruised eye, sat timorously next to him. The fellow was apoplectic; his neck muscles were strained cords as he said, "I don't know why they allow them like that to live. They ought to kill them." He was referring to a television comedian who had recently come out as gay and was on the newscast in the waiting room. What could account for his rage, his putative abuse of his partner, except what he could not face in himself? The Other was so scary to this young man. I was so tempted to despise him for his weakness, but to do so would be to be guilty of the identical Shadow issue—what I disown in myself I might easily despise in him. What we hate in the other is what we hate in ourselves. After the flush of anger I felt, I felt sad for his fears, frightened by his rage, and returned to worrying about my wife in surgery.

---

*Among the many sources that might be cited are: Poe's "William Wilson," Stevenson's "Dr. Jekyll and Mr. Hyde," and Conrad's "The Secret Sharer."

4. Where do you repeatedly undermine yourself, create harmful replications, produce the same old, same old? Where do you flee from your best, riskiest self?

None of us begins the day thinking, "Well, today I shall do the same stupid things I have been doing for decades, but it will all turn out better." Yet, everyday, the complexes, those historically charged energy clusters, operate in their autonomous way, and the same old, same old surfaces. The complexes take over the ego, flood it with their historic scripts, and the familiar, predetermined choices result, even as we believe ourselves free and conscious in any given moment. Even when we have been forced by suffering—ours or that of another—to bring those patterns to consciousness, they have enormous resistance to modification. (This is why "behavior modification," the chief modality of most therapists, can only be partially successful, and then only when addressing issues of limited focus.)

The one message all of us received as children was that the world is big, and we are not; the world is powerful, and we are not. Our subsequent decades are thus frequently dictated by our necessary adaptive patterns, ingrained attitudes toward Self and Other, and reflexive strategies designed to manage anxiety and get one's needs at least partially met. This false self, this adaptive self, is inevitable. All that varies is the magnitude of our adaptation, and the degree to which it furthers our estrangement from the Self. It is tempting and convenient to blame the Other, whether the parent of the past or the partner of the present, but in the end we are led to the humbling conclusion that we are the ones making present choices that reinforce these patterns. Only then can we acknowledge that so many of these choices are self-sabotaging because they bind us to our disempowered past.

I have seen David, a fifty-year-old man, for several years. Child of a fundamentalist family, ridden with guilt, duty, obligation, admonishment, and denigration, he has been afraid to commit to another. While deeply desiring to marry, he finds that the transferred power of his derogated sense of Self renders the Other a demanding, incursive presence whom he is, nonetheless, obliged to take care of. What a double bind! Given this imbalance set up by history, it is no wonder that he has avoided being trapped by the Other again. Yet this aversion keeps him from the caring relationship to the Other that he so deeply desires.

In one of our sessions, David said, "I feel hopeless about my capacity to find someone and then be able to hang in there. I feel that the mother complex floods me. I have been aware of this for twenty-eight years, and it continues to dictate my life. I am paralyzed by it. I get so conflictual when I break 'her' rules and then I run from 'her' and end up running away from women in my life because I am afraid of what they expect, and then I end up isolated and alone."

David is in fact a sensitive, caring individual who deserves a relationship but is tragically held hostage to history, and he simultaneously deprives another person of the relationship they might have with a good soul such as he. In our therapy, I continue to reiterate that this powerful, invasive complex is a psychic phantom, with no more reality than we grant it. The women he meets are simply other people on the planet trying to make their way, not the ogre who once dominated his life. Since he is a highly ethical person, and honestly seeks the right thing in all matters, he is today summoned to remove the Shadow of his history from the women in his life and allow them to be whoever they are. He is learning that he is not in charge of their well-being—they are, although he may wish to support their various struggles. To burden them with the ghosts of his past, those spectral parental presences, is unfair to him and to the one with whom he might engage. "You owe her the good man that you really are," I say, "the man she has been looking for, the one who accepts her for who she is, minus the projections. Don't disappoint her."

For David, staying stuck in this miserable parent complex is, paradoxically, staying safe in the known, resting at anchor in the safe harbor of history. All of us have similar Shadow assignments to redeem reason and volition that have been rendered impotent in the face of the internalized paradigms of Self and Other we acquired. As the recrudescence of our history so frequently undermines the powers of the present, we need to recognize and to struggle daily with the fact that *the enemy we face is the abiding power of our history*, especially the archaic messages of our disempowered childhoods. Claiming our adult capacities, risking service to what wants to come into the world through us, is our individuation imperative. Setting forth upon the high seas of the unknown is where we are meant to be. Allowing our history to prevail is hugging the shore. Kierkegaard noted once that merchant vessels hug the shoreline, but men o' war open their mission instruction packet on the high seas. Setting forth on the high seas is where spiritual enlargement is found, and the only way we find the new land we are meant to occupy.

5. Where are you stuck in your life, blocked in your development? What fears, what familiar issues block your growth?

These are questions I have asked in workshops many times, and then invite persons to reflect on their significance in their separate lives. Interestingly, no one, whether in Sweden, Switzerland, Brazil, the United States, or Canada, has yet asked for an explanation of these questions, nor have they paused very long before beginning to write in their journal. Does this not tell us that all of us know where we are stuck? And if we know we are stuck, why do we not get unstuck? Does mere knowledge of being stuck help us get unstuck? The answer, apparently, is sometimes yes, sometimes no.

Why are we stuck? Why, like David above, do we find the old patterns surfacing in our ever-revolving relationships? In short, we are stuck because the stuck places are "wired" to complexes, energy clusters from our history. Not only do these complexes have a powerful charge of energy and a "fight or flight" plan accompanying them, they are also triggered by multiple stimuli. We often swim in this inner material and do not even recognize it for what it is because the outer situation presents itself as something new, as in fact it is. But we view through the old lens, reiterate the archaic patterning process, and impose it anew.

The critical link in this mechanism that ties us to the past is to be found in the fact that the "wiring" of the complex activates a field of anxiety. The angst need not be perceived by consciousness, but it is registered in the body, has an affective charge that a careful observer may witness, and has the power to affect choice, even shut the person down. Take this common complex, for example: The vast majority of people have considerable anxiety about public speaking. They are not lacking in opinions and are perfectly willing to discourse at length to themselves or to a friend, but they are petrified by speaking in front of others. It is easy enough to trace this linkage of public exposure to a primal threat, the fear of the critical opinion of others. Who has not suffered the loss of approval, the criticism of the Other, at a time when one's own sense of self was most fragile? Thus, the archaic machinery hums below, is activated by a new summons to public exposure, and old anxiety floods the consciousness of the adult. (As a teacher, a frequent public speaker, but a card-carrying introvert, I manage this familiar complex by reminding myself that people are not there to judge me; they are there to engage the common subject that has brought us together. Additionally, I recall the disempowered voice of my parents and tell myself that I am speaking *for* them, using one complex, perhaps, to defeat another complex.)

All of us have these stuck places because all of us are "recovering children." The wiring of our vulnerable psyches reaches back to the archaic and generates enough power to force patterns of avoidance and compliance upon us. Getting unstuck will, of course, demand that we take that anxiety on, even when we do not know what it is. Stepping into the difficult place, wading through it, is never going to be easy. Life is not easy, nor is it fair, so we should dispel these frequent laments quickly. It is here to be claimed, whether one was shown the way by others or not. In fact, one could say, as my analyst in Zurich once said to me, "You must make your fears your agenda." I knew he spoke the truth, and knew what my assignment was. We all know that our frontiers are easily circumscribed by our fears. Pushing back is how we grow up and claim the life we are meant to live.

This push back is Shadow work because it is so much easier to stay stuck. Without enlargement, we do not bring the gift of our unique selves into the world, nor do we live our lives with any integrity. We are creatures of self-protective reflexes to be sure, and understandably so, but if we are nothing more, then we might as well not have been here. Remember Jung commenting that we all walk in shoes too small for us? As constrictive as our psychologies are, they are familiar; they are who we have come to be. Invisibly, we betray ourselves daily with a thousand small betrayals, a thousand collusions with fear. Because of many powerful influences upon us, we get the life we choose, possibly the only one that we could have chosen. Even if our psyche protests, and is dismayed, stuckness can feel like home. But we have to leave home if we are ever to grow up and claim our lives.

6. Where do Mom and Dad still govern your life—through repetition, overcompensation, or your special-treatment plan?

The "mom" and "dad" to which we allude here are not the outer people we once knew, but a massive set of messages that we internalized: first, as template for what the world is about and how one is to act; second, as a set of sometimes explicate, sometimes implicate, messages about yourself, your worth, your script, your entitlement; and third, as a generalized message about one's relationship to the largeness of life.

At the first level, one gets a sense of the "script," the play in which one is acting. What is lived by the parent, as model and accompanying psychology, so frequently forms the paradigm, the normative script for the child, programmed as we are toward repetition. Is this world into which we have been flung safe, inviting, supportive, or harsh, invasive, punitive? What is the core existential message?

At the second level, each of us internalizes messages about who we are, how we are to act, whether we are valued or devalued, and what we must do to gain affection or nurturance. These messages are of course utterly dependent on contingent circumstances—change the family, the socioeconomic milieu, the cultural zeitgeist, and the message is quite different. Consider how David's relational life is sabotaged by those messages about his own lack of worth, and his implicit assignment to find and take care of all the wounded women around him. Why would he not then suffer ambivalence about love? How much those core messages about ourselves and others play out may be modified by alternative lessons from life, as well as intrinsic values of personal character and level of consciousness we bring to bear on such influences. We can learn to trust, to risk, to invest, and to open up, and most of us do, but even our best native resources are cast into a dogfight with the reflexive power of history.

At the third level, one receives elemental messages, perhaps misperceived or misinterpreted, that communicate our relationship to life itself. You will recall Bertha's dream from Chapter Four in which the "witch" steals her doll, an imago of her vulnerable inner child. So much of Bertha's life was lived as a defense against the archetypal losses that history brought her. Having lost her parents, with no comforting parental surrogate, her core perception of life was that it was unsafe, unpredictable, and lacking in nourishment. No wonder that she chose a rigid, controlling lifestyle and an eating disorder to symbolically regain control, to manage the vast sea of angst in which she had always swum. A different fate would have brought her a different "message" about her fragile purchase on life, and a different set of reflexive "choices" in the conduct of her adult life.

We might reasonably argue that we all suffer from "the fallacy of overgeneralization," namely, that what was perceived as true about self and world in its most elemental, archaic form, is generalized as a core message throughout one's life. No wonder we find such repetitions in our separate stories. Our personal Shadow always falls under the penumbra of the shadow of history—at least until it becomes conscious and we take it on.

When we examine the patterns of our lives, we will often find, to our dismay, that we have slipped into repetition, or overcompensation, or our own treatment plan. Repetition is easy enough to see. Overcompensation is common as well. Under every power complex the frightened child is hiding. ("I will be anything except like my mother." "I will be a better dad than my father was." Yet one is still subject to definition by those internalized points of reference.) Sometimes, the wounding of the child leads the adult to convert this history into a gift, a special sensitivity to, or talent for, addressing this sort of problem. Most great art has risen out of anguish of some form or another. Professional caregivers are often, perhaps to their detriment, still working on their own family-of-origin struggles, and can often be helpful to others along the way. The election of a "treatment" plan can range from total repression of an issue, to an addiction that anesthetizes the pain of a wound, to a life of diversion and superficiality, to addressing the issue in a compulsive way in one's adulthood. Who among us has not sometimes eaten too much, drunk too much, worried too much, protested too much, or run toward mindless oblivion as an inviting "treatment" plan?

In all three of these patterns—repetition, compensation, unconscious treatment—one is still a prisoner of the past. Until one can set it down, one remains enmeshed in the thing one wishes to flee. Sometimes a certain wisdom comes to us as we mature. We learn that *we are not our history*, not what happened to us, and how it all got internalized as a *Weltanschauung. We are our aspirations.* We are what wishes to come into the world through us—the will of the gods. We are more than the contingencies of fate, but only if we bring them to consciousness and wage a lifelong struggle for freedom up and out of those shadowy savannahs.

In the end, it is not about "mom" and "dad" at all. They are mere metaphors for our primal messages about self and world. Even the most thoughtful parents leave a Shadow behind, for whatever we choose, however we live, some other energy, some other task of life is left for the child to clean up. So it is not about them. It is about us, about the messages to which we subscribe, whether we know it or not. We are obliged to admit to ourselves that the past persists. (As William Faulkner once observed, the past is not dead; it is not even past.) Our ancestors were perhaps more inclined to believe in ghosts. They weren't wrong. As anyone knows who has worked on a powerful parental complex, even death does not end a life. There are many lingering presences slipping in and out of the sundry guises and disguises of daily life. Failing to see their spectral cerements beneath the surface means that they are playing an often decisive role in our parliament of choices, and this is why we all live in haunted houses. Still . . . even more problematic than ghosts may prove, is the burden such consciousness asks of us. As Jung observed once, "People are afraid [less of ghosts] than becoming conscious of themselves."*

7. Where do you refuse to grow up, wait for magical solutions to the raggedy edges of life, expect rescue, or someone to step forth and take care of it all for you? Where is the guru who will make these choices easy for you?

A colleague of mine once observed that she could usually tell in her first hour with a client whether they were up to the work, whether, in her words, they "were big kids or little kids." As we know, we are all recovering children stumbling about in big bodies, big roles, big consequences, but what varies is our tensile strength, our resiliency, our will to become. Life brings us into this world equipped for the journey. To be sure, our original social and familial environment plays a large role in whether that journey is supported or impeded, but within each of us there is a force that seeks to move through us toward embodi-

*Jung, *Memories, Dreams, Reflections*, pp. 190–1.

ment in the world. At the end of his memoir, *Memories, Dreams, Reflections*, Jung disclaimed any grand conclusions about life and death, or even psychology; however, he affirms that "In spite of all uncertainties, I feel *a solidity underlying all existence* and *a continuity in my mode of being.*"* Notwithstanding the modesty of his claim, this is a profound awareness of how our lives are sustained by a transpersonal force whose name and metaphor varies; moreover, a sober, sensitive reading of our history reveals that unfolding entelechy, even when opposed by the ministries of fate. Even our symptoms, as we have seen, are manifestations of this life force, this psyche, that expresses its anguish whenever we perchance veer from the path of wholeness to that of adaptation.

The legacy of our finitude, our vulnerability before the world around us, leads all of us to diminishing psychologies. At times, perhaps most times, it is hard to imagine ourselves as anything other than our adaptive roles. Our obligatory witnessing and internalizing of our social paradigms, said to us, in so many words: "This is the way it is, who you are, and what you are to do and what to value." A necessary obedience to these paradigms estranges us from ourselves, and tends to cut off, perhaps forever, the connection we once had to the internal guidance system manifested by our instinctual life. Our Shadow is thus accumulated through such implicit admonitions that: 1) we may not oppose our diminishment; 2) we must forlornly seek rescue from others, as every child learns; 3) we might find someone with all the answers to tell us what to do; or 4) magic may be found in self-help groups, itinerant gurus, or the beguiling seductions of popular culture. No wonder the seething masses of the dictators, or the docile audiences of the televan-

*Jung, *Memories, Dreams, Reflections*, p. 358. (Italics mine.)

gelists, sway in unison to the charms of seductive rhetoric. These sibilant speakers tell the child within each of us what it wishes most to hear: that we do not have to grow up, that life is readily manageable, and that someone will fix it for us.*

One thing we can say for our core complexes, they do give us rather clear marching orders, and they have the virtue of familiarity and certainty. By failing to take them on and serve the larger will of our incarnation by the gods, we can continue to blame the ex, indict our parents, or find a simplistic ideology to answer our questions. The frightened fundamentalist inside of us will latch on to totalitarian solutions—all in service to management of the existential anxiety engendered by choice. As Sartre once observed, we are "condemned to be free," and yet we solicit all sorts of ways to flee this freedom. Let us also remember Camus as cited earlier, that the world is meaningful precisely because it is absurd. What he meant was that if it is "meaningful," then it is someone else's package, someone else's meaning. If it is absurd, then meaning is ours to find—or construct if need be—by discerning over time what serves our deepest being.

A fifty-five-year-old woman, Denise, who has lived under the demon of self-doubt all her life, dreamt that she and her husband, Robert, who has further denigrated her for decades, were traveling on some sort of perilous journey together. She typically considered that deferring to her partner's wishes was the most comfortable path, the most confirming of her self-image. This time an inner guide emerges in her dream with a clear message. He says to her: "You can travel with Robert, but

---

*As Dostoevsky illustrates in his parable of "The Grand Inquisitor" in *The Brothers Karamazov*, humankind commonly flees the terrible burden of existential choice and embraces the infantilizing alternatives of miracle, mystery, and authority—treatment plans for the terror of personal responsibility.

it is a long way, and full of misery. Or you can travel with me, and it is a sacred way." As I so often do, I asked her where that dream had come from, whether she had made it up. With vigorous protest she acknowledged its origin from some place within her, yet clearly outside her ego volition. This inner guide, this psychopomp, represented her own, independent capacities that, if she were to trust, would take her where she needed to go. By embracing this inner figure, what Jung called the *animus*, Denise would no longer be dominated by her own negative history within, or Robert without.

Our continuing work revolves around this paradox, that what we are looking for already resides within us. (As St. Augustine averred, that which we are seeking is already coming to meet us). It is the voice of the psyche, the soul, that has been and continues to push for realization through us. Learning to trust, to risk, to deepen the dialogue with that place within from whence the guiding dream comes to us with helpful energies is Denise's project, and ours. Recently, she has taken the bold stride of launching a separate journey, with firm resolve never again to live in service to those old denigrating messages, whether from her history or from Robert.

Finding this inner authority, briefly present to us in childhood but not sustainable, is our common task. Without a connection to inner authority—the discovery of which obliges us to live it with courage in the world—we will only be will-o'-the-wisps and never meet our authentic selves on the road. Why should we think, and continue to collude with the notion, that nature did not bring us into life equipped for the journey? Is it not a form of negative inflation to consider ourselves unworthy of life, or lack the permission to be who we are meant to be? Why should we look to someone else to tell us how to live our life? They are barely managing theirs as it is. Why should we not recover guidance from within ourselves, and then live it in the world? Why should we be jealous or envious of others when we have such richness within? Why should we meddle in the lives of others when we have so much work to do on ourselves? Only by accepting these inherent powers already given us can we begin healing our Shadow split, and thereby contribute our small part to the healing of the world.

SHADOW AS INVITATION

Sooner or later we are obliged to face this paradox: Since the Shadow is composed of *what I do not wish to be*, my deepest, most refractory Shadow will be found in what I most wish to avoid, namely, *becoming me*. That which I seek to avoid is me, for that enterprise feels too risky, obliges tasks too deep for comfort. We find, then, that all our difficulties with the Other begin with and include the Other that is within ourselves. As Jung notes, "This process of coming to terms with the Other in us is well worthwhile, because in this way we get to know aspects of our nature which we would not allow anybody else to show us and which we would never have admitted."*

On the collective level, what the historic personage of the Devil represents symbolically (that is to say, psychologically) is not only a vivid dramatization of the radical Other, but the Other who is within each of us. Recall that when the Devil shows up to tempt Faust, he is attired as a traveling scholar, for only such a person could speak the same language as the scholarly Faust. Only someone who can speak cogently and seductively to our temptations will be persuasive to him, or to us. Or, for example, consider the temptations of Gautama, who became the Buddha. First, he is tempted by Kama, the Lord of

*Jung, "Mysterium Coniunctionis," *CW 14*, para. 706.

Lust, which is an invitation to cling to the tender tendrils of desire. Being fully human we desire, and then are owned by that which we desire, as modern materialism makes so clear for us. Then he is tempted by the Lord of Fear, Mara. Much of our lives, for sure our reflexive defenses, are driven by fear. Fear calls the shots, governs our lives—much of the time. Then he is summoned to the most subtle temptation of all: duty and responsibility toward others. Gautama became the Buddha, the one who saw through* the snares of the senses, the false promises of security, and the summons to power. He transcended his Shadow, not by repressing it or projecting it onto others, but by knowing it fully, and he was therefore not owned by it.

So, too, we see the analogous temptations of Jesus in the desert. In particular, we see the terrific struggle Jesus had with his own shadow issue of legitimacy and the temptation of power. Lawrence Jaffe reports candid, impromptu remarks by Jung at a reception after his last visit to New York City. Asked a question about Jesus, he replies that the Nazarene had a most difficult journey, beginning as an illegitimate child, so to speak, and subsequently rose to be gifted the mantle of Messiah by his follower's claim. Having spurned his three temptations, he nonetheless cried out on the cross that he had been abandoned by his Father. At that moment, his whole life seemed an error, a great, failed collapse. After which, Jung adds:

> We must all do just what Christ did. We must make our experiment. We must make mistakes. We must live out our own vision of life. And there will be error. If you avoid error you do not live; in a sense even it may be said that every life is a mistake, for no one

---

*The word *buddha* comes from the Sanskrit *budh*, which means "to see," to understand that the source of all suffering comes from a dependent attachment to the things of the world. So Gautama *saw*, and in sharing that seeing as an itinerant teacher, he offered to others a path of release from the sorrows of the Earth.

234 • JAMES HOLLIS, PH.D.

has found the truth. When we live like this we know Christ as a brother, and God indeed becomes man. . . . And so the last thing I would say to each of you, my friends, is: carry through your life as well as you can, even if it is based on error, because life has to be undone, and one often gets to the truth through error. Then, like Christ, you will have accomplished your experiment.*

So the life we all conduct from the narrow, biased lens of consciousness is a mistake, a *necessary* mistake. In our adaptations we diverge from the path our nature desires. In our quisling collaboration with fear, we settle for the lesser. But we are bound to and through these errors, and our most profound human struggle is found in standing in the meeting point, the spiritual nexus between our individuation assignment and our human frailties. We are not here to imitate Gautama or Jesus. Those lives have already been done, and much better than we might manage. We are here to meet our summons, *our summons*, on this road of personal brokenness, doubt, despair, defeat, cowardice and contradiction, with only scattered moments of luminosity. There, when from time to time we meet ourselves, when we meet our Shadow, there we are most fully in the game, most completely in the arena in which meaning is won or lost, and life more fully lived.

We may not be thrilled with what we find in this Shadowy struggle, with all its spectral seductions, but we will rediscover the truth of Terence, that "nothing human is alien to me." We can see now that working with the Shadow is not working with evil, per se. It is working toward the possibility of greater wholeness. Wholeness cannot be, by definition, partial, so our theologies and our psychologies cannot remain partial either,

*Jaffe, *Liberating the Heart*, p. 17.

even if our ego is sorely troubled by holding the tension of opposites that wholeness demands of us.

The apparently shadowless person is either naive and superficial, or profoundly immature and unconscious. Our goal, then, is not goodness, but wholeness, as Jung said. Such wholeness is our chief service to our children, our partners, our society, and to the gods who brought us here for this mission. Thus, our Shadow work is an invocation to us, a calling forth, and carries the germ of our possible wholeness. The first place to look for the Shadow is 1) where our fears are found, 2) where we are most ugly to ourselves, or 3) for the many, daily deals we make, the adaptations, and the denials that only deepen the darkness. This challenging paradox remains: We will never experience healing until *we can come to love our unlovable places, for they, too, ask love of us.* Our sick places are sick because no one, especially not us, loved them.

Shadow work requires a discipline, an attitude, a consistency of intentionality on the part of each of us. And none of us can avoid the discipline this work will demand, work for which more rigor than technique will be necessary. As Jung suggested, "If one can speak of technique at all, it consists solely in an attitude. First of all one has to accept and to take seriously into account the existence of the Shadow. Secondly, it is necessary to be informed about its qualities and intentions. Thirdly, long and difficult negotiations may well be unavoidable."*

Only the naive, or highly defended, will believe that he or she can avoid falling into the Shadow, as I hope the reader grasps fully by now. Sometimes we have to embrace this fractious Shadow, acknowledge these darker selves as part of us, and live them more fully in the world. As St. Augustine recom-

*Jung, *Letters, Vol. 1.*, p. 234.

mended, if we are to sin, then sin consciously! In the Gnostic *Gospel of Thomas*, Jesus is reported to have observed to a man working on the Sabbath that if he knew what he was doing— that is, if he was serving a law higher than the law—then he was saved. And if he knew not what he was doing, then he was damned. It is a slippery business to negotiate with the Shadow, and a fool's progress to attempt to outwit the Shadow, but sometimes we are obliged to do so in service to our fuller humanity, or in service to values higher than our ordinary values. And woe unto the person who seeks this transcendence of conventional values without suffering, without sincere struggle to find the right, and without the willingness to pay whatever consequences arrive on his or her doorstep!

In the end, the work we do has a direct bearing not only on our well-being but upon those whom we love and the world around us. The well-being of others depends on *our* work, for the sum of our separate darknesses makes for a very dark world. As William Stafford has written:

> . . . *it is important that awake people be awake.*
> *Or a breaking line may discourage us back to sleep.**

So what if the work seems overwhelming, endless—it makes for a more *interesting* life, and it does not get better than that! As Rilke noted, we only grow "by being defeated constantly, decisively, / by constantly greater beings."† The interplay between conscious life and the Shadow world is rich indeed, for it brings a fuller range of our humanity into play, without which we are superficial, or simply, and dangerously, unconscious. Even

---

*Stafford, "A Ritual to Read Each Other," *The Darkness Around Us Is Deep*, pp. 135f.
† Rilke, "The Man Watching," in Bly, *Selected Poems of Rainer Maria Rilke*, p. 107.

the most conscientious Shadow work will not spare us moments of despair, doubt, and humiliation, but as Jung reminds us:

> The reason why consciousness exists, and why there is an urge to widen and deepen it, is very simple: without consciousness, things go less well.*

Shadow work always challenges the ego, overthrows it, humbles it, sometimes even slays it. That, paradoxically, is its gift, *if* we can bear such a gift. Yet who wants to grow through the gift of egocide, to be slain by the ever-greater, dying unto what we once thought of ourselves, or of the world, or wish still to think? Who wants to really work so hard? But consider what happens to us, to our relationships, to the world, when we do not do our work. It is not enough to say that someone else is not doing their work. We can only affect that small piece of the great mosaic that we inhabit. As the epigraph that opens this book suggests, we do Shadow work not by imagining figures of light, but by making the darkness conscious.

When we do this work, we do it for more than ourselves. When we do this work we find, in the end, that the light is in the darkness itself. We will find that no feeling, even the most turbulent, most contradictory, is wrong, although we are wholly responsible for how or whether we enact that feeling, for feeling is not a choice. Feeling arises from the soul, autonomously; ours is the choice to acknowledge and honor that feeling, or not, without literalizing its meaning. So what if our old concept of ourselves has to go? So what if we have to take on a more differentiated, more complex view of the world than makes us comfortable? Shadow work is troubling, you say?

*Jung, "Analytical Psychology and '*Weltanschauung*,'" *CW 8*, para. 695.

Yes . . . and life without Shadow work is even more troubling. As Shakespeare notes in *Twelfth Night*, no prisons are more confining than the ones we know not we are in. Death, life, and other troubles are our constant companions. Even Prospero concludes in *The Tempest*, "This thing of darkness I acknowledge mine." And, as Goethe reminds us:

> . . . *so long as you haven't experienced*
> *this: to die and so to grow,*
> *you are only a troubled guest*
> *on the dark earth.**

*Goethe, "The Holy Longing," in Bly, *The Soul Is Here for Its Own Joy*, p. 209.

Bibliography

Armstrong, Karen. *Buddha*. New York: Penguin Putnam, 2001.

Arendt, Hannah. *Eichmann in Jerusalem*. New York: Penguin, 1994.

Auden, W. H. *Collected Poems*. New York: Random House, 1976.

Bly, Robert. *The Soul Is Here for Its Own Joy: Sacred Poems from Many Cultures*. Hopewell, NJ: Ecco Press, 1995.

——. *Selected Poems of Rainer Maria Rilke*. New York: Harper and Row, 1981.

Bly, Robert, Hillman, James, and Meade, Michael. *The Rag and Bone Shop of the Heart: Poems for Men*. New York: Harper Collins, 1992.

Campbell, Joseph. *Pathways to Bliss*. Novato, CA: New World Library, 2004.

Caretenuto, Aldo. *The Difficult Art*, p. 54.

Cesarani, David. *Becoming Eichmann: Rethinking the Life, Crimes and Trial of a "Desk Murderer."* New York: Da Capo Press, 2004.

Conrad, Joseph. *Heart of Darkness*. Ed. Robert Kimbrough. New York: W. W. Norton & Co., 1963.

Curtis, Gregory. "Why Evil Attracts Us," *Facing Evil: Light at the Core of Darkness*, p. 96.

Dostoevsky, Fyodor. *Notes from Underground*. New York: New American Library, 1961.

Ecksteins, Modris. *Rites of Spring: The Great War and the Birth of the Modern Age*. New York: Anchor Books, 1989.

Ellmann, Richard, and O'Clair, Robert, Eds. *Modern Poems: an Introduction to Poetry*. New York: W. W. Norton & Co., 1976.

Frey-Rohn, Liliane. "Evil from a Psychological Point of View," Spring, 1965.

Gambini, Roberto. *Indian Mirror: The Making of the Brazilian Soul*. São Paulo, Brazil: Axis Mundi, 2000.

Guggenbühl-Craig, Adolf. *From the Wrong Side: A Paradoxical Approach to Psychology*. Woodstock, CT: Spring Publications, 1995.

Goethe, Johann Wolfgang von, *Faust.* Trans. Walter Kaufmann. New York: Anchor, 1962.

Goldhagen, Daniel J. *Hitler's Willing Executioners: Ordinary Germans and the Holocaust.* New York: Little, Brown, and Co, 1996.

Goldstein, Rebecca Newberger. *Betraying Spinoza: The Renegade Jew Who Gave Us Modernity.* New York: Schocken, 2006.

———. "Reasonable Doubt," *The New York Times*, July 29, 2006.

Hoagland, Tony. *What Narcissism Means to Me.* St. Paul, MN: Graywolf Press, 2003.

Hollis, James. *The Archetypal Imagination.* College Station, TX: Texas A & M University Press, 2000.

———. *Creating a Life: Finding Your Individual Path.* Toronto: Inner City Books, 2001.

———. *The Eden Project: In Search of the Magical Other.* Toronto: Inner City Books, 1998.

———. *Finding Meaning in the Second Half of Life: How to Finally, Really, Grow Up.* New York: Gotham Books/Penguin, 2005.

———. *The Middle Passage: From Misery to Meaning in Mid-Life.* Toronto: Inner City Books, 1993.

———. *Mythologems: Incarnations of the Invisible World.* Toronto: Inner City Books, 2004.

———. *On This Journey We Call Our Life: Living the Questions.* Toronto: Inner City Books, 2003.

———. *Under Saturn's Shadow: the Wounding and Healing of Men.* Toronto: Inner City Books, 1994.

———. *Swamplands of the Soul: New Life in Dismal Places.* Toronto: Inner City Books: 1996.

———. *Tracking the Gods: the Place of Myth in Modern Life.* Toronto: Inner City Books, 1995.

Jaffe, Lawrence W. *Liberating the Heart: Spirituality and Jungian Psychology.* Toronto: Inner City Books, 1990.

Jung, Carl Gustav. *The Collected Works.* 20 vols. Trans. R. F. C. Hull, Ed. H. Read, M. Fordham, G. Adler, and W. McGuire. Princeton: Princeton University Press, 1973. [cited in this work as *CW*.]

———. *Letters*. 2 vols. Eds. Gerhard Adler and Aniela Jaffe. Princeton: Princeton University Press, 1973.

———. *Memories, Dreams, Reflections*. Trans. Richard and Clara Winston. Ed. Aniela Jaffe. New York: Vintage Books, 1965.

Kazantzakis, Nikos. *The Saviors of God*. Trans. Kimon Friar. New York: Simon and Schuster, 1960.

Kelly, John. *The Great Mortality: An Intimate History of the Black Death, the Most Devastating Plague of All Time*. New York: Harper Collins, 2005.

Kinzer, Stephen. *Overthrow: America's Century of Regime Change From Hawaii to Iraq*. New York: Times Books, 2006.

MacLeish, Archibald. *J. B. A Play in Verse*. Boston: Houghton-Mifflin, 1958.

May, Gerald G. *Addiction and Grace*. San Francisco: Harper, 1988.

Mosley, Nicholas. *Inventing God*. New York: Dalkey Archive Press, 2003.

J. Paul Hunter Ed. *The Norton Introduction to Poetry*. New York: W. W. Norton & Co., 1991.

Paulson, Lola. "The Shadow: This Thing of Darkness I Acknowledge Mine," London: The Guild for Pastoral Psychology, #122, 1963.

Rilke, Rainer Maria. *Letters to a Young Poet*, Trans. M. D. Herter Norton. New York: W. W. Norton & Company, 1954.

Robertson, Robin. *Your Shadow*. Virginia Beach: A.R.E. Press, 1997.

Rosenbaum, Ron. "Degrees of Evil: Some Thoughts on Hitler, bin Laden, and the Hierarchy of Wickedness," *The Atlantic Monthly*, February 2002.

Rubin, Harriet. *Dante in Love: the World's Greatest Poem and How It Made History*. New York: Simon and Schuster, 2004.

Sanford, John. *Evil: The Shadow Side of Reality*. New York: Crossroad, 1981.

———. *Jung and the Problem of Evil: the Strange Trial of Mr. Hyde*. Boston: Sigo Press, 1987.

Saunders, Doug. "Children of the War," *The Globe and Mail* (Toronto), May 21, 2005.

"The Shadow," *Parabola: Myth, Tradition, and the Search for Meaning*. Summer 1997.

Shalit, Erel. "The Hero and His Shadow." Solna, Sweden: C. G. Jung Stiftelsen, 1997.

Shattuck, Roger. *Forbidden Knowledge: from Prometheus to Pornography*. New York: St. Martin's Press, 1996.

Slattery, Dennis Patrick. *Casting the Shadows: Selected Poems*. Kearney, NE: Morris Publishing, 2001.

Stafford, William. *The Darkness Around Us Is Deep: Selected Poems of William Stafford*. Ed. Robert Bly. New York: Harper, 1993.

Steiner, George. *Language and Silence: Essays on Language, Literature and the Inhuman*. New York: Atheneum, 1976.

Waley, Arthur. *The Way and Its Power*. New York: Grove Press, 1958.

Woodruff, Paul, and Wilmer, Harry A. *Facing Evil: Light at the Core of Darkness*. LaSalle, IL: Open Court, 1988.

Zorn, Fritz. *Mars*. New York: Alfred A. Knopf, 1982.

Zweig, Connie, and Abrams, Jeremiah. *Meeting the Shadow: the Hidden Power of the Dark Side of Human Nature*. Los Angeles: Jeremy P. Tarcher, Inc., 1991.

Index

abandonment, 78, 87, 88–89, 91,
     93n, 103
acceptance of ourselves, 195–98,
     205
adaptations
     consequences of, 54–58, 69
     development of, 185, 234
     and estrangement from self, 220
     and finding the Shadow, 235
     and neurosis, 75
     and personal growth, 70
     and psychopathology, 60
addiction, 57, 61, 67–69, 89
Africa, 163–65
Agatha (film), 32
agendas, 4, 7–8, 30, 61, 103
aggression, 8, 56, 85–86, 122, 187,
     211–15
agnosticism, 169n, 182n
akrasia, 25
alcohol, 45, 112–13, 115
alone, being, 100–101, 204
anagnorisis (recognition), 28
anger
     about, 50–54
     and caregiving, 207
     and compulsive personality disor-
          der, 78–79
     etymology, 52, 186
     and the positive Shadow, 186–87

in relational dynamics, 104
     and repression, 98–99
     and sexuality, 54
anima, 44–45
animus, 47, 47n, 231
annoyances, examining, 215–19
Answer to Job (Jung), 174, 175,
     177–78
antiheros, 159–63
antisocial personality disorder,
     76–77
anxiety
     anxiety disorders, 65
     and avoidance, 62–65
     basis of, 30
     etymology, 52
     and fundamentalism, 132
     and magical thinking, 70
     management of, 65–70, 220
     and parent-child dynamics, 189
     and personality disorders, 78–79
     and repression, 98
     tolerance of, 201
approval, 89, 205
Arendt, Hannah, 154–55
Armstrong, Karen, 200–201
Arouet, François-Marie (Voltaire),
     128, 153n, 175
artists, 166, 227
Art of the Mind, 17

Auden, W. H., 68
Augustine, 35, 144, 174, 231, 235–36
Auseinandersetzung, 36
authority, personal, 55, 123, 190, 191–92, 193
avoidance
    addressing, 69
    and anxiety, 62–63
    development of, 87
    and employment, 122
    expressions of, 56
    and identification of Shadow, 79
    patterns of, 211–15
    role of, 31

Bacon, Sir Francis, 71, 149
Bailey, Pearl, 104n
"banality of evil," 154–55
behavioral psychology, 28, 220
Bertha (case study), 79–81
bigotry, 11, 17, 65, 118, 167
bin Laden, Osama, 179
Black Death, 144, 147–48
Blake, William, 19, 45, 52, 74
blame
    and complexes, 230
    danger of, 5
    and magical thinking, 70
    as primitive defense, 98, 203, 206–7
    in relational dynamics, 104, 105
    and responsibility, 21
borderline personality disorder, 78
Breuer, Josef, 7
The Brothers Karamazov (Dostoevsky), 230n
Bruno, Giordano, 108n
Buddhism, 24, 35, 181, 200–201, 203, 232–33
bullying, 93, 140
Burke, Edmund, 114
"Burnt Norton" (Eliot), 66
Bush, George W., 19, 116n, 129–30, 141
Butler, Samuel, 107

Campbell, Joseph, 183
Camus, Albert, 182, 196, 230
Candide (Voltaire), 153n, 175
caregivers, 12, 207–11, 227
Carotenuto, Aldo, 203–4
The Castle (Kafka), 138
Cesarani, David, 154
Cheney, Dick, 116n
child
    and adult fears, 81–82
    and adult relationships, 85–86, 102–3
    agenda of, 94
    and personality disorders, 77
    and powerlessness, 193, 220, 238
    and primal bonding experiences, 86
    programming of, 64, 86–94, 194, 211–12
child abuse, 49, 111
Christianity, 35, 48n, 117–18, 181, 199. *See also* religion
Civilization and Its Discontents (Freud), 8
The Cocktail Party (Eliot), 112
codependency, 88, 98
collective Shadow, 107–27
    about, 10
    beneficence in, 109–12
    ecstasies of, 112–19
    and national concerns, 126–27
    and the soul, 126–27
    and violence, 108, 108n
    in the workplace, 119–25
colonialism, 163–66
"The Committee" (Grant), 33–34
compassion, 77, 85, 110, 196–97
complexes
    and adult impasses, 223–24
    and anxiety, 65
    defined, 4, 33–34, 90
    and ego, 184–85, 238
    in groups, 121
    and relationships, 47, 90
    and repetitious behaviors, 220
complexities of psyche, 11–14, 56

compulsive behaviors, 45
compulsive personality disorder, 78–79
conflicts, 87, 103
Conrad, Joseph, 163, 191–92, 219n
consciousness
    assumption of, 26
    and the collective Shadow, 108
    and compassion, 196–97
    and conflicts, 7, 103
    and hidden agendas, 7–8
    humbled consciousness, 36, 203
    and institutional Shadow, 146
    integration of Shadow into, 20–23
    power of unconscious, 28, 61
    and projection, 104
    and splinter selves, xi
controlling behaviors, 89, 99
corporations. *See* work
Cranston, Lamont, 9
Crystal Palace, 157–58
Curtis, Gregory, 132–33

Dante Alighieri, 148–49, 173
Daolin, 24
"Degrees of Evil" (Rosenbaum), 175, 179
delusions, 77, 172
democracies, 137, 146, 158
denial
    and anxiety management, 65
    danger of, 5
    and the examined life, 201
    and finding the Shadow, 235
    Jung on, 79
    pathology of, 65–66
    role of, 31
    and uncertainty, 139
dependency, 95–96, 105
depression
    and adaptations, 185
    and anger, 53
    and caregiving, 207
    and empowerment, 64

and estrangement from self, 196
and parent-child dynamics, 87
and personal growth, 70
in relational dynamics, 104
and repression, 98
and the unlived life, 55
depth psychology, 28–29, 33, 166
desires, 69, 72–76, 88
Devil, 4, 32, 152, 232
Diana, Princess of Wales, 17
Dillard, Annie, 182n
Dissociative Identity Disorder, 32n
dissociative mechanisms, 31–32, 65, 87, 111, 206
doppelgängers, 219
Dostoevsky, Fyodor, 159–60, 195, 230n
doubt, Jung on, 142
dreams, 55, 185, 203

Eastern theological traditions, 34–35, 139n, 168, 181
ecstasy, collective, 112–19
education, 3, 140–41
Edward (case study), 41–48
ego
    and adaptations, 61
    as a complex, 29–30, 184–85
    and consciousness, 12, 21
    defense strategies, 30–32
    and evil, 172–73, 180–81
    in Freudian theory, 33, 161
    of groups, 109, 117
    and hubris, 26
    and intention/outcome gap, 27
    and motives, 7
    and personal growth, 237
    and projection, 16–17
    and religion, 36, 93–94, 168, 181, 201
    splitting of, 178–80
    strength of, 40, 92–94, 93n
Eichmann, Adolf, 114, 154–55
Ekelöf, Gunnar, xi
Eliot, T. S., 66, 112, 156, 165, 196
Emily (case study), 41–48

empathy, 85, 110, 111
employment. *See* work
empowerment, 64, 87–88
enemies, 15, 173, 203
Enron, 125
entitlement, sense of, 77
Eros, 41–50, 188. *See also* sexuality
errors, 233–34
estrangement from self, 55, 101–2,
    185, 196, 205, 220
evil
    and "banality of evil," 154–55
    and ego, 172–73, 180–81
    and Faust and the Faustian age,
        152–57
    and God, 168–69
    nature of, 167–69
    and the Shadow, xii, 9, 56
    and theodicy, 174–75
exploitation, 153, 153n, 195,
    209–10
expression of the Shadow
    through identification, 18–20
    through projection, 14–18
    through unconscious means,
        10–14
extroversion, 31n, 55–56, 101

The Fall (Camus), 196
"The Fall" archetype, 4
false self, 122, 122n
family-of-origin dynamics
    and adult relationships, 86–90,
        91, 102–3, 218, 221–22
    case study, 90–91
    common coping strategies, 87–90
    and corporate life, 122, 123
    examination of, 225–28
    mother complex, 63–64, 221
    and Other, 86n (*see also* Other)
    and the positive Shadow, 188–95
    and the unlived life, 57–58, 87,
        193, 194
fascism, 75
Faulkner, William, 228
Faust and the Faustian age, 151–57,
    232

fear
    and adult impasses, 81–82,
        222–25
    and finding the Shadow, 235
    and fundamentalism, 132
    and personality disorders, 77
    and popular psychology, 201
    in relationships, 93
*Finding Meaning in the Second Half
    of Life* (Hollis), 54
1 Corinthians, 25
food disorders, 67
forgiveness of ourselves, 195–98
France, 136
Freud, Sigmund
    on neuroses, 72
    on prayer, 71
    on psyche's divisions, 33
    on psychopathology, 7–8, 61
    reception of, 161
    on repetition compulsion,
        215–16
    on symptoms, 51
Freudian slips, 8
Frey-Rohn, Liliane, 204
fundamentalism
    and anxiety disorders, 65
    and complexes, 230
    development of, 132, 133
    and ego, 35, 93–94
    examination of, 204
    and fear, 132
    ideology of, 75
    and institutional Shadow, 132,
        133, 138–43
    and magical thinking, 71
    and sexuality, 188
"The Fury of Overshoes" (Sexton),
    106

Galileo, 108n, 149n
Gambini, Roberto, 134–35
Gandhi, Mahatma, 107
gays, 18, 73, 117
Germany, 131–32, 132–33, 135–36
Goethe, Johann Wolfgang von,
    151–52, 155, 180, 238

Goldwater, Barry, 19
goodness, 22–23, 24, 30, 37,
    109–12, 235
Gospel of Thomas, 236
Grant, Martha, 33–34
groups. *See* collective Shadow
Guggenbuhl-Craig, Adolph, 86
guilt, 48, 54, 195, 205

Hafiz, 76
hamartia (limited vision), 27, 174
Hamlet (Shakespeare), 149
happiness, 97–98
hatred of self, 196
Hawthorne, Nathaniel, 4, 183, 184
healing
    guides in, 166
    and prayer, 71n
    and religion, 173–82
    requisites for, 21, 235
    as Shadow effect, 185
    tikkun olam (healing of the
        world), 23
health issues, 55, 120, 185, 186
Heart of Darkness (Conrad),
    163–65
Heine, Heinrich, 136
Hermes Trismegistus, xii
The Hidden Persuaders (Packard),
    15
Hinduism, 35, 181
history
    and adult relationships, 102, 103,
        105
    identification with, 227
    and magical thinking, 106
    power of, 91–92, 212
Hitler, Adolf, 114n, 179
Hoagland, Tony, 84
Hobbes, Thomas, 147
Holocaust
    and culture of Germany, 131–32
    and healing, 118
    and institutional Shadow, 132–33
    perpetrators of, 114–15, 125
    and social progress, 158
homosexuality, 18, 73, 117

honesty, 207, 209
hubris, 26, 27, 37, 172, 174, 195
humanity, 22, 163, 177–78
humor, 56, 117, 118
Huxley, Thomas, 141, 169n

Id, 33, 161
identification, 18–20, 88–89, 110
imagination, 67, 77, 85, 86
imagoes, 84–94, 170–73, 173–74,
    178
impasses, 81–82, 203, 222–25
Indian civilization of South Amer-
    ica, 134–35
*Indian Mirror: The Making of the
    Brazilian Soul* (Gambini), 134
individuation, 75, 94, 99, 185, 193
institutional shadows, 128–46
    criticism of institutions, 145–46
    development of, 137–39
    in education, 140–41
    in France, 136
    and fundamentalism, 132, 133,
        134–35, 138–41
    of Germany, 131–32, 132–33,
        135–36
    and leadership, 132
    power of, 144–45
    regression, institutional, 132, 133
    in relationships, 143
    of United States, 129–31, 132
intention, 25, 27, 85, 99
Internet, 45n, 158–59
irritability, 98, 196
Islam, 35, 181

Jaffe, Lawrence, 233–34
Janet, Pierre, 113
J.B. (MacLeish), 175–77
Jefferson, Thomas, 145
Jesus, 57–58, 233–34, 236
Jews and Judaism, 18, 35, 181
Job (biblical), 7, 36, 71n, 170–73,
    177–78, 199
Johnson, Lyndon, 19
Josey, Alden, 92
Julius Caesar (Shakespeare), 14

Jung, Carl, 229
  on adulthood, 198–99
  on animus, 231
  on *Auseinandersetzung*, 36
  on complexes, 4, 33–34
  on consciousness, 22, 228, 237
  on denial, 79
  on doubt, 142
  on enlightenment, xvii
  on eros/sexuality, 72
  on fundamentalism, 133–34
  on Germany, 135–36
  on Job, 174, 175, 177–78
  on the neurotic, 75
  on the Other, 38, 232
  on parent-child dynamics, 193
  on personal growth, 22, 224
  personality typology, 31n, 55–56
  on power complex, 77, 88, 213
  on the Shadow, xii, 5, 8–9, 206
  on solitude, 78
  on the unlived life, 57, 193
  on wholeness, 235
  on Wotan, 119
justification, 135, 137–38

Kafka, Franz, 138
Kant, Immanuel, 3n
Kazantzakis, Nikos, 69, 147,
    181–82
Kelly, John, 144
Kierkegaard, Søren, 136, 210, 222
Kinsey Reports, 187
Kumin, Maxine, 5–6

leadership, 109, 121, 123–25,
    125n, 129–31, 132
Leibniz, Gottfried, 174
Leopold of Belgium, 163
Letter to the Romans, 24, 32
Levin, Harry, 184
loneliness, 50, 78, 93n, 101
love
  See also desires; relationships
  and the collective Shadow, 111
  and mature relationships, 212
  and paraphilias, 72–73
  and power, 77, 88, 213
  romantic love, 49, 70, 213–14
  as a Shadow task, 94–99
Luther, Martin, 35

MacLeish, Archibald, 175–77
magical thinking, 70–72, 170, 178,
    200, 228–32
manipulation of others, 78, 89, 212
Marlowe, Christopher, 151
marriage, 91, 96–98, 99–100, 143
Mars (Zorn), 53–54
materialism, 89, 109, 181, 233
maturity, 95–97, 99–100, 104–5,
    198–99, 228–32
May, Gerald G., 69
McCain Amendment, 116n
meliorism, 157–58
Melville, Herman, 184
Memories, Dreams, Reflections
    (Jung), 229
Mephistopheles, 152–53, 155–56
"The Metamorphosis" (Kafka), 138
Middle East, 140, 144, 158n
Milgram, Stanley, 115–16
Mill, John Stuart, 139n
Milton, John, 19–20, 33
Mizener, Arthur, 140
modernism, 147–66
  and the antihero, 159–63
  and Black Death, 144, 147–48
  and colonialism, 163–66
  development of, 147–48
  Faust and the Faustian age,
    151–57
  and meliorism, 157–58, 163
  and progress, 157–58, 164
  and sacred/secular order, 148–49
  and science, 149–50
morality, 204
Mosley, Nicholas, 13
mother complex, 63–64, 221. *See
    also* family-of-origin dynamics
"My Shadow" (Stevenson), 162n

narcissism
  and altruism, 110
  and annoyances, 217
  and caring for others, 207–8

narcissistic personality, 77–78
  and relationships, 92, 212–13
  and will, 25
National Holocaust Museum,
  Washington, D.C., 85
Nazi Germany, 131–32. *See also*
  Holocaust
needs, meeting, 94, 121–22, 207,
  213
neuroses and neurotic personality,
  51, 61, 75, 76, 205
New Orleans, Louisiana, 131n,
  210n
Niebuhr, Reinhold, 59
Nietzsche, Friedrich, 8n, 165, 196,
  202, 210
Notes from Underground (Dostoevsky), 27, 195
numbing, 111, 111n, 115

Oedipus, 21, 28, 174
oppression, 87–88
Origen, 15, 35
original sin, 4, 26
Other
  See also relationships
  common experiences with, 87
  and institutional Shadow, 135
  and "Magical Others," 218
  and personality disorders, 76–77,
    78
  and primal bonding experiences,
    63, 86, 87–88, 91
  and projections of evil, 153–55
  as reflection, 205–6, 219, 232
  in religious traditions, 35
  and repetition, 216
outcomes and intentions, 27
overcompensation, 57, 89, 214,
  226–27

Paradise Lost (Milton), 19–20
paranoid personality disorder, 77
paraphilias, 49, 72–76
passive-aggressive behaviors, 79,
  122
Pathways to Bliss (Campbell), 183
Paul (biblical), 24, 25, 32

pedophilia, 48, 73
penal system, 3
perfectionism, 78
persecution, delusions of, 77
personality disorders, 76–79, 185
personality typology, 31n, 55–56
Philo of Alexandria, 212
physical ailments, 55, 120, 185,
  186
The Plague (Camus), 182
Plato, 2–3, 27, 28, 146
Poe, Edgar Allan, 184, 219n
Pogo (cartoon character), 20–21
"A Poison Tree" (Blake), 52
Poland, Jews of, 18
politicians and politics, xii, 16, 19
pornography, 45n, 48, 49
positive Shadow, 183–201
  and anger, 186–87
  and collective beneficence,
    109–12
  and ego, 184–85
  Jung on, 9
  and parent-child dynamics,
    188–95
  and sexuality, 187–88
positive thinking, 200–201
power
  and the child, 193, 220
  and corporate life, 122
  and love, 77, 88, 213
  and parent-child dynamics,
    87–88, 89
  and personality disorders, 76–77
  and powerlessness, 19, 63, 87,
    193
  in relational dynamics, 104
The Power of Blackness (Levin), 184
prejudice, 11, 17, 65, 118, 167
progress, 157–58. *See also* modernism
projection
  about, 103–5
  of absent parent, 103
  and anxiety management, 65
  and consciousness, 45, 104
  and corporate life, 122
  danger of, 5

projection (*cont.*)
  as expression of Shadow, 14–18, 40, 205–6
  and history, 106
  role of, 31
  and self-examination, 197
Prometheus, 76
propaganda, 16
psychological, becoming, 102–6, 166
psychopathology, 60–65
The Psychopathology of Everyday Life (Freud), 7, 61

questions for reflection, 207–32
  annoyances, 215–19
  blocks, 222–25
  maturity, 228–32
  parent complexes, 225–28
  patterns, 211–15
  repetition, 220–22
  virtues, 207–11

rape, 48, 49, 111
rationalizations, 10–11, 20, 24–25, 115
reality, 17, 28, 66
regression, 132, 133
relationships
  See also love; marriage
  case study, 96–97, 102
  and the child's agenda, 94
  constrictive relationships, 85–86
  difficulty of, 83
  and intimacy, 86–87
  mature relationships, 99–102
  and narcissism, 92, 212–13
  and personal growth, 95, 105
  and personality types, 46–47
  principles of, 104–5
  and projection, 65
  recurrent motifs, 103
  Shadow work in, 214–15, 217–18
  and soul, 120
  strength of, 100

and transference, 65
religion, 167–82
  See also specific religious traditions
  and African colonization, 163–64
  and Black Death, 144, 147–48
  and collective Shadow, 117–18
  dualisms, 169
  Eastern theological traditions, 34–35, 139n, 168, 181
  and ego, 36, 93–94, 168, 181, 201
  fundamentalism, 35, 65, 71, 138–43
  and hubris, 62
  and Inquisition, 137n
  and institutional Shadow, 137n
  and intelligent design, 141–42
  Job (biblical), 7, 36, 71n, 170–73, 177–78, 199
  and magical thinking, 70–71, 71n
  monotheism, 169
  polytheism, 34, 168, 169
  popular theology, 199–201
  and prayer, 70–71, 71n
  and psychology, 36–37
  and sexuality, 48n, 188
  and the Shadow, 4
  sin, 4, 25, 25n, 26, 32, 35
  theodicy, 34, 169, 174–75, 180–81
  Western theological traditions, 35, 139n, 168, 181
  zealots, 13
Renoir, Jean, 128
repetition
  examination of, 211–15, 215–17, 220–22, 225–28
  and family-of-origin dynamics, 57, 91
  in relationships, 103
repression
  and anxiety management, 65
  and consciousness, 45
  consequences of, 98–99
  and expression of Shadow, 40
  and parent-child dynamics, 87

and restraint, 74–75
role of, 31, 204–5
and sexuality, 188, 205
and symptom formation, 51–52
The Republic (Plato), 2–3, 123
responsibility, 64–65, 75, 118
Rilke, Rainer Maria, 197, 236
"The River" (Thomas), 38
Roethke, Theodore, 202
romantic love, 49, 70, 213–14
Rosenbaum, Ron, 175, 179
routines, 66–67
Rubin, Harriet, 147–48
Russell, Bertrand, 59, 128

Santayana, George, 21
Sartre, Jean-Paul, 230
Satan, 4, 32
Saunders, Doug, 136
The Scarlet Letter (Hawthorne), 18, 184
Schlessinger, Arthur, 123n
Schopenhauer, Arthur, 202
Schwartz, Delmore, 84
science, 141–42, 149–50
scripts of the past, 64–65
2 Timothy, 25
secret lives, 13, 18
"The Secret Sharer" (Conrad), 191–92, 219n
self-acceptance, 195–98
self-help books, xiii, 200
self-interest, 98, 99, 110–11, 132, 212
self-sabotage, 56, 88–89, 122
Sexton, Anne, 106
sexual abuse, 48, 49, 73, 74, 111
sexuality
and anger, 54
case study, 41–48
cultural emphasis, 49–50
and Freudian theory, 7
and fundamentalism, 188
homosexuality, 18, 73, 117
and perversions, 72
and pornography, 45n, 48, 49

and the positive Shadow, 187–88
and religion, 48n
and repression, 188, 205
virgin/whore complex, 47
Shadow
defined, 9, 30, 185
examination of, 235 (*see also* questions for reflection)
identification of, 79
manifestations of, 1–2, 16–17, 39, 185
scope of, 39–40
The Shadow radio program, 9
Shakespeare, William, 14, 149, 238
shame, 14, 70, 205
Shelley, Percy Bysshe, 67
shelters for abused women, 93
"Shooting Rats" (Slattery), 6
Simon, Carly, 100
sin, 4, 25, 25n, 26, 32, 35
Slattery, Dennis, 6
Smith, Adam, 29
sociopathies, 61, 65
Socrates, 3, 27, 145, 201
Socratic fallacy, 3–4
solitude, 78, 100–101
"Sometimes I Forget Completely" (Rumi), 83
soul, 120–21, 126–27
Spinoza, Baruch, 142–43
splinter selves, xi–xiv, 4, 33–34
Stafford, William, 236
stalking, 93n
Steiner, George, 155, 179
Stevenson, Adlai, 130
Stevenson, Robert Louis, 162, 219n
The Strange Case of Dr. Jekyll and Mr. Hyde (Stevenson), 162, 219n
Studies in Hysteria (Freud and Breuer), 7
suffering, 200–201, 204
suicide, 45, 93, 144
Super Ego, 33, 161
suppression, 31, 65, 87

sympathy, 85, 110
symptom formation, 51–52, 185, 205, 229

The Tempest (Shakespeare), 238
Temple, William, 75n
temptations, 232–33
Tennyson, Alfred, 151
Terence, 2, 36, 234
Theodicy (Leibniz), 174
therapy, 48–49, 68–69, 97–98, 99–100, 203–4
Thomas, Larry D., 38
Thorazine, 28
tikkun olam (healing of the world), 23
Tillich, Paul, 35
torture, 115–16, 116n
The Tragical History of Dr. Faustus (Marlowe), 150, 151
transference, 103–5, 106, 111, 122, 189–90
The Trial (Kafka), 138
Troilus and Cressida (Shakespeare), 149
Twain, Mark, 161, 184, 199
Twelfth Night (Shakespeare), 238
Tyco, 125

"Ulysses" (Tennyson), 151
Unamuno, Miguel de, 27
unconscious Shadow, 10–14. *See also* consciousness
The Underground Man (Dostoevsky), 159–60
United States, 128–30, 132, 135
unlived life
    and anxiety, 65
    case study, 60
    expressions of, 55
    Jung on, 57, 193
and parent-child dynamics, 87, 193, 194
and personal growth, 70

values, 10, 167
violence, 8, 92–94, 108, 108n, 129–30
virgin/whore complex, 47
virtues, 207–11
Voltaire, 128, 153n, 175

war, 8, 108, 113, 129, 130
The Wealth of Nations (Smith), 29
weight gain/loss, 82
Western theological traditions, 35, 139n, 168, 181
"What Narcissism Means to Me" (Hoagland), 84
Whitman, Walt, 23, 29, 68
wholeness, 23, 234–35
Wilberforce, Samuel, 141
Williams, William Carlos, 19
witch hunts, 18, 108, 184
withdrawal, 102, 212
"Woodchucks" (Kumin), 5–6
work
    and collective Shadow, 119–25
    and compulsive personality disorder, 78
    leadership, 121, 123–25, 125n, 126
    work addictions, 67–68
Wotan, the Berserker, 119

Xenophanes, 167

Yeats, William Butler, 145, 177
"Young Goodman Brown" (Hawthorne), 4

Zorn, Fritz, 53–54